John Henry Parker

The Flavian Amphitheatre, Commonly Called the Colosseum at Rome

Its history & substructures compared with other amphitheatres

John Henry Parker

The Flavian Amphitheatre, Commonly Called the Colosseum at Rome
Its history & substructures compared with other amphitheatres

ISBN/EAN: 9783744775168

Printed in Europe, USA, Canada, Australia, Japan

Cover: Foto ©ninafisch / pixelio.de

More available books at **www.hansebooks.com**

JOHN HENRY PARKER C.B.
HON. M.A, OXON, F.S.A, LONDON etc. etc.

THE FLAVIAN AMPHITHEATRE,

COMMONLY CALLED

THE COLOSSEUM AT ROME:

ITS HISTORY AND SUBSTRUCTURES

COMPARED WITH

OTHER AMPHITHEATRES.

BY

JOHN HENRY PARKER, C.B.

Hon. M.A. Oxon., F.S.A. Lond.;
Keeper of the Ashmolean Museum of History and Antiquities
in the University of Oxford, etc.

OXFORD:
JAMES PARKER AND CO.
LONDON:
JOHN MURRAY, ALBEMARLE-STREET.
1876.

PREFACE TO THE COLOSSEUM.

The great excavations carried on in this colossal building in the years 1874 and 1875, have thrown an entirely new light on its history. These were made under the level of the ground, at the foot of the *podium*, which is the same as that of the original *arena*; this large level space had been indifferently called the ground, the floor, the stage, the area, or the arena; no one had any idea that the original pavement would be found 21 ft. below that level, and that the intervening space was filled with walls and passages, dens for wild beasts, places for lifts to send up men, and dogs, and animals: and canals for water, and several other contrivances for the use of the performers on the stage above, for practically the *arena* was the stage on which the performances took place. These excavations have enabled us to ascertain that this had been a boarded floor covered with sand, or *arena* (whence its name), and that this floor could be moved and replaced in a short time, at the word of the Emperor[a]. The evidence of this is brought out clearly in the present work. Large corbels, or brackets, are provided for placing the boards upon when removed, and keeping them out of sight of the people in the galleries; they project from the wall below the *podium*, in the passage over the dens[b].

We had all of us hitherto been taught that this enormous structure had been all built in ten years by the Flavian emperors; this is the uniform modern history, but no ancient author says so. It is only one of the so-called "Roman Traditions," which (as I am obliged to repeat continually) are nothing but the *conjectures* of learned men during the last three centuries, especially Panvinius and his school in the seventeenth. In the present instance it is evident that so far from having been all built in ten years, it was more than a century about from first to last; it was begun in the time of Sylla the Dictator, by his step-son Scaurus, and is described by Pliny in his "Natural History" by the name of the *insane* work of Scaurus, who was called insane because he spent such an enormous fortune upon the work, (equal to more than two millions sterling of modern money). It is true that Pliny calls it a *theatre* and not an *amphitheatre*, and this has deceived scholars, who do not perceive that

[a] See Plate XIII.   [b] Ibid. XVII., XVIII.

the two names were used quite indifferently at that period. Pliny himself contrasts it with the great *theatre* of Pompey, built long afterwards, and when the city had increased so much, yet which only held 40,000 people, while this building would hold 80,000. There is no other site in Rome where 80,000 people could be placed to see a show excepting this and the Circus Maximus, which is never called a theatre. An inscription has been found in the *amphitheatre* itself, in which it is called *theatrum* and not amphitheatrum, which is still *a theatre*, though it has two round ends to it, instead of one being flat. The celebrated Greek theatre at Taormina, in Sicily, which has the most perfect *scena* that is known anywhere, is still called by the people either theatre or amphitheatre indifferently, as I was told by the local guide on the spot, in May, 1876. Either a theatre or an amphitheatre was a place of public amusement.

This great building of Scaurus was three storeys high. On the level of the ground were marble columns by the hundred, on the first floor glass columns (the only instance on record), on the upper floor they were of gilt wood. Pliny says that part of this insane work was only calculated to be of a *temporary* character, and it was in fact all destroyed by fire a few years afterwards, and the glass columns perished equally with those of gilt wood; he also adds that other parts were calculated to be *eternal*, and this equally applies to the part we have remaining, the great substructures, which being underground, and built of large blocks of tufa, would last as long as the hills if let alone. Many of these great blocks of tufa appear to have been used a second time; they were most probably brought from the second wall of Rome, which enclosed the two hills (the Capitoline and Palatine) in one City, and therefore must have passed under the south end of the Palatine, close to this great amphitheatre. Immediately in front of it, and separated from it only by a paved street, the south end of the Summa Sacra Via is supported by a rough concrete wall of the time of Sylla, and on the surface of this concrete wall there are impressions of large blocks of tufa in the plaster with which the concrete is covered. It is well known that Roman mortar is often harder and more durable than stone. A few of the large blocks of tufa also remain in their places, where they were necessary to carry the vault of the platform above. These tufa blocks were used under the *podium* at the bottom, to the height of twenty feet, and parallel to them is another wall of the same kind, with just room enough for a narrow passage between them[c]. In these walls, on both sides, are vertical

[c] See Plates V., VI.

grooves, evidently for lifts to be pulled up and let down, and larger apertures at intervals for the counter-weights.

Behind this wall, under the path in front of the *podium*, are the dens for the wild beasts. At the back of each den, in the corner, is a vertical aperture about four feet square, descending from the passage in front of the *podium*; this descends to ten feet from the ground only, and was for the men to go down and feed the animals below without being exposed to danger. In front of each den is a hole in the original brick pavement, sometimes with a bronze socket remaining in its place. These sockets (of which there are a great number in the pavement) are evidently made for a pivot to work in each, and these pivots must have been the lower end of a post for a capstan to wind the twenty-one feet of cord upon, when the animal in his cage was pulled up to the top, and the trap-door opened by the same cord from below, to let him jump out when required for effect on the stage[d]. It is recorded by contemporary authors that on several occasions a hundred lions leapt on to the stage or arena at once. Some very curious *graffiti*, or scratchings on marble, by the workmen of the third century, have been found, one of which represents a hunt of wild beasts on the arena, in which apparently the dogs have broken loose[e]. Another shews the framework of the netting of gilt wire in front of the lower gallery[f].

There are five different representations of the Colosseum on the coins or medals of the Emperors, one of Vespasian, two of Alexander Severus, and one of Gordianus. These all appear to have been made from the architect's designs before the work was completed; there are slight variations in the accessories, and the upper storey varies considerably. That of Gordianus has for the legend or inscription—

MVNIFICENTIA GORDIANI AVG. [g]

This great tufa wall, on the inner line, has evidently been much shaken by earthquakes in different parts, and the heads of the apertures (which are square-headed when original) have frequently had arches introduced, and are supported by brick walls of different periods[h]. In one instance an arch of tufa had been much shaken, and this is supported by a brick arch of the time of Nero[i]; there are also many other walls and arches of his time in different parts of the building, which make it clear that this building was the amphitheatre for the *gymnasium* and the *naumachia* of Nero. It is

[d] See Plate XVI. [e] Ibid. XXII. [f] Ibid. XXIII.
[g] Ibid. XXIV., XXV. [h] Ibid. X. [i] Ibid. IX., XV.

the natural site for it, close to his great palace, and the remains of that of Scaurus made him excellent foundations to build upon, according to the fashion of his own time, which was of brick, of the finest brickwork in the world. Those whose eyes are accustomed to it can never mistake the brickwork of the time of Nero; his awning is also mentioned; and the first book of the Epigrams of Martial is full of incidents and spectacles in this amphitheatre.

Down the centre of the building, for the whole length, is a wide passage, which was called *the gulf*[k], and which was necessary for sending up the scenery, of which we read frequently, and which must have been put together below, and then sent up to the stage, as wanted, by means of this passage; there is no room for it anywhere else, and there was no place behind the scenes for the actors and workmen, as in a modern theatre. On each side of this great central passage are remains of two canals for water, each about ten feet square, and about the same height from the ground[l]; these were evidently filled with water supplied from the aqueducts, and unmistakable traces of three reservoirs for water from the aqueducts have been found in the first gallery. The four canals are not all quite of the same period, nor on the same plan; one on each side was supported on flat arches of brick of the third century, the other on large beams of wood; the places to receive the ends of the beams are left in the walls on each side of the passage for the workmen under it. These walls are of such a thickness in proportion to their height, that they were evidently made to support the great weight of water; these very thick walls served instead of the great projection of the buttresses of the usual reservoirs of the aqueducts.

There is no bond or junction of any kind between this *brick* theatre, or amphitheatre, and the magnificent *stone* corridors and grand front of the Flavian Emperors; these have evidently been added to a brick building previously existing in the centre[m]. It had long been a matter of wonder to all the great architects of Europe how it could be possible to collect such an enormous mass of material of all kinds, and put them together in ten years; to bring that quantity of travertine stone from the quarries at Tivoli, twenty miles off, cut it, and erect it, was in itself an enormous work. This gigantic building is in round numbers 500 ft. long, 300 ft. wide, and 120 ft. high above the foundations, and the grand corridors are double all round, with the *vomitoria*, or stairs from the seats at short intervals, and there are altogether six storeys, including the *entresols*.

[k] See Plate IV.   [l] Ibid. XV.   [m] Ibid. I., II.

The upper storey was originally of wood, and was destroyed by a great fire caused by lightning, in the time of the Emperor Macrinus; it was rebuilding of stone during the whole reign of Alexander Severus, and was completed by Gordianus III., who commemorated it by a medal, taking the credit of the rebuilding to himself. There was a row of columns in front of the upper gallery; two of the bases remain there, and a number of capitals that belonged to that colonnade[n] have fallen down in an earthquake, and are now lying about on the ground on the level of the arena, but were found in the substructures. These are very rude workmanship[o], perhaps only because they were to be seen from a great distance, but they may possibly have been preserved from the works of Scaurus; they are very different from the finished capitals used in the lower gallery. This rebuilding and addition of the upper storey alone took twenty years in a great building era. Great changes were made at that time to raise the upper storey securely, and this we have pointed out. It is seen that the builders had no faith in the soft tufa for carrying any considerable weight, and provided piers of the hard travertine at short intervals for that purpose[p]. There are altogether six storeys in the present building, but three of them may be considered as *entresols* for passages to and from the *vomitoria*[q]. Gordianus also rebuilt the front of one bay of the lower storey, which had probably been damaged by some of the burning timber falling in front of it. At the bottom of the great central passage was found a very remarkable wooden framework, resembling what is usually called a cradle in a dockyard, and used for a vessel to stand upon[r]. This cradle had the appearance of having been burnt, but it is known that long exposure to extreme moisture will give the same appearance to wood that burning it does. At the east end of the passage, at the lowest level, is the great drain, half above and half below the level of the old pavement[s]. At the entrance to this are the grooves of a sluice-gate in the walls on each side, and an original iron grating to prevent anything being carried through by the rush of water; by this it is evident the water was let off from the canals from time to time through this drain. Unfortunately the old drain, which was at a great depth, was so much damaged that it was found impracticable to repair it, though it was traced the whole length of the building, as far as the Arch of Constantine at the opposite end[t].

[n] See Plate XII.   [o] Ibid. XI.   [p] Ibid. XX., XXI.
[q] Ibid. XIV.   [r] Ibid. VII., VIII., XXVI.
[s] Ibid. XIX.   [t] Ibid. XXXVI.

These interesting discoveries made me think it expedient to pay fresh visits to other amphitheatres, to examine them again more carefully for the purpose of comparison; accordingly, I have been to those of Capua[u], Pozzuoli, Pompeii, and Verona, and found, as I expected, many confirmations of what had been stated in Rome. I took with me Professor Cicconetti, one of the best architectural artists in Rome, to Capua and Pozzuoli[x], and have added some photo-engravings from his drawings. I have also been to Pompeii, and to Sicily, to see Syracuse and Taormina, but did not think it necessary to take him there, or add more plates from them. A great work on the Roman amphitheatres in general would be very interesting, but it would be adding too much to the bulk and to the cost of the present work. I believe that enough has been done to illustrate and explain the Colosseum. I should add, that the common idea that this colossal building is named from the Colossal Statue of Nero, is a mistake. That statue, of 120 ft. high, could not have stood on the basement or *podium* on which the Roman antiquaries would place it, and there is good evidence that a Colossal Statue of Gordianus, about half the size, stood there. The great Colossus was moved by Hadrian from the place on which the Temple of Rome was then built, on the east wall of which the Marble Plan of Rome was fixed (now the church of SS. Cosmas and Damian), to the SUMMA SACRA VIA, where it was used as the statue of Apollo or the Sun, to which Hadrian added one of the Moon. Heliogabalus rebuilt this temple of Egyptian granite, of which the columns are still lying about[y] on the edges of the great platform, in the centre of which now stands the church and monastery of S. Francesca Romana, the campanile of which is of about the same height as the Colossus of Nero, and stands near the same place.

---

[u] See Plates XXVII., XXVIII., XXIX., XXX., XXXI.
[x] Ibid. XXXII., XXXIII., XXXIV., XXXV.
[y] See the Part of this work on the Forum Romanum and the Via Sacra for evidence of this.

CONTENTS.—COLOSSEUM.

	PAGE	PLATE
EXCAVATIONS in 1874 and 1875 shew the foundation to be earlier than the Flavian Emperors	1	
Suetonius mentions it among the works of the Flavian Emperors, and *proposed* by Augustus, but not the *beginning* of the work	ib.	
Part of the Substructures is of the time of Nero . . .	ib.	
It contained the Stagna, or old *Naumachia*, under, and the Gymnasium, on the *arena*	ib.	
Nothing certain about the commencement . . .	ib.	
Modern amphitheatre of Statilius Taurus . . .	ib.	
——————— Julius Cæsar	2	
The building of M. Scaurus the ædile, in part temporary, other parts calculated to be eternal, according to Pliny . .	ib.	
This was on the site of the present amphitheatre . .	3	
The Clivus Scauri leads to this site	ib.	
Cavea, a name for an amphitheatre, applied to the galleries and to the dens and passages under the arena . . .	ib.	
Wild beasts brought into Rome by L. L. Metellus, B.C. 251 .	ib.	
Culprits executed by being thrown to wild beasts . .	ib.	
Amphitheatres a Roman invention (?)	4	
Martial's first book, *De Spectaculis*, relates chiefly to this building	ib.	
Mountain of Rhodope represented as a scene . . .	ib.	
Exhibitions in the Circus Maximus by Julius Cæsar . .	ib.	
A separate building required for these exhibitions . .	5	
Gymnasium and *Naumachia* of Nero on this site . .	ib.	
Remains of Aqueducts and Piscina of Nero . . .	ib.	
——————— Piscina of Alexander Severus . . .	ib.	
The Gymnasium of Nero was on the arena of this building .	6	
Brickwork of the time of Nero in several parts . . .	ib.	IX.
A straight vertical joint between the brick galleries and the stone corridors	ib.	II.
The external wall of three periods, — Vespasian, Titus, and Alexander Severus	ib.	I.
The upper storey an addition and an after-thought . .	ib.	II.
The arena full of trap-doors, through which the wild animals were sent up in cages on lifts	7	XVI.
Grooves in the walls for the lifts, and sockets in the pavement for the pivots of the capstans, to wind the cords upon, were visible below	ib.	
The original walls of tufa are interfered with by later walls of brick	ib.	
Inscriptions record the dates of these later walls . .	ib.	
Another inscription gives the word THEATRUM for this amphitheatre	ib.	

	PAGE	PLATE
Supper of Nero in this amphitheatre	7	
Exhibitions of Titus at the dedication	8	
Sea water (?) used in the canals	ib.	
The *Naumachia* were in this amphitheatre	ib.	
The *stagna Neronis* are the canals or reservoirs supplied by aqueducts	ib.	
They are called by Tacitus *Stagnum Navale*	9	
———— by Suetonius a "sea," that is, when the surface was flooded	ib.	
The new *Naumachia* were those of Augustus in Trastevere	ib.	
Stagnum of Agrippa near the Pantheon, supplied by the Aqua Virgo	ib.	
Stagna of Nero supplied by three aqueducts	ib.	
The old *Naumachia* in this building	10	
No *Naumachia* in the amphitheatre of Statilius Taurus	ib.	
The *stagna* were boarded over for the gladiators and the wild beasts, but the boards could be removed easily	ib.	
The canals brought to light in 1812, and more clearly in 1875, with the substructures	ib.	III.
Open channels for running water in many parts of the corridors	11	
Water supplied by aqueducts.—Remains of two *piscinæ*	ib.	
The arena was of wood covered with sand, and full of trap-doors	ib.	
Corbels, or brackets, provided for placing the boards upon when removed	ib.	XVII.
Gymnasium and *Naumachia* of Nero in this building	ib.	
Exterior of the brick theatre left unfinished by Nero, finished by the Flavian Emperors in stone	ib.	I.
Upper gallery of wood destroyed by fire, A.D. 217	12	
The original restoration in stone completed, A.D. 240, under Gordianus	ib.	II.
Vertical piers of travertine introduced to support this upper floor	ib.	
Names of *Stagna* and *Naumachia* used indifferently	ib.	
The *Stagnum* of Nero, "like a sea," was in the Colosseum, when the surface was flooded	ib.	
Some of the walls of the substructures are of brick, of the time of Nero	ib.	
The arches of the dens under the *podium* are of Neronian brickwork	ib.	
The walls of tufa in the substructure are older than the time of Nero	13	
In the superstructure the walls of the front and of the corridors are of travertine	ib.	
At Verona and at Capua are similar remains of aqueducts	ib.	
At Pozzuoli (Puteoli) the arena is of brick, and full of holes for trap-doors	ib.	
———— The surface there seems to have been flooded for the *Naumachia*	ib.	
At Tusculum are canals, as in Rome	14	
In the Colosseum the two sides appear to have been flooded, but not the central passage	ib.	
The two *stagna* would be each 300 ft. long, and about 50 ft. wide	ib.	

CONTENTS.

	PAGE	PLATE
The canals were great cisterns or reservoirs under the boarding	14	
These are 10 ft. deep, but not always the same width	ib.	
The walls to support the canals are unusually thick	ib.	
Canals were lined with lead, one supported on arches, the other on great beams of wood, 8 ft. above the pavement	ib.	X.
The lofty walls of tufa round the edge of the substructure were for the lifts, *not* for the canals	ib.	XV.
Other lifts for men and dogs on each side of the central passage	ib.	
An arch of tufa shaken by an earthquake, supported by a brick wall of the time of Nero, and another half-arch of the same period abutting against it	ib.	IX., XV.
Two small square chambers of Nero are enclosed in the travertine walls of the Flavian Emperors	15	
Augustus intended to build an amphitheatre here, but did not	ib.	
The tufa walls are probably the work of Scaurus, in the time of Sylla	ib.	V.
In these walls are vertical grooves for the lifts and cages	ib.	
Animals were brought from the *vivaria* outside the walls in cages, called *pegmata*	ib.	VI.
Podium protected by wire netting and bars	16	
Seneca describes the *pegmata* in this theatre	ib.	XVI.
One *vivarium* was at the Prætorian Camp, the other at the Sessorium	ib.	
A small stream of water ran in front of the dens	17	
A pit 4 ft. square, for a man to descend to feed the animals, behind each door	ib.	
The tufa walls were in some parts supported by brick walls of the Flavian Emperors	ib.	IX.
Curious wooden framework on the floor of the central passage, believed to have been a cradle, or dry-dock	18	VII.
The general plan of the Colosseum is oval, with galleries, *vomitoria*, &c.	ib.	VIII.
A large part destroyed by having been used as a stone quarry	ib.	
The north side the only part at all perfect	ib.	I.
A great deal of tufa used to fill up between the piers of travertine	ib.	XXI.
The tufa taken from the second wall of Rome close at hand	ib.	
Travertine piers cut through the older wall to carry the upper gallery	19	XX.
The front is of three periods, the upper storey added a century after the rest	ib.	
A great mixture of stone and brick in the construction	ib.	
Name of the the architect not known; Gaudentius only employed upon it	20	
Views on coins, and in sculpture on the tomb of the Aterii, of the first century	ib.	
Machine for raising stones for the walls	21	
No open space under the arena	ib.	
A large number of broken columns and capitals have fallen from the upper gallery on to the arena, and into the *cavea*	ib.	XI.
Representation of the amphitheatre on coins	ib.	XXI.

CONTENTS.

	PAGE	PLATE
Acts of Commodus in this building described by Dion Cassius	22	
The awning of Nero mentioned by Pliny	23	XIII.
Contrivances for supporting it. Masts and corbels	ib.	
Awning of the amphitheatre at Pompeii—shewn in a fresco	24	
Castra Misenatium, for the sailors employed here in furling and unfurling the awning, or *vela*, or *velaria*	ib.	
The wooden upper storey burnt, A.D. 217	25	
A.D. 217. Restored by Heliogabalus, Alexander Severus, and Gordianus	ib.	
The number of wild beasts kept for the shows, A.D. 244	ib.	
100 lions killed at once in the shows	26	
A.D. 320. The building damaged by lightning; restored by Constantine	ib.	
—— 357. Amphitheatre described as perfect by Ammianus Marcellinus	ib.	
—— 445. Restored by Lampadius, after being much damaged by an earthquake	27	
—— 508. Again restored by Venantius Basilius	ib.	
—— 519. Used for shows of wild beasts by Theodoric	ib.	
—— 523. Again used. This is the last occasion mentioned	ib.	
The building apparently perfect in the time of Bede	ib.	
A.D. 1130. The building made part of the fortress of the Frangipani	28	
—— 1227. Half of the fortress given to the Annibaldi by Frederic II., but the grant rescinded by Innocent IV., in 1244	ib.	
—— 1349. The building much damaged by an earthquake	ib.	
—— 1362. It is made common property as a stone-quarry for the great families	29	
———— Several palaces built of stone from this quarry	ib.	
—— 1540. Miracle plays performed there	ib.	
———— The view of Jerusalem belongs to this time	ib.	
—— 1575. Sixtus V. began to make it a cloth manufactory	ib.	
—— 1703. The building again damaged by an earthquake	30	
—— 1728. Benedict XIII. consecrated the whole area as a church	ib.	
—— 1749. The cross and the stations erected by Benedict XIV.	ib.	
—— 1756. A grand mass celebrated here by the Cardinal Vicar	ib.	
———— Palaces built out of the ruins	ib.	
The construction of the inner part is made visible by the demolition of the outer corridor	ib.	
The north-eastern side is nearly perfect	ib.	
One arch of the lower storey restored by Gordianus, A.D. 220—238	31	
A.D. 1810. Excavations begun by the French	ib.	
—— 1812. The walls weeded by them; this was repeated in 1870	ib.	III.
The excavations of the French shew the channels for water	32	
Upper wall hastily built under Gordianus	33	
A.D. 1864-5. Excavations made in search of treasure	ib.	
Many remains of shallow open channels for water	ib.	
Also remains of three reservoirs in the principal gallery	ib.	
And of two *piscinæ* under the Cœlian, on the same level as this gallery	ib.	

	PAGE	PLATE
The excavations of the French were not deep enough for historical purposes	34	
When the boards were removed from the arena they were placed on the corbels or brackets, or large consoles provided for them below	ib.	XVII.
Apollodorus tells Hadrian that he *ought* to have provided space for all this machinery	ib.	
A long and large passage found at the south-east end	ib.	IV.
The original pavement is 21 ft. below the level of the arena	35	
In the ancient tufa walls are vertical grooves for the lifts, on which the *pegmata*, or cages for wild beasts, were placed	ib.	VI.
There are also sockets for the pivots of the capstans	ib.	XVII.
Under the passage is a large drain	ib.	
An ancient iron grating at the mouth of the drain	36	XIX.
The place for the flood-gates is plainly visible	ib.	
Large corbels and brackets for placing the boards of the arena upon, remain in many parts	ib.	XVIII.
The martyrdom of the early Christians took place on the sand of the arena, not on the soil, 21 ft. below it	ib.	
The results of the excavations of 1874-75 were a great surprise	37	
Many of the lower walls belong to the repairs after earthquakes in A.D. 442 and 508	ib.	
A narrow and lofty vaulted chamber on each side of the central passage under the galleries, with six sockets in a line	38	
The wooden frame-work, cradle, or dry dock, fully described	ib.	
The old substructures were evidently retained and used when the upper part was built	39	
Piers of travertine run from top to bottom of the building to carry the upper gallery, and the old tufa walls were cut through	ib.	
THE EVIDENCE OF THE CONSTRUCTION, AND COMPARISON	40-54	
Comparison one of the first principles of Archæology, especially useful for this enormous amphitheatre	40	
AMPHITHEATRE AT CAPUA is almost the same size as that of Rome	40, 41	XXVII.
——— The substructures more perfect than in Rome	41	
——— Aqueduct and drain	ib.	XXVIII.
——— Dens under the *podium*	ib.	
——— Sockets for the pivots for the cages	ib.	XXIX.
——— Arena of brick, not wood, but had apertures for the trap-doors	ib.	XXX.
——— Grooves for covers over them to make them water-tight	ib.	
——— The building is of the time of Hadrian	40	
——— Inscription	41, 42	
—— PUTEOLI, OR POZZUOLI	42, 43	XXXII.
——— Building much smaller than those of Rome or Capua	42	
——— Substructures more perfect and more highly finished	ib.	
——— Arena of brick, with apertures for trap-doors	ib.	
——— Arrangement for fixing the masts or poles for the awning, as in Rome	43	XXXIII.

CONTENTS.

	PAGE	PLATE
Amphitheatre at Puteoli, or Pozzuoli—The building also of the time of Hadrian	43	XXXIV.
——— The vaults preserved and used	42	
——— Verona	43, 44	{XXXI., XXXII.
——— The outer wall almost destroyed	43	
——— Arcade of two lower storeys preserved	44	
——— Comparison of the number that each amphitheatre would contain	ib.	
——— The seats remarkably well preserved	ib.	
——— Dimensions of all the three principal amphitheatres at Rome, Verona, Capua	45	
——— Pola, in Istria	45, 46	
——— Built in white stone, like marble	ib.	
——— Two tiers of arches remain	ib.	
——— And a curious stone parapet, with indications of the awning	ib.	
——— Built against a rocky mountain on the slope	ib.	
——— Substructures in the lower part	ib.	
——— Canal for water visible	ib.	
——— Square towers (for the musicians?)	46	
——— At Nimes there is still a wooden floor, with trap-doors in it	ib.	
——— But the arrangements below are quite different	ib.	
——— At Arles, no substructures visible	ib.	
——— At Bordeaux, the remains are called the *Arènes*, it had a boarded floor	ib.	
Substructures compared	47-52	
Space required for the actors is usually given behind the scenes in theatres, in an amphitheatre under the stage	47	
Vessels employed in the *Naumachia* were usually *rates*, or rowing-boats	ib.	
The battles were of the sailors with swords, not with the boats	ib.	
At Pozzuoli an intermediate passage for messengers	ib.	
In the Colosseum such a passage for the sailors to manage the awning; the corbels that support it are all that remain	ib.	
A great central passage or gulf in all the amphitheatres	ib.	
Traces of a great machine for lifting up vessels at Capua, as in the Colosseum	ib.	
Machines required were numerous and large	48	
Apollodorus told Hadrian that he *ought to have* provided a place for them, but he had not done so	ib.	
Cords for the awning, strong enough to carry an elephant, were called *catadromus*	ib.	
An actor playing the part of Icarus, leaping from the upper gallery, fell dead at the feet of Nero	ib.	
Pegmata were not only cages but wooden machines; these are mentioned by Josephus, Calpurnius, Apuleius, Claudian, Vopiscus, and Martial	49	
The Colossus (on the Summa Sacra Via) was visible from the gulf	ib.	

CONTENTS.

	PAGE	PLATE
That a hundred lions leaped on to the stage or arena, at once, is mentioned not only by Herodian, but by Vopiscus, Julius Capitolinus, Lampridius, Ammianus Marcellinus, Statius	50	
The netting to protect the lower gallery was of gold (or gilt) wire, and was called *retia*, as mentioned by Calpurnius	ib.	
Naval fights sometimes held in the Circus Maximus	ib.	
———— but must have been in the canals of the Colosseum, because Heliogabalus filled them with wine	51	
They were called Circensian games, because sometimes held in the circus	ib.	
Martial clearly distinguishes them	ib.	
That the vaults under the arena were called *caveæ*	ib.	
THE ARENA	52	
Criminals torn to pieces by wild beasts upon it	ib.	
The gladiators and other actors often killed	ib.	
Celebrated gladiators were called for by the people	ib.	
Usually four gates to each amphitheatre	53	
The names of these not easily ascertained	ib.	
One was called *sandapila*, or *sanavivaria*, or *libitinensis*, from *libitina*, "death"	ib.	
Others—Porta Prætoria, Porta Sacra, Porta Cochlea	54	
THE GAMES ON THE ARENA	55	XXII.
———— Great importance attached to them	ib.	
The Emperor went to see the wild beasts fed	ib.	
Tacitus gives an account of games performed under his own direction	ib.	

APPENDIX.

	PAGE	PLATE
SCAURUS	56	
———— The name means club-footed, from the first member of the family, but it was a great family, the *Gens Æmilia*	ib.	
One of the family built the Basilica Æmilia	ib.	
The insane works of Scaurus, their enormous cost	ib.	
His theatre, to hold 80,000 people, could only be on the site of the Colosseum	ib.	
No other theatre is three storeys high	ib.	
Extract from Pliny, relating to Scaurus and his works	ib.	
The amphitheatre of Nero not in the Campus Martius	58	
The great drain	59	XXXVI.

LIST OF PLATES.

I. Exterior—General View.
II. Views of Parts—Upper Gallery, and remains of Reservoir in first gallery.
III. General View in 1812.
IV. View in the Substructures in 1874.
V. View in the Interior in 1874.
VI. Interior—View at the South-east End.
VII. General View in the South-east Part, with the Cradle.
VIII. Plan of the Part Excavated.
IX. Arches in the Substructure, of the first and second century.
X. Canals for the Naval fights.
XI. Two Capitals, one from the upper gallery the other from the lower one.
XII. Restoration of one Compartment.
XIII. Section and Details of one Compartment.
XIV. Section of one Bay, and Plans of the Six Storeys.
XV. A. Probable Restoration of the Stagna, &c. B. Brick arches of Nero supporting a tufa wall and arch.
XVI. Probable Restoration of the Lifts and *Pegmata*, or cages, with the animals leaping out.
XVII. View in the Substructures, shewing the Consoles for placing the boards upon.
XVIII. View and Plan of one Division, shewing the great consoles inserted into the old tufa wall.
XIX. View in the Substructure, with the mouth of the Great Drain, and the iron grating and the grooves of the sluice-gate.
XX. Portion of the Superstructure in the principal gallery.
XXI. View in the Upper Part, with the aperture from which a travertine pier has been carried away.
XXII. The Graffiti: A. and B. Athletes; C. A hunt of wild beasts.
XXIII. A Graffito of the framework of the netting or gilt wire on the *podium*.
XXIV. Representations of the Colosseum on Coins.
XXV. Diagrams of the Coins.
XXVI. A Roman Galley on a Cradle.
XXVII. I. Amphitheatre at Capua. II. Amphitheatre at Pompeii, from a fresco of the first century.
XXVIII. Amphitheatre at Capua—Perspective View and Details.
XXIX. Amphitheatre at Capua—Details.
XXX. Amphitheatre at Capua—Plan of Substructures and Superstructures.
XXXI. Amphitheatre at Verona—A. Exterior. B. Interior.
XXXII. Amphitheatre at Pozzuoli—Arena.
XXXIII. Amphitheatre at Pozzuoli—Plan.
XXXIV. Amphitheatre at Pozzuoli—Views and Section.
XXXV. Amphitheatre at Pozzuoli—Views in the Interior, subterranean part.
XXXVI. Colosseum—Plan of the Great Drain.

THE FLAVIAN AMPHITHEATRE,

COMMONLY CALLED

THE COLOSSEUM.

The importance of the great excavations made in 1874 and 1875 in this colossal building, and the evidence obtained by them for the history of the fabric, can hardly be overrated. It is now evident that the substructures under the level of the base of the *podium* are (when not rebuilt) the earliest part of it, and considerably earlier than the time of the Flavian Emperors, who built the magnificent front and corridors around a theatre previously existing on that site.

This great amphitheatre is indeed enumerated by Suetonius[a] among the works of Vespasian, and he adds that an amphitheatre in the centre of Rome had been projected by Augustus. But he does not say that it was then begun, and it seems evident that it was in use in the time of Nero in connection with his great golden house, and was partly built by him, but the exterior left unfinished. It contained the *stagna*, or *stagnum navale*, called also *Vetus Naumachia*, made at a still earlier period on the same site, which was called the old *naumachia*, when Augustus made new and larger ones in the Trastevere. It also contained his gymnasium on the boarded floor, or *arena*, of the theatre, over the *stagna maritima*, or canals for the sham naval fights. We know nothing certain as to the exact date of the commencement, but the building was continued during the reign of Vespasian and till the second year of Titus, namely A.D. 80, when it was dedicated. There is no evidence to prove that it was *commenced* even under Nero.

Pliny gives an account of a wooden amphitheatre built by Statilius Taurus, which was in the Campus Martius; he says[b] that

"he made two large theatres of wood, morticed together in a singular manner, and suspended so as to turn freely, in which on both sides were exhibited the afternoon shows of plays, then turning them round—nor were the scenes interrupted by the turning—quickly turning to face each other, and (intermediate) boards falling down; and the two parts held together by horns. He made an amphitheatre and exhibited the gladiatorial shows, carrying with him

---

[a] "Fecit et nova opera ... item amphitheatrum urbe media, ut destinasse compererat Augustum." (Suetonius, Vespasianus, c. 9.)
[b] Plinii Nat. Hist., lib. xxxvi. c. 24, s. 8.

the consent of the greater part of the Roman people. For which was most to be admired, the inventor or the thing invented? The work or its author? To have thought of such a thing, or to have carried it out? To exhibit it, or permit it? Upon all these points there was a *furor* of the people, to dare to sit on such an unsafe and unstable seat."

This gave the form of an amphitheatre, or a theatre round at both ends, and not with one side flat, as in the other theatres, but the two names are often used indifferently; this set the fashion, and Julius Cæsar followed it a few years afterwards in his great wooden amphitheatre; but the turning round had been abandoned, and the advantage of substructures under the stage would become apparent for making the shows still more popular. It is mentioned as being very large, to admit of naval fights with large vessels, but this was in the Campus Martius, and was a temporary structure only, as stated by Dio Cassius[c].

The Theatre of M. Scaurus, the ædilis, is mentioned by Pliny[d] as being on an enormous scale,—the *scena* of triple height, with 360 columns, and he enumerates it among the *insane* works that were made at his private cost. The upper part was of wood.

"He made, during the time that he was *ædile*, the greatest work that ever was made by human hands, not for temporary use only, but destined for eternity also[e]. This was *a theatre*; the *scena* of it was *triple* in height. There were three hundred and sixty columns in that building, of which six were brought from Hymettus, not without reproach at the sumptuousness of a citizen. The lowest part of the *scena* was of marble, the middle part of glass, an unheard-of luxury in that kind of work; the highest part of gilt wood. The columns were at least thirty-eight feet high; the images between the columns were three thousand in number; the *cavea* itself held eighty thousand people."

Scena usually means the stage for the actors to perform upon, but how could this be triple, and three storeys high? To what other site in Rome, excepting this great amphitheatre, which held 80,000 people, could all this possibly apply?

This was in the time of Sylla; the site is not mentioned. Dio

---

[c] Dionis Hist., lib. xliii. c. 25.

[d] "Non patiemur duos Caios, vel duos Nerones, ne hac quidem gloria famæ frui: docebimusque etiam insaniam eorum victam privatis operibus M. Scauri, cujus nescio an ædilitas maxime prostraverit mores civiles, majusque sit Sullæ malum, tanta privigni potentia, quam proscriptio tot millium. Hic fecit in ædilitate sua opus maximum omnium, quæ unquam fuere humana manu facta, non temporaria mora, verum etiam æternitatis destinatione. Theatrum hoc fuit. Scena ei triplex in altitudinem, CCCLX columnarum, in ea civitate, quæ sex Hymettias non tulerat sine probro civis amplissimi. Ima pars scenæ e marmore fuit: media e vitro, inaudito etiam postea genere luxuriæ: summa, e tabulis inauratis." (Plinii Nat. Hist., lib. xxxvi. 24. 7.)

[e] The meaning of this appears to be that the upper part was temporary, and was removed shortly afterwards, as is related in another place; but the substructures were permanent, or eternal.

mentions[f] a great flood in the time of Julius Cæsar, A.U.C. 694 (B.C. 59), extending as far as the great wooden theatre. The *clivus Scauri* descends from that part of the Cœlian Hill on which the Claudium was afterwards built, to the level of the road or street that leads from the Circus Maximus to the Colosseum. All this was under water at the time of the great flood in 1871.

The name of *cavea* is said by Lipsius[g] to be applied to the amphitheatre by several classical authors. He cites Ammianus Marcellinus[h], Prudentius[i], and others, as using that name for it; but they probably meant not only the hollow where the seats were placed, but also the hollow space under the arena, with the dens for the wild beasts, to which that name was also applied. Statius[j] uses the word *cavea* for the cages for lions, with doors round them, the closing of which frightened the lions. Livy mentions iron cages (*caveas*), but Claudian says that the animals were shut into wooden houses[k]; probably the cages in which they were brought from the *vivaria* were of iron, but wooden cages (*pegmata*) were sufficient to place upon the lifts, and send the animals up to the trap-doors[l].

Long before this time wild beasts had been brought into Rome for exhibition, in the year 502 of Rome[m] (B.C. 251). Lucius Cæcilius Metellus, the pro-consul, when he had conquered Sicily from the Carthaginians, brought into Rome 142 elephants taken from them, which he exhibited in the Circus Maximus. The custom of sending culprits to execution by being torn to pieces by wild beasts is very ancient in the East, as the well-known history of Daniel and the lions clearly shews. The invention of circuses and amphitheatres for the exhibition of hunts is attributed to the Athenians by Cassiodorus[n]; but it is generally thought to be a Roman invention, although the name is Greek. Livy[o] records that in the

---

[f] Dionis Hist. Rom., lib. xxxvii. c. 58.

[g] Justi Lipsii de Amphitheatro liber, 1684; *et apud* Grævii Thesaurus Ant. Rom., Lugd. Bat. 1699, folio, vol. ix.

[h] "Alter in Amphitheatrali *cavea* cum adfuturus spectaculis introiret." (Ammiani Marcellini, lib. xxix. 1, Valentinianus, &c., A.D. 371.)

[i] "Quid pulvis *Caveæ* semper funebris et illa Amphitheatralis spectacula tristia pompæ." (Prudentius contra Symmachum, lib. i. l. 384-5.)

[j] ". . . . stat cardine aperto
Infelix *Cavea* et clausis circum undique portis
Hoc licuisse nefas pavidi timuere Leones."
(Statii Silvæ, lib. ii. 5; Leo Mansuetus imp., l. xi.)

[k] Claudianus de laudibus Stilicho, lib. iii.

[l] Lipsius has collected a host of extracts from the classical authors respecting this great amphitheatre, and the arrangement and amusements in it; but as the substance of these is given in the usual classical dictionaries, especially Dr. Smith's, and they do not affect the history of the building, it is not necessary to repeat them here.

[m] Polybii Hist., i. 84.

[n] Cassiodori Variar., lib. v. epist. 42.

[o] Livii Hist., xxxix. 22.

year 568 of Rome (B.C. 217), Marcus Fulvius Nobilior, after the war with the Ætolians, exhibited for the first time "the athletes, and the hunting of lions and panthers."

In the year 586 of Rome (B.C. 227), Livy[p] also relates that "P. Cornelius Scipio Nasica and P. Lentulus, the *Ædiles Curules*, exhibited 63 African wild beasts, 40 bears and elephants." Martial, who was a contemporary of Vespasian and Titus, Domitian and Trajan, has numerous epigrams on the subject of scenes that took place in the Amphitheatre of the Cæsars, by which he obviously means the Colosseum; a large part of his first book, *de Spectaculis*, relates to such scenes on this spot[q]. On one occasion, he mentions that a representation of Rhodope (a mountain in Thrace), where Orpheus sang, with the rocks and woods, was given upon the stage. It is evident from this, and from many other passages in the classical authors, that the stage, called the ARENA, was on the level of the *podium*, and visible to the people in every part of the great theatre; and not at the bottom of a pit twenty feet deep, where only a small number could have seen it, although some persons maintain this opinion.

We are told by Suetonius again[r] in the life of Julius Cæsar, that—

"these spectacles were exhibited in the Circus Maximus, in the circuit of the Euripus, with races of *bigæ*, and *quadrigæ*[s], and horses, with the young nobles for riders or drivers. Hunting of wild beasts for five days, and sham fights, castles being made over the *metæ*; a *stadium* or stage was made in the Campus Martius for the athletes, and naval fights in the smaller *codeta*[t]," (which was in the Trastevere, and probably on the site on which Augustus afterwards made his great Naumachia,) "and in the lake then dug out, *biremes*, and *triremes*, and *quadriremes*[u] of the Tyrian and Ægyptian fleets, in great number, fought together. The whole population of Rome was attracted by those exhibitions, so that the streets and houses were quite empty; and from the pressure of the crowd several persons were crushed to death, including two senators."

These attractive exhibitions obviously required a building especially prepared and calculated for them, which Augustus proposed to provide, but left for his successors to carry out the plan. It is probable that in the time of Nero the great work was commenced on the site of that of Scaurus[v], and making use of his substructures,

---

[p] Ibid., xliv. 18.
[q] Sig. Fabio Gori has collected all these passages, and given an Italian translation of them in his work entitled *Le memorie storiche, i giuochi e gli scavi dell' anfiteatro Flavio*. Roma, 1874.
[r] Suetonii Julius Cæsar, cap. 39.
[s] That is, chariots on two wheels and others on four wheels.
[t] "In minore *Codeta*, defosso lacu."
[u] Vessels with two, or three, or four rows of oars.
[v] See Plate IX.

was carried on gradually, and eventually completed in this colossal building.

We are told that Nero made a Gymnasium and Naumachia in connection with his great palace, or golden house, and no vestiges of any such buildings have been found [w], unless both were combined in the great building called the Colosseum from its colossal size. The amphitheatre at Capua, being also a very large one, is said to have been called a Colosseum, but on rather doubtful authority. It is, however, certain that the name had nothing to do with the Colossus of Nero. It is evident that Nero made a great reservoir of water on this spot, which was supplied from his aqueduct on the Cœlian [x]. The *specus*, or channel for this water, remains in the wall of the Claudium, on the northern side, opposite the Palatine; and at the north-east corner of that part of the Cœlian Hill on which the Claudium stood, are remains of a *piscina* of the time of Nero, obviously intended for the filtering-place before the water went across into the Colosseum. At a short interval only, about a hundred yards to the south of this, is another *piscina* of the time of Alexander Severus, when the upper storey was added, and the whole building repaired after the great fire. It is quite possible that Nero made a large oval reservoir on this spot, adjoining to his palace, supplied by an aqueduct, similar to the great oval reservoir on the Palatine, near the house of Augustus, excavated in 1872. The Romans were fond of the oval form for a sheet of water; the basin of the fountain of Domitian, also on the Palatine, is oval; and the remains of the fountain of Juturna in the Forum Romanum shew the same form [y]. The long canals for the vessels to float in, which are ten feet deep, about the same width, and the same height

---

[w] Every square yard of this part of Rome has been trenched in the search for statues in the seventeenth and eighteenth centuries, and records of these numerous excavations are carefully preserved in the Miscellanea of Fea. Had there been any such building as would be required for this purpose anywhere near his palace, it must have come to light, and nothing of the kind has been found.

[x] See Plate II.

[y] The basin of Nero was possibly cut through the layer of tufa, which underlies the whole soil of Rome, down to the clay under it. In some excavations made under my direction in a cave under the Aventine, near the Marmorata, which was the mouth of the Aqua Appia, a level bed of white clay was found under the tufa rock of which the Aventine Hill consists; this would account for the walls in the central part built of concrete and brick, on this clay foundation, having been frequently damaged by earthquakes, while the great stone arcades, being built upon the tufa rock, did not suffer from the shocks. Clay is always a bad foundation to build upon, and there are always settlements in buildings that rest upon it. The objection to this theory is, that the surface of the water would be twenty-one feet below the arena and the foot of the *podium*.

above the original pavements, are not so early as the time of Nero; they are of the third century, with many later repairs.

To include the Gymnasium in the same building, Nero made a wooden floor over the reservoir, which he could remove and replace at pleasure; this was covered with sand for the athletes to wrestle upon, and became THE ARENA. Around this great oval basin galleries were erected for the spectators, which were gradually enlarged and raised higher as the seats were further off; and the great stone arcades of the Flavian Emperors, with the corridors in them, are built round those older galleries, which were chiefly faced with brick. Several of the arches of the galleries, in the fine brickwork of Nero, remain in the Colosseum[z]; and the stone arcades were evidently built up against them without any junction between the two in any part. The bricks on the side of the arch next the stone piers of the corridors, are in many places cut in half, to make way for the stone piers. The straight vertical joints between the brick galleries and the stone arcades are often two or three inches wide; this may be the effect of an earthquake, but there is no bonding between one and the other. The enormous arcades and corridors are in themselves a gigantic work, and it was evidently difficult to obtain so great a supply of materials.

The external wall and corridor are of three periods. The first is the ground floor only, with the Doric order of columns; the first and second floor, with the Corinthian columns, belong to the second period, and it is a little later than the lowest part, but not with any long interval; the upper floor is an addition of the third century, and replaces a wooden storey.

In the interior of the building, as we are told in the anonymous chronicle published by Eccard, which is good authority [a], Vespasian dedicated the three lower steps, and Titus added two others to the three placed by his father. The wooden gallery, built upon the top of the great corridors or arcades (for the plebs), appears to have been an afterthought, not part of the original design, but an addition obviously called for. The large space at that height gave accommo-

---

[z] See Plate IX.

[a] In the ancient catalogue of the Emperors and their works, known as "Catalogus Viennensis Impp. Rom. apud Eccard.," under Vespasian, it is stated that he dedicated the first three steps of the amphitheatre, implying that three were already finished even in his time.
[A.D. 70.] "Hic prior tribus gradibus amphitheatrum dedicavit;"
That Titus added two more.
[A.D. 81.] "Hic amphitheatrum a tribus gradibus patris sui dura adjecit."
And further, that Domitian completed the building up to the clypea, that is, the top cornice at that time, when the upper storey was of wood.
[A.D. 92—96.] "Domitianus Imp. ... Amphitheatrum usque ad clypea."

dation for an enormous number of people, which could not have been given before, to see what was going on upon the ARENA or STAGE during the performance. This had numerous trap-doors in it, under which were lifts for the wild beasts in their cages to be sent up on to the stage when wanted. The performance was in many respects like our pantomimes. There are evident traces of the lifts below, by the vertical grooves in the tufa walls for them to slide up and down [b]; and recesses remain in these walls for the counter-weights also to work in, with holes in the pavement for the sockets of pivots for the capstans necessary to wind up the cords, and loose them as required. These original walls, with the grooves for the old machines, are in many parts interfered with by more modern walls built up between them, probably in the fifth and sixth centuries, when great repairs were made after earthquakes, or perhaps rendered necessary by the weight of the water under the wooden floor in the central part.

Two important inscriptions relating to the history of the building have been preserved [c]: one found in 1810 on the western side, recording the repairs after an earthquake by the præfect Basilius, A.D. 445; the other in 1813, recording similar repairs by Lampadius, A.D. 508. Three of the marble seats were also brought to light, one with the number XVIII., another with the word EQUITI, the third, with an inscription, the beginning of which is broken off:—

```
         tr IB IN . THEATR . LEGE . PL . VI
         vind ICET . P . X . II.
```

. This is important, because it shews the use of the word THEATRUM [d], and not AMPHITHEATRUM, for the colossal building; which agrees with the usage of Dio and other contemporary authors, who always call it THEATRUM *par eminence*, or the great theatre of Rome, there being no need to distinguish it further.

The following extracts from Dio Cassius can only apply to the great amphitheatre:—

"Such was the shamelessness of Nero, that he himself drove chariots in public; and, sometimes, having slain wild beasts, and having suddenly introduced water into the area, he made a naval battle; and then withdrawing the water, he introduced the gladiatorial strife. Then again introducing it, he gave in public a sumptuous supper. Tigellinus was the prefect (or overseer) of the supper, and it was a supper of the grandest magnificence, arranged in this manner. In the middle of the amphitheatre and in the water great wooden wine-casks were

---

[b] See Plates V., VI., XV., XVI.
[c] Photos., Nos. 3136, 3137.
[d] Photos., No. 3204.

placed, and upon them a floor of planks[e] was laid, and around this, booths and small chambers were erected[f]."

"Nero had various kinds of shows in the amphitheatre, sometimes filling it with sea-water, in which fishes and sea monsters swam, and made a naval fight between the Persians and the Athenians; then suddenly withdrawing the water, and drying the ground, he ordered a number of men on foot to rush in, not singly, but in numbers and close together[g]."

"When he (Titus) dedicated the theatre for hunting, and the thermæ called after him, he exhibited many wonderful things. Cranes fought and four elephants, nine thousand wild boars and other beasts were killed, which women, even some of noble rank, had brought together. Many contests, also, on foot, and naval fights took place, for suddenly filling the amphitheatre with water, he introduced horses and bulls, and other tame animals, who had been taught to act in the water as on land. He also introduced men in ships, who, in the guise of Corcyrians and Corinthians, imitated a naval battle[h]."

In another chapter Dio repeats the same account, with the addition of "a public supper[i]." This shews that the arrangements in the amphitheatre were the same in the time of Nero as in the time of Commodus, when Dio was himself present, and describes what he saw. If the water was really *sea*-water, it could only have been in the canals. The fact of three aqueducts having converged to this point to bring water to the great building, makes it most probable that the water was not *really sea-water*, but perhaps had *sea-weed* inserted in it to suit the fishes and the sea monsters. Suetonius also mentions the *naumachia* in the amphitheatre[j] in the time of Domitian, among the magnificent shows that he provided for the people. Dio clearly distinguishes between the Amphitheatre of Nero and that of Statilius Taurus in the Campus Martius, which he also calls *Theatrum Tauri*[k].

The word *stagnum* is commonly translated *pond*, but it does not necessarily mean *only* a pond; any reservoir of water might be so called; the *castellum aquæ*, or large cistern for the water supplied by the aqueducts, was also a *stagnum*. The "Stagna Neronis[l]"

---

[e] This platform was, perhaps, constructed of a great number of timbers fastened together. Lucan has described such a platform with a tower on it. (Pharsal., lib. iv. 420, sqq.)

[f] Dionis Hist., lib. lxii. cap. 15.

[g] Ibid., lib. lxi. Nero, vi. c. 9 and 17.

[h] Ibid., lib. lxvi. c. 25.

[i] Ibid., lib. lxii. Nero, iii. c. 15, and 20, 22.

[j] "Spectacula magnifica assidue et sumptuosa edidit, non in amphitheatro modo, verum et in circo . . . ac in amphitheatro, navale quoque." (Suetonii Domitianus, c. 4.)

[k] Dionis Hist., lib. lxii. c. 18.

[l] "Omnis Cæsareo cedat labor Amphitheatro:
 Unum pro cunctis fama loquatur opus. . ."
  (Martialis, De Spectaculis, Epigr. 1.)
 "Hic, ubi conspicui venerabilis Amphitheatri
 Erigitur moles, stagna Neronis erant." (Ibid., Epigr. 2.)

are mentioned by Martial, as well as by Tacitus [m], who also mentions a *stagnum navale* among the games in the public theatre of Augustus [n].

Suetonius [o] compares the Stagnum of Nero to a "sea" surrounded by the buildings of a city: a strong expression, which shews that there were some buildings immediately round it. The Claudium on the Cœlian, the Porticus Liviæ on the Summa Sacra Via, and Porticus of Nero himself on the Esquiline, would be visible on three sides of it. The representation of this great building on the coin of Titus was evidently taken from the design of the architect. It represents a building of two storeys only, with gigantic statues under each of the arches of the corridors.

The *new naumachia* made by Augustus in the Trastevere were larger reservoirs for the same purpose; this *naumachia* is also called a *stagnum* by Tacitus [p], who describes a similar scene in the *stagnum* of Agrippa [q] (which was in his *thermæ*, near the Pantheon), with the letting in the water suddenly for a naval battle; and then letting it off again as suddenly, and having a supper in the same place; he also mentions the *stagna* of Nero [r], and the *stagnum navale* of Augustus [s]. The *stagnum* of Agrippa was supplied with water by his aqueduct (the Virgo), and it has been mentioned that those of Nero were supplied by three aqueducts, two from the Cœlian and one from the Esquiline. The remains of the *specus* and of the *piscinæ* have been already mentioned [t]. There are slight remains of three reservoirs in the gallery, lined with the peculiar cement used only for the aqueducts, called *opus signinum*. From the Esquiline the water was brought to the Amphitheatre in leaden pipes, after serving the Thermæ of Titus; a quantity of these leaden pipes have been found in excavations at different periods [u], as recorded at the time by eye-witnesses, and some of them are still preserved as mementoes in the office of the Municipality.

---

[m] Taciti Ann., xv. 42.
[n] Ibid., lib. xiv. c. 15.
[o] Ibid., c. 31.
[p] "... lacu in ipso navale prælium adornatur, ut quondam Augustus, structo eis Tiberim stagno; sed levibus navigiis et minori copiâ ediderat." (Taciti Annal., xii. 56.)
[q] "Igitur in stagno Agrippæ (Tigellinus) fabricatus est ratem, cui superpositum convivium aliarum tractu navium moveretur.... volucres et feras diversis e terris, et animalia maris Oceano abusque petiverat." (Taciti Annal., lib. xv. c. 37.)
[r] Taciti Ann., lib. xv. c. 42.
[s] Ibid., lib. xiv. c. 15.
[t] See p. 5.
[u] Santi-Bartoli (in a paper printed in the *Miscellanea*, by Fea, vol. i. p. ccxxiii.) states that in his time a quantity of leaden water-pipes, which carried water from the Thermæ of Titus to the Colosseum, were found in an orchard north of the Colosseum.

Suetonius[v] mentions that some of the amusements for the people provided by Nero were held in the wooden amphitheatre of Statilius Taurus in the Campus Martius, but he mentions the *naumachia* separately, and we have no account of any *stagnum* having been there, nor is it probable, as it could only have been supplied with water by the aqueduct of Agrippa, and it was originally built before that aqueduct was made. The *naumachia* were an essential part of the amusements of many Roman amphitheatres, and there are considerable remains of the canals for them at Capua and at Tusculum.

Suetonius, in his life of Titus, thus writes :—

"Having dedicated the *Amphitheatre*, and having quickly completed the Thermæ hard by, he provided the most magnificent and expensive entertainment [for the people]. He exhibited a naval fight *in the old Naumachia*, and also a combat of gladiators; and, in one day also, five thousand wild beasts of all sorts [w]."

Those *stagna* were boarded over for the gladiators and for the wild beasts, but the boards could be moved and naval fights exhibited at other times, as had previously been done on the same spot in "the old Naumachia[x]." The account of the scenes that took place here, described by Dio Cassius, agrees with this. The excavations made in 1814 shewed that there were canals built of brick running parallel to each other the whole length of the area, as at Capua, and in several other amphitheatres; these were, no doubt, for the naval fights. The vessels were probably towed along from the opposite ends, and where they met were lashed together, and the sailors of one of them tried to board the other: to prevent this was the naval fight. Probably the space between these two canals was flooded when the water was let in. These canals, reservoirs, or *stagna*, were brought out more clearly in 1875, and the substructures which supported them were then made visible[y].

---

[v] Suetonii Nero, c. 12.

[w] This dedication is referred to by Eutropius thus,—

"Hic [Titus] amphitheatrum Romæ ædificavit, et in dedicatione ejus quinque millia ferarum occidit." (Eutropius, lib. vii. c. 14. See also Cassiodorus, Variar. l. v. op. 42. Opera omnia, ed. 1679, fol. vol. i. p. 94, c. 2.)

The account by Suetonius, writing some eighty or ninety years previously, is very clear :—

"Amphitheatro dedicato, thermisque juxta celeriter exstructis, munus edidit apparatissimum largissimumque. Dedit et navale prœlium in veteri naumachia: ibidem et gladiatores : atque uno die quinque millia omne genus ferarum." (Suetonius Titus, c. 7.)

These old *naumachia* were the same as the *stagnum natale*, the old place for such amusements on the spot. They have been supposed to be the Naumachia of Augustus in the Trastevere, but without authority ; and the mention of the gladiators in connection with them implies that it was at the same place.

[x] See Photos., Nos. 3268, 3269, and the drawing of this restored in Plates VII. and XV.

[y] See p. 37, and Plate X.

In the corridors are many remains of the open channels for the water brought from the aqueducts. They are not more than a foot deep, often not so much, being frequently much worn: when perfect they are nearly of that depth, and are lined with the peculiar cement used only for the aqueducts, called *Opus signinum*, and in Italian, *Coccio-pesto*. This is an invariable mark of an aqueduct; this open channel must have been brought across from the Cœlian reservoir on the colonnade, shewn upon the coin of Titus. The system of drainage for the rain-water is quite distinct from the channels for the aqueducts.

The floor of the ARENA for the gymnastics and the slaughter of wild beasts was of wood covered with sand; on one occasion (as we have shewn) placed upon wine-barrels in the parts that had been flooded; the boards could be removed or replaced with facility. It was full of trap-doors with lifts under them, some large for the animals to jump through, these are over the passage round the outer line, in front of the dens under the *podium*; others smaller for men and dogs for the hunt; these are on each side of the central passage. Large corbels, with bold projections for placing the boards upon when removed from the floor of the stage, are provided over the stream of water, in front of the *podium*, but at a lower level; they are in pairs six feet apart, and also served to stiffen the lower end of the masts or poles for the awning; on the surface of them a notch is cut to place the boards upon, and ready access was given by the passage in front of the *podium*. The gymnasium and the *stagna* were in one and the same building used for both purposes, and Nero probably built galleries of brick round it for the accommodation of the people, according to the fashion of his time. The exterior was left unfinished for some years, and completed of stone by Titus and the Flavian emperors on a more magnificent scale. The space for the upper galleries was afterwards very much enlarged by building them upon the magnificent double arcades of stone round it, and so completing the great building known as the Colosseum. The straight vertical joint, which is plainly seen between the old brickwork within and these stone galleries and corridors, and the want of any bond between them, is thus accounted for[z]. The upper gallery for the common people was an addition to the original design over these arcades and corridors, and was originally of wood; it was destroyed by fire caused by lightning in the time

[z] Photos., Nos. 1761, 1762.

of the Emperor Macrinus, A.D. 217, and restored in stone in about twenty-three years, having been completed by Gordianus III., A.D. 240. To support this upper gallery of stone at that enormous height vertical piers of travertine are introduced, cutting through the walls of the lower galleries from top to bottom [a]; these walls are of tufa, faced with brick. In several instances portions of these piers of travertine have been removed for building purposes in the Middle Ages, and the space that had been occupied by the piers is left empty. The brick facing of the walls on either side stands just as firm without these travertine piers as with them, a clear proof that their object was to support the upper gallery when it was rebuilt in stone, and not to support the brick walls of the lower one through which they were cut, although they appear to do so. This accounts for the fact that in the brick arches of construction (as they are called), the bricks, originally two feet square, are cut down to a few inches [b].

The names of *stagnum* or *stagna*, and *naumachia*, are evidently used indifferently by the classical authors. It has been already mentioned that in the description of the far-famed palace of Nero, reaching from the Esquiline to the Palatine Hill, Suetonius also speaks of it having "a lake (*stagnum*) like a sea surrounded by buildings, after the fashion of cities [c]." This could only apply to the Colosseum, and from this it would appear that in the time of Nero the surface could be flooded when required for theatrical display. Probably in two parts, divided by the great central passage or the gulf, and these two parts were called the *stagna*. It must always be remembered that the one object of the whole building was a theatre for the amusement of the people, very much like the Crystal Palace for London.

The probability is that some of the walls of the buildings of Nero round his *stagna* were used as part of the lower galleries of the Colosseum; these walls and arches are a mixture of stone and brick, and some of the brickwork has quite the character of the time of Nero, so well known to Roman antiquaries as the finest brickwork in the world [d]. The excavations of 1874 and 1875 have confirmed

---

[a] Photos., No. 3279, and Plates II. and XX.

[b] It is important to notice this, because some able architects did not see it at first sight, and imagined that these brick arches rested upon the stone piers, which was evidently not really the case, though it appears to be so.

M. Viollet-le-Duc, one of the most eminent architects of our time, says that an experienced architect would cut through old tufa walls of this kind as easily, and with as little scruple, as he would cut through cheese, and the brick facing made no material difference.

[c] ". . ., item stagnum maris instar, circumseptum ædificiis ad urbium speciem." (Suetonii Nero, c. 31.)

[d] Photos., Nos. 3282, 3285.

this opinion; there is a series of arches over the entrance to the dens for wild beasts, under the *podium*, which are distinctly of the well-known brickwork of Nero. Some of these walls of the substructure are earlier than the time of Nero, others are later, with large repairs of the fifth and sixth centuries. The great external corridors are entirely built of stone, and are evidently added on to the galleries; there is a straight joint from top to bottom in all parts, and no junction with ties anywhere in the original construction. The construction of the walls of the Colosseum in the interior shews such evident patchwork of different periods, that it is impossible to believe they were all built within ten years, as is commonly said.

In many other places besides Rome, part of the amphitheatre was at times filled with water for the exhibition of naval fights, indeed the actual remains of the conduit for the water are shewn in more than one place. At Verona, where the area of the amphitheatre is considerably below the level of the adjacent ground, the conduit or *specus* is shewn at the level of the second gallery, and below that of the upper one, and the water seems to have gone down a cascade into the end of a corridor or passage at the lowest level. At Capua the aqueduct for bringing in the water and a large drain for carrying it off rapidly, are shewn, both at a low level[e]. In either of these cases, the substructure is to a great extent filled up with vaulted brick chambers separated by passages, but the walls and vaults are lined with that peculiar cement that resists water, and thus a great part of the surface may have been covered with water to a sufficient depth for the purpose. At Puteoli or Pozzuoli, near Naples, the underground chambers of the amphitheatre are unusually perfect, and the brick floor over them, with numerous trap-doors, with deep grooves round the edge for a cover to fit tight over them when the surface was flooded[f]; at Tusculum one of the canals has been excavated, the other is still buried. From these it appears that the naval fights were represented as in a river, rather than in the sea. There are two long straight passages, the whole length of the central space, with no doors in them; and the walls are faced with the peculiar water-cement. These passages are wide enough for a trireme to pass along, and it seems more probable that the naval fight took place on this sort of river than on the whole surface, which would have been necessary for a sea-fight.

This obviously applies equally to the Colosseum, where the great

[e] See Plate XXI.   [f] See Plate XXII.

excavations in 1875 shewed that there were *two* canals on each side of a great central passage, parallel to it and to each other, with an interval of about six feet between them, which was flooded when the water was let in to make two fine sheets of water the whole length of the arena, each about three hundred feet long and fifty feet wide[g]. These were just under the boards, which were carried away and placed on the corbels provided for them in front of the *podium*, but below the level of the base of it. The walls to support this body of water are unusually thick, and have buttresses on both sides for greater strength[h]. The two canals were not of the same width, but of the same depth, ten feet, with passages, ten feet high, under them. The most narrow canal is nearest to the centre, and has been supported on great beams of wood resting upon the massive walls; the places for the ends of the beams are left at short intervals in the walls. The other and wider canal had brick arches to support it, which remain, though the great leaden cistern in the form of a canal has been destroyed.

The two great lofty walls of tufa are independent of the brick walls supporting the canals. The lifts, or *pegmata* for the wild beasts, were placed in the outer passage between the two tufa walls, just under the edge of the *podium*[i]. On each side of the central passage are a series of small square closets for lifts, for men and dogs to ascend from the passages at the lowest level to the floor above, through the trap-doors. These continue visible for the whole length of the surface and central passage. The pavement of these passages is of brick in herring-bone fashion, such as was common in Rome during the first three centuries. Some persons have imagined that the walls are built upon this pavement, but if this is the case anywhere, of which there is no evidence, it would only be a part of the later repairs of the fifth or sixth century.

There are some portions of a third wall of tufa parallel to the other two, and within them; this has been much damaged, and very little of it remains. In one place, near the south-west end, there is an arch in this tufa wall apparently much shaken by an earthquake, and consequently supported by two brick arches of Nero, one under it, the other abutting against it, like a flying

---

[g] See Plate XV.
[h] Photos., No. 3268, 3269.
[i] Photos., Nos. 3203, 3205, 3282, 3283. In some parts a brick wall of the fifth or sixth century has been introduced between the two old tufa walls, during the repairs after the earthquakes. This is at first sight rather puzzling, until it is examined and properly considered.

buttress in a medieval church [j]. The long, thin bricks of the time of Nero are perfectly well known to all Roman archæologists, and are only met with in buildings of his time. Two other small square chambers, one on either side of the great central passage, also remain at the south end, with an arch of the brickwork of Nero on each side [k]. These chambers are enclosed in stone, so that half the thickness of the wall is of brick, the other half of travertine. This wall, therefore, affords conclusive evidence that there was a great theatre on this spot before the time of Vespasian, and that the tufa walls are *earlier* than the time of Nero.

We are expressly told that Augustus had intended to build an amphitheatre here, but had not done so. We have no mention of Claudius having built one, we are therefore driven back to an earlier period (probably to the amphitheatre of Scaurus, in the time of Sylla) for the date of the tufa walls, with the grooves for lifts, or *pegmata*, in them, as has been mentioned. Outside of these great walls of tufa, and under the path in front of the *podium*, are a number of dens for lions, or other wild beasts of that size [l]. And in front of each is an opening large enough for the animal to pass through into a cage placed on a lift in the passage between the two tufa walls, and in each of these walls are vertical grooves cut in them for the lifts to work up and down; also deeper grooves, about a yard long, for the counter-weights [m]. Behind the place for each cage, in the passage, is a socket let into the pavement for a pivot to work in [n], apparently for a capstan or post to wind the cord upon to pull up the lifts and cages. These cages were of wood, and called *pegmata*. The word *pegma* is used in different senses by Pliny, Martial, and others for a wooden box, cage, or framework; and the wild beasts were brought in such cages from the places where they were kept outside the walls, called *vivaria*.

There were two *vivaria*, one on the southern side of the Prætorian Camp, of which there are some remains. The evidence for this is an inscription of the time of Gordianus III. (A.D. 241), which mentions a keeper of the *vivarium* [o] belonging to the sixth

---

[j] Photos., No. 3271.
[k] Photos., Nos. 3285, 3286.
[l] For elephants there are four larger dens provided, two on either side of the central passage. See the Plan.
[m] Photos., No. 3282.
[n] See Plates XVI., XVII.

[o] This *vivarium* is a triangular piece of ground, the wide end of which touches the wall of the Amphitheatrum Castrense; the narrow end is only just wide enough for the body of a man to pass through an aperture made in it, as the ground is between a wall of

Cohort of the Prætorian and Urban[p] Guards. The other was on the southern side of the Sessorium, which was both a palace and a Prætorian Camp.

The *podium* was protected by nets[q]; and there were projecting bars for rollers, which turned round when touched, so that the claws of an animal could have no hold upon them: these are mentioned by Calpurnius. Seneca, in his Epistle (88) uses the word *pegma* for "a wooden machine in the theatres," which raised and lowered itself *imperceptibly*—evidently what we now call a lift—the machinery of which was not seen by the spectators. Wooden towers used on the stage in sham fights were also called *pegmata*[r]. The following account given by Seneca[s], who wrote about A.D. 20, of these machines, clearly applies to the Colosseum and the substructures under it. As that was before the time of the Flavian Emperors, it is probable that the wooden amphitheatre on this spot was in existence in his time, and that the tufa walls for the lifts now remaining were then standing and in use. He says—

"There are games that give pleasure to the eyes and the ears. Among these we may enumerate the machines which cause the cages to raise themselves, and silently rise to the top of the wooden floor (or stage), and others in unexpected variety, either gaping open or coalescing again, others which were distant drawing together again spontaneously, or those which were near gradually retiring from each other. The eyes of the silly people are astonished at all these sudden movements, the causes of which they do not understand."

Aurelian on the inner side, and a wall of the Sessorium on the outer side, preserved by Aurelian as an outwork. This was the scene of the celebrated ambuscade of Belisarius, by means of which the Goths were driven away from Rome, as described by Procopius (De Bello Gothico, lib. i. c. 22.)

[p] PRO S. IMP. M. ANTONI . GORDIANI . PII
FELICIS AVG. ET TRANQVILLINAE SABI
NAE AVG. VENATORES IMMVN. CVM CV
STODE VIVARI PONT. VERVS MIL. COH
VI. PR. CAMPANIVS VERAX. MIL. COH. VI
PR. FVSCIVS CRESCENTIO ORD CVSTOS
VIVARI. COHH. PRAETT. ET VRBB
DIANAE AVG. D. S. EX. V. P.
DEDICATA XII. KAL. NOV.
IMP. D. N. GORDIANO AVG. ET POMPEIANO COS.

(Inscription found in Rome in 1710, and printed by Nibby, Roma Antica, vol. i. p. 386.)

[q] A compartment of this is shewn in one of the *graffiti*, found in the excavations of 1874.

[r] "Caius princeps in circo pegma duxit." (Plinii Nat. Hist., xxxiii. 16.)

[s] "Ludiviæ sunt, quæ ad voluptatem oculorum atque aurium tendunt. His annumeres licet machinatores, qui pegmata per se surgentia excogitant, et tabulata tacite in sublime crescentia, et alias ex inopinato varietates, aut dehiscendentibus quæ cohærebant, aut his quæ distabant, sua sponte coeuntibus aut his quæ eminebant paulatim in se residentibus." (Seneca, Epist., 88, s. 19.)

Juvenal, writing about A.D. 100, also mentions the *pegmata* in the Colosseum [t], with the *velaria*.

There is a small stream of water in front of the dens, supplied by the aqueducts, from which the animals could drink. Behind each den is a small cell, four feet square, descending from above, called *catabolicus* [u], but not lower than ten feet from the ground, apparently for a man to go down and feed them safely.

In what seems the earliest part of the two tufa walls, near the south-west end of the building, the apertures in the inner part are square-headed doorways, and not arches [v]. These are filled up with brick walls of the time of the Flavian emperors, or later [x]. In other parts of these tufa walls there are arches in the inner wall, also supported by brick arches of the time of the Flavian emperors, in which the bricks are thicker, and there is more mortar between them than in those of the time of Nero.

On the floor of the central passage is a remarkable piece of ancient wooden framework lying on the ground [y], which has the appearance at first sight of having been burnt, but long exposure to wet will have the same effect on wood that fire has. (The Irish bog-oak often appears as if it had been burnt, and wood has been dug from under the foundations of an Irish round tower that had the same appearance.) This framework is a good deal worn, as if it had been much used; it has all the appearance of a dry dock, or a cradle for a vessel to stand upon. When the *stagnum navale* of Nero was in use, there must have been some machinery for lifting up the vessels and placing them on the canals. They must also have been removed out of the way when the water was let off, and the boarded floor of the stage or arena replaced [z].

On each side of this wooden framework is a series of slabs of stone about a yard square, placed upright, with a hole through each

---

[t] "Sic pugnas Cilicis laudabat, et ictus ;
 Et pegma et pueros inde ad velaria raptos."
 (Juvenal, Satyr iv. 121, 122.)

[u] See p. 49.
[v] Photos., No. 3283.
[x] Photos., No. 3286, and Plate VII.
[y] Photos., No. 3263.
[z] Those English people who remember Sadler's Wells Theatre in London about 1820, must know that there was always a sheet of water or reservoir under the stage, and trap-doors in the floor by which sea-monsters could be introduced. The amusements of the old Roman people seem to have been frequently of this kind. Naval fights in boats might have been performed in the Colosseum, and a great deal of machinery must have been required to remove the floor and replace it.
 A wooden Roman bridge still remains under water near Compiègne in France, of which M. Peigné Delacourt has published an account, with engravings of it, so that wood under water is preserved in the same manner as when it is buried in a wet soil. This is well known in the case of piles for bridges, and in those under the city of Amsterdam.

for a water-course. These seem to have been for fixing the wooden frame of a *cradle* for the vessels to stand upon, and to keep them upright. This plan is well shewn in a drawing of a trireme that was made for Napoleon III., to shew the French people what a Roman trireme was like[a].

It is well known that the general form of the Colosseum is oval, and that it had four principal entrances, one of which only remains; this is said to have been the entrance for the emperor and his suite, it is not numbered as the other entrances and seats were[b]. The theatre, as we are told in the Regionary Catalogues, was calculated to hold 87,000 people, and was admirably adapted for its purpose. There were four principal staircases, by which the spectators could ascend to the highest tier of seats, and these were so arranged that the different orders could disperse without meeting each other. The numerous places of egress, called *vomitoria*, and the windows to light the staircases, were contrived with great skill.

Vast as this amazing edifice still is, the whole of the outer wall with the arcades and corridors, on the south and west sides, have been destroyed, having been used as a stone quarry for building some of the largest palaces in Rome, but on the north and east sides it is tolerably perfect. A correct idea of the whole can only be formed by mounting to the top, and surveying the whole extent from thence. The finest view of the exterior is from the Thermæ of Titus, or the windows or the garden of the monastery of S. Pietro in Vincoli, on the hill opposite the north front.

The great mass of the building under the corridors is of tufa, and was probably taken from that part of the second wall of Rome which passed under the south end of the Palatine close at hand; each block of tufa, being of large size and a ton in weight, was likely to be brought from the nearest point. It has been mentioned that

---

[a] See Plate XXVI.

[b] It appears evident from the inscriptions from the College of the Arvales that the seats were regularly and permanently allotted to different persons holding different offices, according to their rank. The lower seats being of marble, the upper ones of wood.

There are many inscriptions relating to the seats in the different theatres and amphitheatres in Rome:

LOCA . ADSIGNATA IN AMPHITEATRO
L . AELIO . PLAVTIO . LAMIA . Q . PAC-
TVMEIO FRONTONE . COS .
ACCEPTVM . AB . LABERIO . MAXIMO
PROCVRATORE . PRAEF . ANNONAE
L . VENNVLEIO . APRONANO . MAG .
CVRATORE . THYRSO . L
FRATRIBVS . ARVALIBVS . MAENIANO .
I . CVN . XII . GRADIBVS . MARM . VIII .
GRADVI . P . V = GRAD . VIII . PED .
V = £ . F . PED . XXXXII S . GRADV . I . VNO .
P . XXII S . ET . MAENIANO . SVMMO .
II . CVN . VI . GRADIE . MARM . IV .
GRADV . I . VNO . P . XXII S . ET .
MAENIANO . SVMMO . IN . LIGNEIS .
TAB . LIII . GRADIBVS . XI . GRADV .
I PED . V = GRAD . XI . PED . V = = —)
F . PED . LXIII S = = — SVMMA . PED .
CXXVIIII S = = —

(Gius.-Ant. Guattari, Roma descritta ed illustrata, &c. Roma, 1805, 4to., vol. ii. p. 13.)

there are piers of travertine at short intervals, as if the builders were afraid to trust the soft tufa to carry so great a weight[c]. These piers go right through the walls from top to bottom, to carry the weight of the upper gallery when full of people; tufa is too soft a material to be trusted for this purpose, and the brick facing did not add materially to the strength. It is faced with cut stone (travertine) on the exterior, and with brick on the interior. The work, as said before, was evidently carried on for a long time. Three periods may be perceived[d] in the stonework, with apparently an interval of some years between them. The upper storey is of a later date, of the time of Alexander Severus and Gordianus, and was evidently completed in great haste, of materials previously prepared, (as may be distinctly seen in the interior); this upper wall is built also in the most slovenly manner, with portions of cornices and of columns, or fragments of old tombs, built into it as mere pieces of stone[e]. On the interior of this wall large corbels remain distinctly visible, which could only be for the floor of the wooden gallery.

In the lower series of seats the vaults under them are not original, except those on the ground-floor; and in the corridors the large corbels for wooden floors and galleries still project from the face of the wall very distinctly[f]. The mixture of stone and brick in the construction is curious, and in several parts indicates the great repairs in the fifth and sixth centuries recorded by inscriptions found during the excavations.

There is a series of arches on the first floor within, some of them begun, and some completed, in stone, but the greater part have springing stones only upon the stone jambs, the arches afterwards being completed in brick, and brick vaults introduced in place of the original wooden floors and galleries; above, nearly all is brick, except the corridors and the outer facing. The construction of this part is very good throughout; the stones are in large oblong blocks, closely fitted together, originally held with iron clamps, fragments of which remain, as may be seen or felt in the interior of the building in apertures of the wall: the holes where other iron clamps have been, are left all over the face of the building, and in the corridors, always at the edges of the stones, where in rusting they have split the stone and fallen out. They were of this

---

[c] Photos., No. 3279.
[d] See p. 6, and Plates II. and XX.
[e] See Photos., Nos. 367.
[f] One series of these corbels in the upper corridor seems to have been for a wooden gallery, for the use of the sailors going to furl or unfurl the awning.

form ⌐¯¯¯⌐[g]. On the west side, where the outer wall is gone, the inner wall (now external) shews distinctly the flat pilasters of stone carried up nearly to the top, but left unfinished, and continued with brick afterwards.

Nothing is known with certainty of the architect of the work; an inscription found in the Catacomb of S. Agnes, in memory of Gaudentius, has given rise to the legend that he was the architect[h], and that he afterwards suffered as a martyr within its walls. Twelve thousand Jewish slaves are said to have been employed upon it during five years, and ten million Roman scudi expended upon it in the same time.

The fine tomb of one of the family of the Aterii found at Cento Celle, and now preserved in the Lateran Museum, is covered with panels of sculpture of numerous buildings packed closely together, of which there is reason to believe some are only designs, and were never executed. This makes it probable that it was the tomb of an architect, and one of the sculptures represents the Summa Sacra Via as he thought it ought to have been. One building is a triumphal arch, with a colossal figure under it, and an inscription on the cornice—ARCVS IN SACRA VIA SVMMA; another triumphal arch has the inscription ARCVS AD ISIS. Between these two is seen the Colosseum looking down upon it, represented as of two storeys only, and not quite the same as the existing building, but the figures under the arches are shewn as on the coin. Another sculpture on the same tomb represents the machine for raising large stones to the top of a high wall or building, described in Part III. of this work (Construction, p. 91). From the circumstance of this machine being represented upon the tomb, it seems most probable that the person here interred was the inventor, or had made some improvement in it, and that it was especially intended for the Colosseum, for which it certainly would have been very useful. The date of the tomb is of the first century[i]. Such a machine is mentioned by Vitruvius, and similar machines are still in use in some parts of Switzerland.

---

[g] Some clamps of the same form were found, in 1870, in the interior of the wall of Servius Tullius, (in the part destroyed for the railway,) where the stones were joined together by them.

[h] SIC PREMIA SERVAS VESPASIANE DIRE PREMIATVS ES MORTE GAVDENTI LETARE CIVITAS VBI GLORIE TVE AVTORI PROMISIT ISTE DAT KRISTVS OMNIA TIBI QVI ALIVM PARAVIT THEA-TRV̄ IN CELO. This inscription only shews that he was employed upon the work; it is preserved in the church of S. Martino a Monti. See Nibby, Roma nell' anno MDCCCXXXVIII. parte i. Antica, p. 400.

[i] See Photographs, Nos. 1500 and 1501, and the Photo-engraving, Plate XXIII. of Supplement to vol. i.

The numerous walls that intersect the space under the stage shew clearly that there could be no area in this theatre, that there is no open space excepting on the stage itself, and this was the boarded floor, called the *arena*, from the sand with which it was covered. The latter is quite a different thing from an *area*, and yet almost all the modern writers on the antiquities of Rome fall into this mistake. The passage cited in a previous page from Dio Cassius, who describes what he saw, is quite decisive that the arena was a boarded floor covered with sand.

A great number of large marble columns and capitals of the Composite order, rudely worked, as if on purpose to be seen from a great distance only, have rolled down from the edge of the upper gallery to the arena below, probably in an earthquake. They must have fallen before the substructures were filled up with earth, as many of them were found at the bottom on the old pavement, which they had damaged by falling upon it, and some have made holes through great walls, and were found lying with half the column on the inner side of the wall, and the other half on the outer one. Probably the cords for the awning were caught on the entablature of this colonnade as they passed, the length from top to bottom being too great to keep them tight. There must have been at least a hundred of these columns; possibly there were two colonnades, the second on the edge of one of the lower galleries, but they are work of the third century, not earlier, and as the upper gallery was added at that time, they must have belonged to that period.

The Flavian Amphitheatre and Meta Sudans are represented on four coins of the emperors, one of Vespasian[j], A.D. 80, with the head of Titus, and inscription on the obverse. This is a bird's-eye view, represented with the walls of the two storeys, and with the Meta Sudans on one side, and a double range of columns on the opposite side, one over the other. This medal was used by Fontana in his plans and drawings of a restoration[k], though he does not give an engraving of it. The upper storey is very different from the existing building; in the interior the upper gallery is evidently represented on this medal as of wood; the colonnade or arcade, of two storeys, connecting the amphitheatre with the Cœlian, seen on the coin, was most probably to carry the shallow open channel of water from the Aqueduct[l]. The second of Domi-

---

[j] See Photos., No. 488, and Plates XXIV., XXV.

[k] L'Anfiteatro Flavio descritto e delineato dal cavaliere Carlo Fontana. Nell' Haia, M.DC.XXV. fol. max.

[l] These views of buildings on coins appear to have been made from the architect's designs before they were car-

tian, nearly the same as the last, but with a double arcade instead of colonnade; the third of Alexander Severus, with the Meta Sudans[m] on the right, and a group of figures on the left. There are two coins of this emperor with the same subject on the reverse, not of the same size, and not quite alike. The fourth of Gordianus III., with the legend on the obverse, IMP. GORDIANUS. PIVS. FELIX. AVG.; on the reverse the view of the Colosseum, as if looking down upon it, with the masts for the awning, and a wild-beast hunt going on at a high level, certainly not at the bottom (as has been said). On the left, standing behind the Meta Sudans, is a colossal figure about fifty feet high[n]. On the right is a small building which is just below, and a gable end to the roof, probably the *piscina* of Alexander Severus, of which we have remains. Over the Colosseum is the legend MUNIFICENTIA GORDIANI AVG.[o] In this the upper storey is represented as of stone.

A.D. 150. By the time of Antoninus Pius the amphitheatre needed repairs, as we learn that it was restored by him[p].

In A.D. 191, Dio Cassius, who was a Roman senator in the time of Commodus, was an eye-witness of the games, and gives an account of the manner in which that emperor amused himself in this amphitheatre.

"He used to put on, before he entered the amphitheatre, a tunic with sleeves made of white silk embroidered with gold, and thus habited we (the Senators) saluted him; but on entering it he put on his purple robe sprinkled with gold, like a Greek *chlamys*, and a gold crown with Indian jewels; he was also accustomed to carry a *caduceus* like Mercury. In the street some one carried before him a lion's skin and a club. But when he went into the theatre he sat on a gold seat. He also entered the theatre in the costume of Mercury, and threw aside the other things which he had carried except the tunic.

"On the first day he alone killed a hundred bears with javelins thrown from the paths in the upper part. For the amphitheatre being everywhere divided by diametrical partitions, each division having a roof, round which he could go, he could the more readily strike down the wild beasts, who were themselves divided into four divisions. . . . .

"These things being done on the first day, on other days he descended from the upper place into the area of the amphitheatre, and killed the fatted beasts

---

ried out, and were sometimes altered. There is no representation of the Colossus of Nero in any of them. For the shallow channel of water, see Photos., No. 1759.

[m] See No. 302, and 488 c.

[n] On bad impressions of this coin the Meta Sudans looks like a second smaller figure, or of a youth; but on good impressions the Meta Sudans is distinct, and the figure behind it overtops it by the head and shoulders only.

[o] See No. 488 c.

[p] ". . . Romæ templum Hadriani, honori patris dicatum, Græco-stadium post incendium restitutum, instauratum amphitheatrum," &c. (Jul. Capitolinus-Antoninus Pius, c. 8, ap. Script. Hist. Aug.)

when they came near to him, or were led to him, or brought in cages; he killed a tiger, and an hippopotamus, and an elephant: having done these things he went away. Then after dinner he went through the gladiatorial exercise armed as a gladiator, with the shield on his right arm, and holding the wooden sword in his left hand, of which he was very proud, as he was left-handed. . . . For fourteen days exhibitions of this kind were continued, and I can certify that we senators always came with the knights, except Claudius Pompeianus, the senior, he never was there, but sent his sons to see the shows. . . . .

"But of the rest of the people many did not go into the amphitheatre, and some after they had seen a little went away, some from being ashamed of what they saw done there, others from fear, because it was reported that the Emperor wished to kill some of them with arrows as Hercules formerly killed the Stymphalidæ. . . . This fear was common to all, belonging not more to others than to us; for even to us Senators he did things in such a manner, that for any cause we expected to be killed. He even killed an ostrich and cut off its head, when he came to the place where we were seated, holding in his left hand the head and in his right his bloody sword, and saying nothing, he moved it grinning, to shew he would serve us in the same manner; and which many people laughed at seeing our fear, &c. . . . These things being done he comforted us, and ordered us, when he was fighting in the manner of a gladiator, to go into the theatre in our habits and cloaks as knights: in which costume we were not accustomed to go into the theatre except on the death of the Emperor. It happened also to him that on the last day of the games his helmet was carried through the door by which the dead were usually carried, which things, in the opinion of many, were done to indicate to every body his approaching death. It is certain that soon after he died, or rather was killed [q]."

The spectators were protected from the heat of the sun by a great awning, which was suspended from masts or poles at the top by cords. Pliny mentions an awning painted in imitation of the sky, with stars in it, in the amphitheatre of the Prince Nero [r]. There were similar poles at the bottom also, to support the lower end of the cords over the heads of the spectators in the galleries [s]. These are likely to have had the great beams of the screen in the front of the *podium* fixed to them. The contrivances for supporting them at the top were very ingenious, and can still be seen. On the exterior there is a row of corbels, ten feet below the summit, for the ends of the poles to rest upon, and holes are left in the cornice for them to pass through. These masts stood full twenty feet above the walls; and on the inner side of the upper wall are also corbels for the cords to be fastened to, to keep them upright. At the bottom of the galleries, in front of the *podium*, there are similar contrivances

---

[q] Dionis Cass. lib. lxxii. c. 17—22.

[r] "Postea in theatris tantum umbram fecere: quod primus omnium invenit Q. Catulus, cum Capitolium dedicaret. Carbasina deinde vela primus in theatro duxisse traditur Lentulus Spinter Apollinaribus ludis. . . . . Vela nuper colore cæli, stellata, per rudentes iere etiam in amphitheatro principis Neronis." (Plinii Nat. Hist., lib. xix. c. 6.)

[s] See Plate XVII.

to support the poles for the awning, a recess in the wall of tufa, with a piece of travertine let in for the lower ends to stand upon, and long corbels on each side to support and stiffen the lower part[t]. The central space was not covered over, and the athletes were exposed to the weather. There is an excellent representation of an amphitheatre, with the awning partly closed and partly open, in a fresco-painting of the first century at Pompeii, which has been engraved in the valuable Journal of Pompeii, edited by the learned Keeper of the Museum, Sig. Com. Fiorelli[u]. The construction of the upper walls is quite different from, and very inferior to that of the great arcades; this belonging to the third century, not to the first; and part of it has all the appearance of having been completed in a great hurry, as we see in the interior many pieces of stone evidently prepared for other parts of the building, and used as blocks of old material only, some with inscriptions on them, apparently taken from tombs[v]. The tradition is that the Emperor Gordianus insisted on the completion of the building-contract by the time appointed, which was done with great difficulty.

A large number of sailors were kept continually employed in furling and unfurling the great awning, and attending to the machinery. They had a camp provided for them near at hand, called Castra Misenatium, because the sailors came originally from the fleet at Misenum (in the bay of Naples). The exact site of this camp has not been ascertained. Some suppose it to have been on the Cœlian, near where the *navicella*, or model of a galley in marble, now stands[w], but it was not in that Regio; it must have been on the Esquiline, immediately to the north of the great building, or on the Velia. The awning was called *vela* or *vehela*, an old Latin word, from which came also the name of *velabrum*, meaning "sails." The modern name "veil" is supposed to come from it.

Calpurnius[x] describes a visit to Rome by a country lad, and gives an account of the amphitheatre:—

"We saw the theatre (amphitheatre) with interwoven beams rising to heaven, so high as almost to overlook the Tarpeian rock, and the immense steps and the sloping passages gently descending. . . . What shall I describe further? I saw all kinds of wild beasts, . . . not only those carniverous monsters of the forest, but sea-monsters together with fighting bears. I saw seals, and herds of shapeless animals bearing the name of horses (hippo-potami), but deformed, the off-

---

[t] Photos., No. 185.
[u] This is reproduced in Plate XXI.
[v] Photos., Nos. 167, 185.
[w] See Regio III., Castra Misenatium.
[x] Calpurnius has usually been considered as a writer of the third century, but the most recent editor of his Eclogues (Haupt) shews that he was contemporary with Nero and Titus, and Dean Merivale is of the same opinion.

spring of the Nile. Oh how often have we trembling seen the arena sinking in parts, and a gulf burst open in the ground from which wild beasts have emerged [?]."

In A.D. 217, the amphitheatre was struck by lightning and burnt under Macrinus, as we are told by Dio Cassius. This passage shews that the upper storeys were of wood, and that there was much woodwork about the galleries and corridors.

"The amphitheatre also was struck by lightning on the very day of the Vulcanalia (23rd of August), all was consumed to such an extent that the upper precinct and whatever was on the area was burned, and all the remaining part shivered in pieces by the heat; nor could the fire have been extinguished by human means, although there was plenty of water, had there not also been copious and vehement rain from the heavens. All the gladiatorial games, consequently, for many years were transferred to the Stadium [a]."

The restoration was begun in the time of Heliogabalus [a], and continued through the whole reign of Alexander Severus [b], A.D. 222—235; and finished under Gordianus III., A.D. 244, as has been shewn by his coin. In A.D. 248 the games, which had been transferred for a time to the Circus Maximus, were again celebrated here.

In A.D. 238-44, we learn that the number of wild beasts kept in Rome for the use of the amphitheatre during the time of the Emperor Gordianus was as follows: 32 elephants, 10 elks, 60 tame lions, 10 tigers, 30 leopards, 10 hyenas, 1 hippopotamus, 1 rhinoceros,

> [?] "Vidimus in coelum trabibus spectacula textis
> Surgere, Tarpeium prope despectantia culmen,
> Immensosque gradus, et clivos lene jacentes. . . .
> Ordine quid referam? vidi genus omne ferarum. . . .
> Non solum nobis silvestria cernere monstra
> Contigit: aequoreos ego cum certantibus ursis
> Spectavi vitulos, et equorum nomine dignum,
> Sed deforme pecus (i.e. Nilo).
> Ah trepidi quoties nos descendentis arenae
> Vidimus in partes ruptaque voragine terrae
> Emersisse feras!
> Et coit in rotulam teretem quo lubricus axis
> Impositos subita *vertigine* falleret ungues
> Exciteretque feras auro quoque torta refulgent
> Retia, quae totis in arenam dentibus extant,
> Dentibus aequatis: et erat mihi crede Lycota
> Si qua fides, nostro dens longior omnis aratro."
>   (T. Calpurnii Siculi Bucol. Ecloga vii.)

[a] Dionis Cass. lib. lxxviii. c. 25.

[a] "Opera publica ipsius praeter Aeden Heliogabali Dei . . . et amphitheatri instauratio post exustionem . . . nulla extant." (Lampridius, Antoninus Heliogabalus, c. 17, ap. Script. Hist. Aug.)

[b] ". . . sumptibus publicis ad instaurationem theatri, circi, *amphitheatri*, et aerarii, deputavit." (Lampridius, Alexander Severus, c. 24.) There are coins of this emperor with the amphitheatre on the reverse. See Plate XXV.

10 wild lions, 10 camelopards, 20 wild asses, 40 wild horses, and many other wild animals, besides two thousand hired gladiators[e]. All these, the Chronicler adds, were exhibited or slain by Philippus, at the Ludi Sæculares which he celebrated with great pomp for the thousandth[d] anniversary of the foundation of Rome, A.D. 248, when he had gladiatorial and wild-beast exhibitions in the amphitheatre[e].

Herodian[f], the Greek historian, writing about the middle of the third century, says that a hundred lions, killed in the amphitheatre by Commodus, appeared to leap out from under the earth. More strictly speaking, they came from under the sand on the stage, as they were sent up in cages which opened at the top, and naturally sprang out as soon as liberty was given to them.

In A.D. 250, another fire took place under Decius, but the damage was speedily repaired.

In A.D. 280, the Emperor Probus in his triumphal shows again had a hundred lions killed in the amphitheatre[g].

In A.D. 320, the amphitheatre was again damaged by lightning, but was soon restored by Constantine[h]. An attempt was made, A.D. 325, to abolish the barbarous combats, and the exposure of convicts, but this was not effected until the martyrdom of Telemachus, an Oriental monk, A.D. 403, who made a pilgrimage from the East on purpose to be martyred here, and during one of the sanguinary shows he rushed into the midst, and falling on his knees, entreated the spectators to have mercy on their victims. He was immediately stoned to death, but so great a sensation was caused by this martyrdom, that the emperor Honorius was able to take advantage of it to suppress the shows.

In A.D. 357, the amphitheatre is described by Ammianus Marcel-

---

[c] "Fuerunt sub Gordiano Romæ elephanti triginta et duo, quorum ipse duodecim miserat, Alexander decem: alces decem, tigres decem, leones mansueti sexaginta, leopardi mansueti triginta, belli, id est hyænæ, decem, gladiatorum fiscalium paria mille, hippopotamus et rhinoceros unus, archoleontes decem, camelopardali decem, onagri viginti, equi feri quadraginta, et cetera hujusmodi animalia, innumera et diversa: quæ omnia Philippus ludis sæcularibus vel dedit vel occidit." (Jul. Capit. Gordianus Tertius, c. 33.)

[d] This celebration shews that the chronology then accepted by the Roman people is the same as that of Livy, which is used as the chronological table of buildings prefixed to this work.

[e] Suetonius in Gordiano III., c. 33.

[f] Herodian, lib. i. c. 8. Ammianus Marcellinus mentions the same exhibition, and the same number of lions leaping out at once, lib. xxxi. c. 19. See Plates VI. and VIII.

[g] "Centum jubatos leones." (Vopiscus in Vita Probi, c. 19.)

[h] "Eam autem denunciationem adque interpretationem, quæ de jactu amphitheatri scripta est, de qua ad Heraclianum Tribunum, et magistrum officiorum scripseras, ad nos scias esse perlatum." (Codex Theodosianus, lib. xvi. tit. x. lex 1. Imp. Constantinus ad Maximum, A.D. 321.)

linus as perfect, and as a marvellous work, from its great height, and its immense size. He also mentions the massive walls of rough stone, or concrete (*moles*), bound together by travertine (*lapis tiburtinus*)[i].

A.D. 445. The amphitheatre was much repaired by the Prefect Rufus Cecina Felix Lampadius, under Theodosius II. He restored the seats, the arena, and the podium, as appears from an inscription[k] dug up on the spot in 1814, and fixed on the wall within the building to preserve it. These repairs are supposed to have been required in consequence of the damage done during the siege by the Goths under Alaric, or more probably from the effect of the earthquake mentioned by Paulus Diaconus[l] as taking place in that year, when he says that many of the great buildings in Rome were damaged.

A.D. 508. The Prefect Venantius Basilius also repaired the arena and the *podium*, which had been damaged by an earthquake[m].

It was again used for the show of wild beasts under Theodoric in A.D. 519[n], and under Anicius Maximus, A.D. 523. These were the last occasions on which we have any mention of these savage exhibitions. In the beginning of the eighth century it appears to have been still perfect, from the well-known proverb preserved in Bede's *Exceptiones patrum, Collectanea*, &c.; that the Colosseum and Rome would stand or fall together[o]; but during that century it was again seriously damaged by an earthquake, and it was then so much in ruins that it was not used until the eleventh, when it was converted into a fortress, and the southern side is said to have been much damaged by Robert Guiscard and his Normans, but more probably by the travertine stone being carried away for building materials.

---

[i] "Amphitheatri molem solidatam lapidis Tiburtini compage, ad cujus summitatem aegre visio humana conscendit." (Ammianus Marcellinus, lib. xvi. c. 10.)

[k] SALVis. dd. NN. THEODOSIO. ET. PLACIDO. valentiniano. augg. RVFVS CAECINA. FELIX. LAMPADIVS. VC. et. int. praef. vrb. HAReNAM. AMPHITEATRI. A. NOVO. VNA. CVM. Podio. et. portis. posticis. SED. ET. REPARATIS. SPECTACVLI. GRADIBVS restitvit.

[l] Paulus Diaconus, Miscell., lib. xiv.; ap. Murat. Rer. Ital. Script., vol. i. p. 96, c. 1, A.

[m] This appears from another inscription found in 1813:—
DECIVS MARIVS VENANTIVS BASILIVS V C et INL. PRAEF VRB PATRICIVS CONSVL. ORDINARIVS ARENAM ET PODIVM QVAE ABOMINANDI TERRAEMOTVS RVIN PROSTRAVIT SVMPTV PROPRIO RESTITVIT.

[n] "Muneribus amphitheatralibus diversi generis feras, quas praesens aetas pro novitate miraretur, exhibuit. Cujus spectaculi voluptates etiam exquisitas Africa sub devotione transmisit." (Cassiodori Chronicon, A.D. 519; inter opera ejus, ed. 1679, fol., tom. i. p. 195, col. 2.

[o] "Quamdiu stat Colyseus, stat et Roma; quando cadet Colyseus, cadet et Roma; quando cadet Roma, cadet et mundus." (Bedae Opera, Basileae, 1563, fol., vol. iii. col. 651.)

In 1130, it became the chief fortress of the Frangipani family, and Pope Innocent II. took refuge here from the anti-pope Anacletus[p].

In 1142, the Roman people had driven out the barons, and had possession of this with their other fortresses, as appears from the records of the Roman Senate at that period[q]. But the Frangipani[r] soon recovered it, and the pope of their party, Innocent III., A.D. 1180 (called by the opposite party the anti-pope), was their guest; and from hence he fulminated his excommunication against the emperors, but he was soon afterwards captured and banished.

In 1160, Alexander III.[s] (Bandinelli of Siena, called the orthodox Pope) in his second year, being besieged by the Emperor Frederic Barbarossa, abandoned the Lateran Palace, and took refuge in the stronghold of the Frangipani, with his brothers and their families. He there held courts, treated causes, and also waited for opportunities. At that time the Colosseum gave its name to the district around it. The fortifications included part of the Palatine Hill, with the Arch of Titus, on which was a large tower.

Under Gregory IX., A.D. 1227, the Annibaldi family obtained a decree from Frederic II., requiring the Frangipani to cede to them one-half of the Colosseum fortress, which might have led to its entire destruction; but Innocent IV., in 1244, rescinded the engagement, and declared this building to be under the direct dominion of the Holy See. During the residence of the Popes at Avignon, the Colosseum belonged to the Annibaldi or Annibaldeschi, who were then in the ascendant[t]. In 1312, the Emperor Henry VII. obliged them to give it up, and placed it under the care of the municipality, who appropriated it to bull-fights; but this only lasted until 1332, when eighteen youths of noble families were killed by the infuriated bulls, of which a minute account is given in the chronicle of Monaldeschi, printed in Muratori's collection[u].

In 1349, it was again damaged by the earthquake described in Petrarch's letters; after this the great families entered into a com-

---

[p] Card. de Aragonia, Vita Innocentii II. apud Muratori, Rerum Italicarum Scriptores, vol. iii. p. 1, p. 435 B.

[q] Cont. de Senatu Romano, lib. vii. c. 1, §. 168.

[r] Delle Memorie Sacre, e profane dell' Anfiteatro Flavio di Roma, &c., dal Canonico Giovanni Marangoni Vicentino. In Roma, 1745, 4to. Cap. I. p. 49, Codice pergameno, Scritto dal celebre Onofrio Panvino inedito ed intitolato, de Gente Frogapanica.

[s] Card. de Aragonia, Vita Alexandri III. ap. Muratori, Rerum Ital. Script., tom. iii. p. i. p. 459.

[t] Albertino Mussato, Hist. Aug., lib. v.; ap. Murat. Rerum Italic. Script., tom. x. c. 454. Nibby, Roma nell' anno MDCCCXXXVIII, parte i. p. 413.

[u] Rainaldi Annal. an. 1244; Panvin. de gente Frangipani; Muratori, Rerum Italicarum Scriptores, tom. xii. col. 535, 536. Nibby gives a more complete and accurate version of this occurrence from a better text, though modernized. See Roma Antica, part i. p. 414.

pact, in 1362, to make the ruins common property as a quarry, by which all might profit[x]. In 1381, the senate gave a portion of the arcades to the Chapter of the Lateran, for a ward to their hospital. Their badge, the head of Christ between two candlesticks, is carved over some of the archways.

In 1438, Eugenius IV. built two walls to connect the Colosseum with the monastery of S. Pietro in Vincoli, in order to prevent the evil doings that were going on there; but after the death of that Pope, the Roman people went in a crowd and pulled down those walls which had shut them out of the great building. The monks stated to Flaminius Vacca that they had preserved the deed of gift, and if they ever had a pope from their monastery, it would be acted upon[y].

In the fifteenth century, the great palace of S. Mark of Venice, built by Paul II., 1464—1471, at the south end of the Corso, the Farnese in 1534, the Cancelleria in 1495, the Borghese in 1590, and many other edifices[z], were built out of this quarry.

In the sixteenth century it was used for miracle plays; this practice began under Paul III. in 1540[a], a purpose to which it had previously been applied on Good Friday in each year by the "Confraternity of the Gonfalone;" this is mentioned as early as 1263.

We have one vestige of this remaining, a view of Jerusalem with the Crucifixion, painted on the wall over the principal entrance then in use at the north end over the arch, and seen in going out as we look up. It shews to what a height the earth had then been raised to make this a convenient place for such a picture.

Sixtus V. proposed to turn it into a cloth manufactory, and drawings for that purpose were actually prepared by his architect, Fontana[b], in 1590; but the design was abandoned at the death of the Pope.

---

[x] "... et præterea se omnes emendarent de faciendo tiburtinam (travertini) quod esset commune id quod judicitur." (Fea, Dissertazione nelle Ruine di Roma, p. 398.)

[y] F. Vacca, Memorie ap. Fea, lxxiv. p. 72.

[z] Poggio the Florentine, writing in 1425, says that a large part of the building was reduced to lime by the stupidity of the Romans:—"... atque ob stultitiam Romanorum majori ex parte ad calcem delatum." (Poggio, de Varietate Fortunæ, lib. i.)

[a] Flaminio Vacca, Memorie, 72; Marangoni, Memorie dell'Anfiteatro Flavio,
p. 57, quoted by Nibby, Roma nell' anno MDCCCXXXVIII, parte i., Antica, p. 418.

[b] Belloni, Vita di Domenico Fontana. Roma, nell' anno MDCCCXXXVIII, &c., parte i., Antica, pp. 414—417. (Le Vite de pittori, &c., Roma, 1728, 4to. p. 93.)

The space enclosed within the outer walls is six acres, and there is an extraordinary difference of climate between the northern and the southern side. Dr. Deakin published a work on the Flora of the Colosseum: he found 423 *species* of plants, belonging to 253 *genera*.

Over the door now generally used is a painting of the heavenly Jeru-

In 1703 it was again damaged by an earthquake, and soon afterwards Clement XI. destroyed the lower arches of the western side of the corridor, and used some of the stone to build the steps at the Port of Ripetta, on the Tiber. He employed other parts as a warehouse for saltpetre for the neighbouring manufactory of gunpowder, on the hill adjoining, near the church of S. Pietro in Vincoli, still indicated by the name of the street, and this manufactory continued in use until 1811.

In 1728, Benedict XIII. consecrated the whole area, at the instigation of a Carmelite friar, Angelo Paoli. A small chapel was made under one of the archways, and dedicated to *S. Maria della Pietà*. In 1741, a hermit was appointed to reside here, but in the following year he was stabbed by an assassin, and although the wound did not prove fatal, the Pope ordered the closing of every ingress by gates locked and barred. About the same period, Leonardo da Porto Maurizio, a Minorite friar, drew immense congregations to his sermons in the Colosseum.

In 1749, Benedict XIV. ordered the erection at his private expense of the central cross, and the fourteen stations of the *Via Crucis*, which remained until 1874, when they were removed for the ground to be excavated.

In 1756, a grand mass was celebrated here by the Cardinal Vicar of Rome under Benedict, in the presence of a very numerous assembly. The same ceremony was repeated a few years afterwards under Clement XIII.

The outer arcade on the south-western side of this colossal building was entirely destroyed in the middle ages by the Pontifical families, who used it as a stone-quarry for building their great palaces. This enables us to see more clearly the construction of the walls of the corridors and front of the three periods :—

First, the arches on the ground-floor, built of travertine.

Second, the first-floor, also of travertine, not long after the other.

Third, the upper storey, of brick on the inner side, of the beginning of the third century.

We also see the numerous holes left by the iron clamps with which the edges of the stones were bound together, according to a Roman fashion which has been in use from the time of Servius

---

salem and the Crucifixion, of the time of Paul III., A.D. 1534-50, in the style of the older pilgrimage pictures. At the time it was painted the passage appears to have been filled up with earth to such a height as to make the picture a conspicuous object in leaving the building; at present it is quite above the heads of the passers-by, and is seldom noticed or seen.

Tullius to the present time. On the north-eastern side the front is perfect, and we see the ornamental columns and cornices in the two lower storeys, and in the upper one the corbels for the masts to carry the awning, with holes in the cornice to let them pass through. One of the arches of the lower storey has been restored in the time of the Gordians, A.D. 220—238, and is a good example of the still good construction of that period, though not so good as that of the time of Titus and Vespasian [c].

In 1810, when Rome was incorporated in the French Empire, the Governor, Baron Daru, placed the Colosseum under the direction of the Roman architect Valadier, to carry on regular excavations, which were continued for four years, from 1810 to 1814; of these works the Comte de Tournon [d], then prefect, has written an account.

In 1812, under the French, the ruins of the walls and the surface of the vaults were weeded of the vegetation which threatened their ultimate destruction, and the uprooting of the shrubs had become necessary to save the walls. In sixty years they had again grown up so vigorously that another weeding was absolutely required, and in November, 1870, the whole of the ruins of the Colosseum were cleared of weeds and shrubs, under the direction of Signor Rosa, who was appointed by the Italian Government to superintend the works, and to carry on excavations on a large scale, from that building to the Forum Romanum. There is no doubt that it was quite time this clearing should take place, as the roots of the plants were in many parts displacing the stones, and would soon have done serious mischief. There was a great outcry against this necessary work by the botanists and the lovers of the picturesque, but archæologists must approve of it. Many things are now brought into view more clearly than they were before.

A view of these excavations was taken and engraved in 1813.

---

[c] The interior of the building is still grand in its ruins. This is well shewn in the photograph (No. 1195,) with the cross, and the altar, and the stations erected by the pope about 1750, and destroyed in 1874, in order to excavate the whole of the area. A restoration of the interior according to Canina can also be seen in another photograph (No. 724).

[d] Etudes Statistiques sur Rome, par le Conte P. N. C. de Tournon. Paris, Didot, 1821, 8vo., 4 vols., and deuxième edition, 3 Volumes en 8vo avec atlas, Paris, 1858.

The fine set of drawings made for the French Government at that period are now preserved in the British Museum, and fully bear out what I had stated before I had seen them. They clearly shew that the French excavations were not carried down more than ten feet. The tops of the arches of the lower passage are shewn in the drawings, but these excavations appear to have been stopped by water rising to that height. See Plate III.

It represents clearly the passages round it, and two straight parallel channels down the middle of it for the naval fights, which were in reality not a representation of sea-fights but of river-fights. In 1814, and again in 1867, the subterranean passage leading from the Amphitheatre on the side next the Cœlian was excavated as a private speculation in search of treasure, which was not found; but the passage was left open as we now see it [e].

In 1864-5, considerable excavations were made between the Colosseum and the Cœlian, in search of treasure supposed to have been buried there, but only a subterranean passage was found. The work was interrupted by water gushing out in great abundance,—to such an extent that the area of the Colosseum was completely inundated, and the water was obliged to be drawn off by a steam engine [f]. The passage then discovered is still left open; the upper part of the vault only is removed, which formed the floor, or rather supported the floor, of another passage on the present level of the ground, leading from the *podium*, or lowest storey, towards the Cœlian. The point where the water gushed out and stopped the work was just outside of the site of the outer wall, long since destroyed on that part of the building. The great excavations of 1874 shewed that this passage turned to the left or south when it reached the outer wall, and followed the line of it until it joined the outer end of the long straight passage down the centre of the building.

The upper wall on the north side, where it remains perfect, formed the back of the wooden gallery over the corridors for the common people, and was faced with brick, but the greater part of the ancient brickwork had fallen down, and has been copied in modern times; a great deal of the back of the stone wall, left exposed, shews the hasty construction [g], in the time of Gordianus.

The remains of Aqueducts and *Piscinæ* have already been mentioned [h], but some further account of them seems to be requisite. A *piscina* always consists of four vaulted chambers, two above and two below, and the middle wall of the two lower chambers has

---

[e] See No. 1742, and Plate III.
[f] Probably the aqueduct which passes there had a hole made in it; the same aqueduct goes on from this side of the building to the south-east end. This occurred again in 1874, and a steam engine had again to be employed. This passage, before it turns, goes in the direction of the *castellum aquæ* of the time of Alexander Severus, of which there are considerable remains between this point and the Cœlian. The *specus* of an aqueduct of the same period passes along between the Cœlian and the amphitheatre, near the surface of the ground; a portion of this was visible in 1874.
[g] See Photograph, No. 367.
[h] See p. 5.

small holes in it, for straining the water as it passes through. The lower chamber of a *piscina* is also known by having no windows in it, and the lining being of the water-cement (*opus signinum*). The lower chambers of two *piscinæ* only remain; of the northern one the middle wall between the two lower chambers is the only part now visible, this is faced with *opus reticulatum* of the time of Nero, and has the usual small holes for water-pipes through the wall. The southern one is of brickwork of the third century, of the time of Alexander Severus; of this there is much more remaining, one end with the usual boldly projecting buttresses to support the weight of water, and part of two other chambers of the reservoir.

The excavations which had been made in the time of the first Napoleon and of Pope Pius VII., 1810—1814, were filled up again after drawings and plans had been made of them. They were not considered satisfactory by scholars because the excavations had not gone deep enough, having been stopped by water, as very often happens in Rome at certain periods of the year, when the springs are high. They were again suspended by the same cause in the spring and summer of 1874, but Signor Rosa, with his usual energy, obtained machinery and a steam-engine to pump the water out[i]. The whole area was found to be undermined by chambers and passages, with walls chiefly of brick, but some of tufa, with indications of several different periods[j].

When the Pontifical Government returned to power in 1815, Pope Pius VII. ordered the enormous buttress to be built, for supporting one end of the wall then left broken, and preventing the ruin from extending further. We have already lost forty-seven out of the eighty arches, which have been destroyed for using the materials by previous Popes to build their family palaces, or monasteries and churches, so that there remain only thirty-three of the external arches of travertine. The other end of the wall, near the Meta Sudans, was left in a dangerous state until that was also supported by the great buttress of Leo XII. In 1828, Gregory XVI. followed the example of his immediate predecessors, and rebuilt in brick some arches of what had been the internal corridors, but had become external, owing to the demolition of the great outer arcades in earlier ages. In 1852, Pius IX. repaired the principal entrance from the Esquiline side, and some more of the arches of the inner arcade.

---

[i] In the summer of 1875 they were again suspended for want of funds to pay for the steam-engine, which costs a pound a-day.

[j] Of which an account has been given in pages 5, 6, 10, 13, 14, 21, 35, of this chapter.

Under the arena was all the machinery usual under the stage of a large theatre; and much space was required for it. When the boards had to be cleared off the central part, to leave open the four long channels of water, which are seen in the view of the Colosseum taken in 1812[k], and the space between them which was probably flooded to the depth of a few feet for effect, the boards removed from the centre must have been piled up at the sides, and on the large corbels before mentioned[l]. Apollodorus, the architect, in his celebrated reply to the Emperor Hadrian, told him that *he ought to have* prepared a place for the machinery of the great amphitheatre under the platform, and in such a manner that the great building should have been visible from the Forum Romanum. The site intended by him for the temple evidently was the large level platform on the Summa Sacra Via, on which S. Francesca Romana now stands; and the place for the machinery intended by him was obviously that excavated in the spring of 1874, under the south-east end of the platform immediately opposite to the Colosseum, a very convenient place for the purpose. There still remains a rude rubble vault, of the time of the Republic, with a small aqueduct introduced in the time of the early Empire to carry water to the fountains at each corner of the Porticus Liviæ, which must have been on this site, but which did not extend to the end. There is an excellent place for a temple at the end of the *porticus* or colonnade; and the platform could easily have been extended several yards nearer to the Colosseum: it is evident that this is what Apollodorus said that Hadrian *ought to have done*, but that he had not done so.

At the south-east end, under the old entrance, at the present level of the ground, a long passage has been found, with a series of square-topped arches, at about fifteen feet below that level. This has been traced further to the south, beyond the limits of the building; it must have led from the great foss-way in that direction. There is a large and deep drain extending from the south end of the Colosseum, turning at an angle and passing at the foot of the Claudium to the Meta Sudans, near the arch of Constantine. It was continued under the present Via di S. Gregorio, and the southeast end of the Palatine[m].

---

[k] See Plate III.
[l] See Plate XV.
[m] About the year 1865 a new drain was made by the Municipality under that road, and when it was nearly finished the old drain of the Empire(?), or of the time of Sylla(?), was found under it at a considerably lower level. It is fifteen metres below the surface of the ground, and so much filled up with earth that it is considered (in 1876) quite impracticable to have it cleared out and repaired.

In one part, near the south end, on the western side of the central passage at the lowest level, which is twenty-one feet below the present level of the ground and the top of the walls of the substructure, the two ancient tufa walls (before mentioned) remain nearly perfect, with the vertical grooves opposite to each other, evidently for lifts to slip up and down, and in each instance in the wall on one side a hollow is cut, for the counter-weight to work up and down [n]. These lifts are very near together in the outer passage, in front of the *podium*, but far below the bottom of it. Behind each of them is a small square chamber under the passage in front of it, with a narrow entrance to it, and a small stream of water running in front for the use of the animals, as these are plainly the dens for the wild beasts to be placed in temporarily, and there is just space enough for the animal to pass through into the wooden cage (*pegma* [o]), which had two doors, one at the side, the other at the top. When the cage on the lift was pulled up to the level of the floor of the stage or arena, under one of the trap-doors, the upper part was pulled up by a cord from below along with the trap-door, and the animal thus placed at liberty sprang out on to the stage. In the original pavement, which remains round a great part in the passages, behind the place for each of the lifts, is a round hole for the socket of a pivot to work in, evidently for the windlass for winding up the cord [p]. It is calculated that there was one of these lifts in front of each arch, and a den behind each, all round the *enceinte* of the building, so that all the wild beasts could spring on to the stage at once with tremendous effect. The persons in the lower gallery were protected by strong nets, and by bars that turned round on pivots, so that the claws of wild beasts had no hold upon them.

Under the long passage which comes in at the south end is a large drain at a considerably lower depth; there are gratings in the paved floor of the passage above opening into it, which had unfortunately been stopped up in some of the great floods, but was partially cleared out as far as the Meta Sudans in 1875. The paved floor of the passage over the drain under the arena is three feet above the level of the pavement, which is of herring-bone brickwork (*opus spicatum*), and the passage before mentioned goes all round the building nearly under the edge of the *podium*. Modern iron steps have been placed for people to descend to the bottom of the

---

[n] Photos., Nos. 3203, 3283.
[o] For the *pegmata*, see p. 14, and the authorities quoted in the note.

[p] See Plates XVIII., XIX., and Photos., No. 3283, and the graffito of the net, Plate XXIV.

building, and under these is seen the ancient iron grating to prevent anything being carried off by the rush of water[q]. From this it is evident that the great drain was to carry off the water used in the canals for the *naumachia*, when the Emperor " ordered the water to be let off and the boards to be replaced." There are evident marks of a great flood-gate or sluice drawn up, as a portcullis, at the entrance to this drain. It also appears that the vessels were floated down on the wooden framework on which they were dragged along, now made visible, but it does not appear that they could have been floated up also to the level of the canals. The space between the wooden floor of the *stage*, called the arena, and the original pavement being twenty-one feet, the canals were ten feet deep, and yet room is left for the passages and machinery under them. Possibly, but not probably, the whole central space could be floated, excepting just at the south end, where room was left for the machinery. The vessels were probably never removed from the building, but left under the vaults, and dragged out when required.

The tufa walls with the grooves for lifts belong to the earliest part of the building, and must be earlier than the time of Nero[r], as has been shewn; and his *stagnum navale*, or *naumachia*, his *venationes*, or wild-beast hunts, and gymnasium, which are recorded as belonging to his great palace, could have been nowhere else but on this spot.

We now see distinctly the large corbels[s] all round the building at a certain height, about six feet below the present level of the soil, for carrying the boards of the great floor covered with sand called the arena, upon which the athletes wrestled, the wild beasts were killed, and the persons condemned to death were torn to pieces by wild beasts; so that the martyrdom of the early Christians who were condemned to death in this manner took place on the sand of the *arena*, and not on the soil of the *area*. These corbels, in some instances, at the south end of the building, have the ends of them built into the old tufa wall, which is cut away to receive them. This old wall is not so regular in plan as the great work of the Flavian Emperors, the architect of which probably intended to destroy these old walls ultimately. Dio Cassius (himself a Roman senator) gives a vivid description of scenes which took place in this Amphitheatre[t] in his presence, in the time of

---

[q] See Photos., No. 3201, and Plate XIX.
[r] See the evidence of this, p. 13.
[s] See Plates XIII. and XVI.
[t] Dionis Cass. Hist. Rom., lib. lxxii. c. 17, 18, 19, 20, 21.

Commodus (as has been said), which leaves no doubt about the matter. Similar scenes are described in the time of Nero. The whole of the arena was, in fact, supported in all directions by the walls of the chambers or passages not more than ten feet apart; one object of which, no doubt, was to carry the great boarded floor, that could be removed at pleasure by the order of the emperor, and replaced as readily [u].

The excavations of 1874 and 1875 [x] very much astonished the people in Rome, and more especially the English visitors, who had been long accustomed to consider the *area* and the *arena* to be the same thing; they were amazed to see the whole of the area undermined with walls [y]. The walls that were first seen are for the most part brick walls of the fifth century, and the inscription [z] found there in 1814 records that they had been repaired by Lampadius, prefect, A.D. 442. This was after they had been much damaged by an earthquake. Another inscription records repairs of the *arena* and the *podium* by Basilius, prefect and consul, A.D. 508, after another earthquake. A long subterranean passage [a] at a considerable depth, leads out at the south-east end in the direction of the church of S. Clement; this passage passes under a number of square-topped arches or doorways, and has rather the appearance of having been a state entrance at the time that the level of the street was as

---

[u] Some scholars say that those scenes could not have taken place on this site, because the Flavian Amphitheatre was not built in the time of Nero. But it has been shewn that an awning in the *amphitheatre of Nero* is described by Pliny, writing at the time, during the life and reign of Nero, as he uses the expression *principis Neronis*, which he could hardly have used after his death. No other site but this can be found for such a large building as an amphitheatre, and this is close to the Golden House of Nero. In any case athletes or wrestlers, and *naumachia* or naval fights, are part of the tradition of many Roman amphitheatres, and there are sufficient remains of the substructures in many places to prove that this tradition is well founded. The *corridors* of the Flavian Emperors, though splendid additions to this great theatre, were not *necessary* for the performance of those pantomimes. It has also been shewn that the old tufa walls *must be* earlier than the time of Nero, and are probably of the time of Sylla.

[x] See Plates IV. to X.

[y] They were made at the suggestion of the author of this work, rather sooner than would otherwise have been the case, in order that he might be able to see them. Signor Rosa unfortunately began pulling down the walls of the substructure, calling them "Frangipani walls." The Frangipani family had possession of the Colosseum in the twelfth century, but the construction of that period is totally different from any of the walls in the Colosseum, either above or below the level of the *arena*. The Minister of Public Instruction fortunately arrived in Rome in time to stop their demolition, and obtained an Act of Parliament, in 1875, appointing a general Archæological Commission for all Italy, with Signor Fiorelli, from Pompeii, at the head of it; and no individual will in future be permitted either to destroy antiquities, or to build anything new, without the consent of the Commission.

[z] See No. 3202, and p. 27.

[a] See No. 3201.

low as that passage, that is, before the filling-up of the foss-ways, which began in the second century. On each side of this passage is a long narrow vaulted chamber parallel to it, under the corridor, and in the pavement of each of these chambers is a series of six round holes lined with hard copper or bronze, for a pivot to work in; they are somewhat worn, and in a straight line one behind the other. The most probable use for these was for a windlass or capstan to be worked in each, and by these means to drag along the vessels in the canals before mentioned, as extending down the centre of this colossal building.

It has also been mentioned that a very ancient wooden frame, calculated for the keel of a vessel to slide upon, remained on the ground in 1875, just within the passage at the south-east end of the building, as if the vessels used in the sham fights could be placed out of sight in the lofty central passage. This is said by those accustomed to dockyards to have all the appearance of a dry dock, or a cradle for vessels to stand upon [b]. We read of the vessels being divided into two nations or sides, there were probably six on each side, and each nation occupied one of the canals. It is probable that the surface between the two canals on either side of this central passage, just under the level of the arena (which was twenty-one feet above the brick floor), was flooded with two or three feet in water, but the keels of the vessels were in the canals. On either side of the passages before mentioned [c] are remains of other walls of tufa, with vertical grooves in them, as if for lifts; the brick walls, between those of tufa, have been introduced at a later period, and in these instances the grooves are not opposite each other. This shews that great alterations have been going on at different periods in these subterranean works, some of which are earlier than the existing building, and others considerably later [d]. In one place, near the south-east entrance, the two old stone walls, with the vertical grooves, remain in their original places facing each other, so that lifts might work up and down in them.

Architects had long wondered where the builders could possibly have obtained such an immense mass of materials in so short

---

[b] See No. 3263, and Plate VII.
[c] See No. 3203.
[d] The plan of one section of this enormous building (see No. 183 and Plate XIV.), and those of the six different floors or storeys, shew the admirable arrangement of the seats and passages, and *vomitoria* for the rapid exit of the people, as well as the plan of the whole building would do. The magnificent stone arcades of the Flavian Emperors, A.D. 80, appear in many parts to be built against brick walls and galleries of the time of Nero, originally built for the spectators of the old Naumachia. (See No. 3205, 1762.)

a time, it was therefore evidently natural that they should make use of anything that served their purpose. It appears that in some parts the galleries for the spectators of the old Naumachia were thus made use of as they stood, without actually rebuilding them. The great tufa blocks of the second wall of Rome were also used as old materials for the substructure of the great stone arcades; but the builders, who had to add the upper gallery, were afraid to trust the soft tufa to carry so great a weight[e], and therefore built piers of travertine about four feet wide[f]. These piers to support the upper gallery go right through the walls of all the lower galleries, from the top to the bottom of the building (as has been said on p. 12).

The architectural details of the Colosseum are much admired by architects; the cornice-mouldings of the lower storey are good examples of the style of the latter part of the first century[g]. The supply of water for the naval fights must have been from the Aqueducts; the water was brought from the Cœlian in a shallow channel, carried upon a lofty double colonnade, or arcade[h]. It has been mentioned[i] that there are slight remains of three reservoirs to receive it, which can be traced by remains of the particular cement used only for the aqueducts[k]. The continuations of the shallow channel along the corridors can be seen in many places, and are shewn in the photographs[l].

In the upper storey of the third century, on the exterior, the corbels for the masts to rest upon, and the holes in the cornice for them to pass through, have been mentioned[m]. On the interior of this wall, now that it has been stripped of plaster, and the wooden gallery that had been built up against it has been destroyed, we see clearly how hastily it has been built of old materials[n]. In other parts it has been cased with modern brickwork, but the corbels for fastening the masts on the inside are preserved[o].

---

[e] The amphitheatre is 1,837 Roman feet in circuit, 638 long, 535 wide, and 165 high from the ground, besides 21 feet for the substructures, so that the whole height was 186 feet. The Roman foot is not quite so long as the English foot, but the difference is trifling. The number of spectators was 87,000 according to the Regionary Catalogue; modern authorities say that the measurement shews this number to be rather exaggerated.

[f] See Nos. 1081, 1762.
[g] See No. 1346.
[h] A coin of Titus shews a colonnade, and one of Domitian also. See Plate XXV.
[i] See p. 11.
[k] See No. 1761.
[l] See Nos. 1758, 1759, 1760, 1763.
[m] They are more clearly shewn in another photograph, No. 827.
[n] See No. 367.
[o] See No. 185.

THE EVIDENCE OF THE CONSTRUCTION, AND COMPARISON.

It is well known that the first principle of the modern science of archæology is comparison. To compare small remains of one place with more perfect remains of the same kind, and as far as may be, of the same period, in other places. By these means, what has been destroyed in one is frequently supplied by the corresponding part in another. This is remarkably the case with regard to the amphitheatres, which are very numerous; there was one to every Roman town of importance, and such large buildings have almost invariably left remains visible [p]. It appears nearly certain that the Colosseum in Rome was the earliest, and that this was the type generally followed more or less closely by the others. This was a gradual development, and not merely one original design; the magnificent front and stone corridors of the Flavian emperors, which constitute what is usually considered to be the amphitheatre, were in fact built round a theatre previously existing [q]; that the names of theatre or amphitheatre were used indifferently is implied in many instances, and is distinctly shewn by an inscription found in the Colosseum itself, and preserved on the spot, in which it is called *theatrum*, and not *amphitheatrum* [r]. The theatre, or amphitheatre, round which the corridors were built, has been shewn to have been in parts of the time of Nero [s], and other parts earlier, most probably the work of Scaurus in the time of Sylla [t]. This colossal building was finished and consecrated by Titus in the year 80 [u].

CAPUA.

The great amphitheatre at Capua is almost of the same size as the Colosseum in Rome, and a remarkably exact copy of it; some say that it was called by the same name, but this is rather doubtful,

---

[p] They were, however, not always of stone or brick; in places where stone was scarce, they were frequently of wood only.

[q] See p. 1.   [r] See p. 7.

[s] See p. 6.   [t] See pp. 2, 9, 23.

[u] See pp. 1, 8. That the amphitheatres were among the finest buildings of the Romans in all their cities it is hardly necessary to say; it seems clear that they were first built for the favourite amusement of the hunting of wild beasts, and that the first name for them was *Theatrum Venatorium*; but the gladiators were soon introduced, for the further amusement of the people in the same buildings. Both amusements are believed to have been used in Greece before they were introduced into Rome, but they were in use in Rome before the time of the Empire. At first, the amphitheatres were temporary buildings of wood only (as has been shewn), but there were several of these. After the great Flavian amphitheatre was completed, this seems to have been the only one in Rome; but those of several other cities, such as Capua and Verona (see the learned work of Scipio Maffei, *Verona Illustrata*, Milano, 1876, parte quarta) must have been nearly equal to it.

as persons who have resided at Capua for years say they have never heard it so called; the name is not of much importance: the plan and arrangements are identical, and although the superstructure has been almost entirely destroyed, the substructures at Capua are far more perfect than in Rome; and here we have the mouth of an aqueduct perfect in these substructures, and remains of canals for water, with the very massive walls to support them, exactly as in Rome. The great drain to carry off the water also remains, but on rather a different plan; instead of being carried under a low arch at the end of the great central passage, as in Rome, the water is conveyed into a large and deep well in the centre of the building, with four small channels running into it, beside the great central opening. From this well there is a large and deep drain leading to the river. There are the same dens for wild beasts under the *podium*, and in the pavement the same sockets for pivots to work in, to pull up the cages, or *pegmata*, or lifts. The arena, instead of being a boarded floor, is of brick, carried on vaults, with numerous square apertures for the trap-doors. The central passage is vaulted at the two ends, but open in the greater part. Round each of the openings there is a deep groove, as if a wooden cover had been fitted tightly over each and made water-tight, so that the surface of the arena might be flooded for naval fights; but there is reason to believe that only rowing-boats, drawing little water, were used in this instance, and not galleys.

The earliest part of the building at Capua is of the time of the Emperor Hadrian, but only a small part of that period remains, as shewn by the construction (reticulated work with a framework of brick). Most of the walls in the substructure are faced with brick of the second or third century, with later repairs [v].

---

[v] The following inscriptions, found upon the spot, agree with the construction, as is always the case when the true date can be ascertained. The first is of the time of Hadrian, A.D. 120, (No. 43 in chapter vii. of the work of Francesco Alvino, which contains the ancient inscriptions found upon the spot); the second (No. 48 of the same collection) appears to be of Septimius Severus and Pertinax, A.D. 192; the third in point of date (No. 16 in the collection) records restorations by Lampridius:—

XLIII.
IMP. CÆS. T. ÆLIO
HADRIANO AVG
PATRI PATRLE
SVBLEVATORI ORBIS
RESTITVTORI OPE
RVM PVBLICORVM
INDVLGENTISSIMO
OPTIMAQ. PRINCIPI
CAMPANI
OB INSIGNEM ERGA EOS BE
NIGNITATEM D. D.

Puteoli or Pozzuoli.

This amphitheatre is very much smaller than either the Colosseum in Rome, or the amphitheatre at Capua; the superstructure is in a very ruinous state, but the substructure is almost perfect, and the work is much more highly finished than in either of the others. There are considerable remains of rich stucco ornament on the vault over the passage to one of the side doors. The arena is nearly intact, and is of brick, carried on vaults, what the Italians call *pensile;* this word does not mean literally hanging, but hollow underneath; and this brick floor is full of square holes for trap-doors; round the edge of each is a deep groove, as if for a cover to fit into, which may very well have been made water-tight. Signor Scherillo, a native of Pozzuoli, and now a canon of the cathedral at Naples, has published several papers on this amphitheatre in the *Atti dell' Accademia di Archeologia, Letteratura e belle Arti di Napoli.* He is of opinion that the arena was flooded to the depth of about three feet, or about half way up the *podium;* the water would only cover the two or three lower steps, and there were probably also water-tight doors at the foot of them. At a short distance in front of the *podium* is a channel about a foot deep, in which probably a beam of wood has lain, and at intervals of ten or twelve feet is a square hole, evidently for a beam of wood to have stood in, no doubt the lower part of the frame for the netting to keep off the wild beasts from the people in the lower gallery, as in the Colosseum, and probably carried up as poles or

XLVIII.
IMP. CÆS. DIVI M. ANTONINI
GERM. SARM. FIL. DIVI COMMODI
FRATRI DIVI ANTONINI PII NEPOTI
DIVI HADRIANI PRONEPOTI DIVI
TRAIANI PARTHICI ABNEPOTI DIVI
NERVAE ADNEPOTI
SEPTIMIO SEVERO PIO PERTINACI
ARABICO ADIABENICO P.P. PONT. MAX
TRIB. POT. IIII. IMP. VIII. COS II. PROC
COLONIA CAPVA

XVI.
POSTVMIO LAMPADIO
V. C.
ET INLVSTRI CON. CAMPANIAE
RESTITVTORI PATRIAE
ET REDINTEGRATORI OPERVM IVBLICORVM

By a singular coincidence, Lampadius was also the name of the Prefect who restored the Flavian amphitheatre in A.D. 445; but though the surname is the same, the prename is not, he was probably of the same family.

masts to receive the lower ends of the cords to carry the awning; there are also remains at the top of the outer wall of the same arrangement of fixing the masts there as in the Colosseum, and the same thing can be seen in many other amphitheatres where the outer wall remains perfect. This amphitheatre is entirely of the time of Hadrian, a beautiful piece of construction. It seems to have been a favourite show-place of the Emperors on state occasions, for the upper classes and foreigners, when the fleet was assembled in the Bay of Naples, in which the Cape of Misenum is one of the promontories near this spot. The enormous reservoir of water for the supply of the fleet, called the *Piscina Mirabilis*, is also not far off; and the amphitheatre belonged to the great imperial villa, originally of Nero, in the bay adjoining.

This amphitheatre has been shamefully used in the Middle Ages, the arena having been made into a cabbage garden, with a deep bed of earth upon it. The upper parts of the walls had probably been damaged by the great earthquake, and in order to get rid of the numerous broken columns and capitals lying about, the gardeners threw them down the openings into the vaults below, where they are stacked up under the arches like so many mere blocks of stone, to put them out of the way. Fortunately it is owing probably to the vaults having thus been made use of, that they have been so well preserved, and also because there was not much call for building-stone in the neighbourhood, as the ruins of the villa and the temples had supplied as much as was wanted.

VERONA.

In many of the Italian cities, as well as in Gaul and Britain, the amphitheatre was made of earth and wood only, the seats cut out in banks on the slope of a hill or of an *agger*, in districts where stone was scarce. In the Circus Maximus also the seats for the *plebs* on the Aventine seem to have been made in that manner, the stone galleries were on the Palatine only.

At VERONA, as in many other instances, the outer wall has been almost entirely destroyed; two bays, or four arches of it only remain, but these are sufficient to shew the plan, and that it was three storeys high, the Tuscan order of columns being used throughout. The upper storey seems to have been for the passage round the seats over the corridors; the two lower ones with the seats remain nearly perfect, forming a fine double arcade on the outer side without columns, now made visible by the demolition of the outer corridor and wall. In its present state it is one of the finest buildings of its class. There seems to be no historical evidence of its date; in Murray's Handbook it is said to be of the time of the Flavian Emperors, but no authority for this is given, and it is not probable. The measurements given by Maffei do not *quite* agree with those taken by Alvino [a], but the variations are not great; and as one is taken in Neapolitan palms of ten inches, the other in Veronese feet, the apparent variation probably arose only from the different mode of calculating. None of them agree with those in Murray's Handbooks, which are taken from the Lectures of Mr. Woods. The general proportions may be judged of by the number of persons that each would contain; Publius Victor states that the Colosseum had 87,000 places, and Maffei states that this at Verona had 77,000, this would make it one-eighth less. The variations are not of much importance. The outer wall was partly destroyed by an earthquake in 1184, and the stones were then used as building material, as in other places, but this was soon stopped. The unusually perfect state of the seats arises from the care taken of them in the Middle Ages, very much to the credit of the inhabitants at that period. As early as 1228, it was agreed that each *podesta* (or mayor) should expend 500 lire (about £20 [b]) on the repairs of this building; and in 1435 penalties were inflicted on any one who removed any of the stone. This shews that the people of Verona were more civilized than the Romans at that period. In 1545 a special officer was appointed to take charge of it. The restoration of the seats has been carefully done, and is not perceived without some examination. This restoration was begun by voluntary subscription as early as 1568, and continued as late as 1805. The arches were numbered on the exterior, as in the Colosseum; the four that remain have the numbers LXIIII to LXVII over them. The arrangement of the masts and poles for the awning are the same as in Rome, and were managed in the same manner. The plan of the *vomitoria* is also nearly the same. No excavations appear to have been made *under* the arena; a plan and section of the substructures under the galleries is given by Maffei, they are similar to those in Rome. He does not appear to have been aware that there was likely to have been anything under the arena; he mentions the conduits of aqueducts, and drains for carrying off the water, which seem to shew that *naumachia* were held here, but we have no information as to how they were managed.

---

[a] See p. 45. [b] This would be at least equal to £200 of modern money.

The proportions of the three principal amphitheatres, as given in the work of Alvino[a], in Neapolitan palms[b] of ten inches are:—

	Colosseum.	Verona.	Capua.
Length of interior	639	522	645
Breadth of interior	527	417	530
Length of arena	298	252	289
Breadth of arena	186	149	174
Height of first order	35	29	36
Entire height of interior	174	91	169
No. of orders[b]	4	3	4
Actual height of ruins	171	62	75
No. of arches	80	72	80
Circuit	170	134	178
Gates	2	1	2
Width of arches	15	$12\frac{1}{2}$	15
Breadth of pilasters	8	$6\frac{1}{2}$	8

THE AMPHITHEATRE AT POLA, IN ISTRIA.

THIS fine structure is built of beautiful white stone, almost marble, in large blocks without mortar, but it had metallic fastenings, which have all disappeared, and left their marks behind them. There are two rows of arches, and above a line of square windows; also a curious stone parapet, with very distinct indications of arrangement for spreading the *velarium* or *vela* (the awning). There is only one line of columns, but there was originally a second, and most of the bases of them are still *in situ*. The amphitheatre is built against a rocky mountain, which causes the northern part of the ellipse to be much lower than the outer one. There are numerous passages and substructures, except on the rocky half of the building. There are two principal entrances facing each other, and in a line with them is a trench exactly similar to the one in the Colosseum, and at Capua, &c. These canals for conducting water into the arena can still be seen, and there seems no doubt of its having been used for *naumachia*. There are but few remains of the seats, except a large accumulation of *débris*, and traces of the stairs and *vomitoria*. The whole line of the *podium* is also perfectly preserved, but no trace of the concentric *euripus* found in other

---

[a] Anfiteatro Campano illustrato e Restorato da Francesco Alvino terza edizione col paragone di tutti gli anfiteatri D'Italia ed un cenno sugli antichi monumenti di Capua. Napoli, 1842.

[a] The Neapolitan *palm* is ten inches English measure. If the measurements of Signor Alvino are reduced to English measure, they do not agree with those of Messrs. Taylor and Crecy for the Colosseum; as he used the same scale for all three, the proportions are the same.

[b] In Rome these are Doric, Ionic, Corinthian, Composite; at Verona, all Tuscan; at Capua, all Doric.

amphitheatres. The most puzzling parts of the structure are four rectangular towers, which appear to have had no special staircases leading to them from the ground; antiquaries, with all their ingenuity, have not yet given any satisfactory explanation of these objects. They were most probably for the music, as in the circus of Maxentius on the Via Appia, near Rome, where one tower remains at each end of the *carceres* [e].

The amphitheatre at Nimes, in Aquitaine, still has a wooden floor with trap-doors in it; the present floor is not ancient, but no doubt replaces an old one; there is no staircase, and the only access to the passages below is by a step-ladder, and the arrangement of the substructures is quite different from that in Rome, or at Capua, or Puteoli. There are large masses of stone at intervals to support the floor, and wide passages between them. On two of these massive piers are inscriptions, with the name of the architect, the same inscription repeated twice, in characters of the third century. There are no signs of *naumachia*, or of aqueducts; the seats and the superstructure are more perfect than usual, and have a very fine effect.

At Arles the superstructure also is very grand, but there are no substructures under the arena visible. It is partly cut out of the rock, the lower part supported by massive substructures, but no passages in them are visible. Excavations have not been made there, and the doorways appear to be filled up to half their height, as at the Porta Tiburtina in Rome.

At Bordeaux the ruins of the amphitheatre are called the (*arènes*) arena, and it evidently had a boarded floor covered with sand, as in the Colosseum; and the superstructures, with the seats, are more perfect than in Rome. There is a great general resemblance, but the details are not the same. The Colosseum is the only amphitheatre which has *double* corridors round it, and the absence of this outer passage makes a different arrangement of the stairs to the *vomitoria* necessary in this and other amphitheatres, where the people went straight out through each archway.

[e] I am indebted for this clear account of the amphitheatre at Pola to Lord Talbot de Malahide, who was there in October, 1875. The excellent drawings of Mr. Arthur Glennie, who resided at Pola for one whole summer, also agree perfectly with the excellent account of that remarkable building, which further contributes to illustrate the Colosseum at Rome. An excellent account of Pola appeared about the same time in the *Saturday Review*, but this is more general, not so specially written with this object in view.

Substructures compared.

In treating of the amphitheatres in general, and corroborating the account given in this work of the Colosseum, it must be borne in mind that in every theatre a considerable space is required behind the scenes for the use of the actors. The performances in an amphitheatre would equally require such space for the performers when off the stage, and the only space to which they could possibly retire is under that stage which is called the *arena*, because it was covered with sand; and it has been shewn that in these substructures there are numerous passages and contrivances for the machines to send up the wild beasts to be hunted, the men and the dogs to hunt them, and the athletes for the wrestling matches; we have also canals for water for the keels of the vessels, in some instances, but not in all; in some cases, the vessels employed could only have been rowing-boats, *rates*. We have also mention of battles with swords in the *naumachia*, and of many men being killed. This seems to make it clear that the principal amusement consisted in the crew of one vessel trying to board the other, and the defendants preventing their doing so in every way that they could, either by throwing them off into the water, or with swords and spears.

At Pozzuoli, where the substructures are nearly perfect, there are remains of an intermediate passage, as if for men to run along; and this has been traced to communicate with the Emperor's seat, and is thought to have been for messengers to go with orders, and to give the necessary directions. All that remains of this intermediate passage are the corbels for carrying a wooden gallery upon. There are similar corbels for an intermediate passage between two floors in the Colosseum, but here in the upper part, apparently for the sailors to run along to furl or unfurl the awning, not in the substructures; there also appear to have been separate stairs and *vomitoria* for that passage, and as we know that several hundred sailors were employed in the Colosseum, such an arrangement would be quite necessary.

Mention has frequently been made of the great central passage, which exists not only in the Colosseum, but in all other amphitheatres where substructures were made. This passage appears to have served for several useful purposes; there are traces of machines in it for lifting up some large object, not only in the Colosseum but also at Capua; and the things to be lifted up in all probability must have been the vessels for the naval fights. This central passage is mentioned or implied in several instances in the classical authors; it had the appearance of a gulf dividing the earth or *arena* into two parts. Apuleius calls it *vorago terræ* (a gulf of the earth); Martial, the *via media*, or middle way; and Petronius, *ruina terræ*, from the appearance of a swallowing-up the machines and the gladiators.

The machines used for these public amusements were evidently numerous and important, and required a good deal of space to stow them away, more even than was afforded by the vaults and passages under the arena in the Colosseum. This is implied by the celebrated letter of Apollodorus, the architect, to the Emperor Hadrian, in which the architect told the Emperor that he *ought to have* built the Temple of Roma at the south end of the Summa Sacra Via, and to have made room for this machinery of the amphitheatre in vaulted chambers under it (as before mentioned); *that he did not do so* is evident, for the excavations of 1874 brought to light rude concrete walls of the time of the Republic, with a small aqueduct of the time of the Early Empire, made to carry water to the fountains at the corners of the *porticus* above. The accounts which we have in classical authors, of the machinery employed in the amphitheatre, remind us very much of that used for a Christmas pantomime in one of the London theatres, and all these great shows were very much of the character of a pantomime. To begin at the top, the cords which carried the *velarium*, or awning, were strong enough for a rope-dancer, and were called by the name of *catadromus;* and we have an account in Suetonius, in the time of Nero, of an elephant being taught to walk upon these cords with a Roman cavalier on his back [d]. We also have an account of an actor trying to play the part of Icarus, and fly down from the top, falling dead at the feet of Nero, and sprinkling him with his blood [e].

The *pegmata* have been mentioned as cages for wild beasts, and this was evidently one meaning of the word, as used by Seneca in his Epistles, quoted in a previous page, but this was one meaning only; the same name was applied to a wooden framework of any kind, sometimes evidently what we now call scenery, either fixed or moveable. Josephus mentions *pegmata* used in the triumphal procession of Titus, one of which was three storeys high, and another

---

[d] "Notissimus eques Romanus elephanto supersedens per catadromum decucurrit." (Suetonii Nero, cap. xi. Xiphil. lxi.)
"Ego eo vocabulo funem intelligo, qui summo theatro alligatus, declinis ad imum theatri pertinebat solum defigebaturque, per quem descendere maximi periculi et artis atque adeo miraculi erat." (Turnebo, Adv. xxvii. 18.)

[e] "Icarus, primo statim conatu, juxta cubiculum ejus (Neronis) decidit, ipsumque cruore respersit." (Suetonii Nero, c. 12.)

four, on which were representations of the capture of Jerusalem. Another is mentioned by Calpurnius as representing the Tarpeian rock [f], and the victims were thrown from the top of it on to the arena, or into the gulf, and killed on the spot. Apuleius also describes one as representing Mount Ida, with trees, and shrubs, and fountains, on which appeared from time to time Paris and Mercury, and the three goddesses, Juno, Pallas, and Venus, with a number of animals to complete the scene [g]. Another is described by Claudian as representing Mount Etna [h], with the flames burning at the top. Others representing Vulcan and Cyclops; these were in the shows of Carinus and Numerianus, and are mentioned by Vopiscus [i]. It is evident that this scenery must have been prepared below and sent up from the central passage, as there was no room anywhere else for sending it up. Martial [k] also mentions *pegmata* as rising from this middle way, and that a person could see from thence THE COLOSSUS among the stars. As the Colossus stood on an elevated platform on the Summa Sacra Via, just in a line with this middle way, and was itself 120 ft. high, it is quite probable that the head of it could be seen from below, over the upper gallery.

The dens for the wild beasts in the substructures under the *podium* are found both at Capua and at Pozzuoli, just as in the Colosseum, and the technical name for such a den was *catabolus* [l].

---

[f] "Vidimus in cœlum trabibus spectacula textis
Surgere, Tarpeium prope despectantia culmen."
(Calpurnii, Ecloga vii. v. 23.)

[g] "Erat mons ligneus ad instar incliti montis illius, quem vates Homerus Idæum cecinit, sublimi instructus fabrica, consitus viretis et vivis arboribus summo cacumine, de manibus fabri fonte mœnante, fluviales aquas eliquans." (Apulei, Metamor., lib. x. c. 30.)

[h] "Mobile ponderibus descendat Pegma reductis
Inque chori speciem, spargentes ardua flammas
Scena rotet: varios effingat Mulciber orbes
Per tabulas impune vagus, pictaque citato
Ludant igne trabes, et non permissa morari
Fida per innocuas errent incendia turres."
(Claudianus, De Consulatu Mallii, v. 325.)

[i] "Memorabile maxime Cari et Carini et Numeriani hoc habuit imperium, quod ludos populo Romano novis ornatos spectaculis dederunt, quos in Palatio circa porticum statuti pictos vidimus . . . centum pantomimos et gymnicos mille pegma præterea, cujus flammis scena conflagravit quam Diocletianus postea magnificentiorem reddidit." (Vopiscus in Carino, cap. 18, ap. Script. Hist. Aug.)

[k] "Hic ubi sidereus propius videt astra Colossus,
Et crescunt media Pegmata celsa via,
Invidiosa feri radiabant atria regis."
(Martialis, De Spectaculis, Ep. 2.)

[l] "Catabolum erat locus, in quo feræ crudiebantur sive ad mansuetudinem sive etiam ad crudelitatem, quam in bestiarios exercerent." (Papias.)
"Catabolum est clausura animalium, ubi desuper aliquid jacitur." (Vossii, Lexicon Etymologicum.)
The Catabolensis or Catabolici were

Besides the mention by Herodian of a hundred lions leaping on to the arena at once, as "if out of the earth," (mentioned in page 26), the same thing is mentioned by several other authors at different periods, both of lions and of other wild beasts. Vopiscus mentions this in the life of Probus[m], and that all the doorways were stopped for a time; and he distinctly mentions the animals coming out of the caves below. Ammianus Marcellinus[n] also mentions the doorways being often stopped for the wild beasts. Statius mentions the same[o], and Julius Capitolinus, both in the time of Antoninus Pius and Marcus Aurelius. In each case a hundred lions are mentioned, and in the latter that they were killed with arrows; and in the time of Probus, not only a hundred lions, but also a hundred Lybian leopards, a hundred Syrian ones, a hundred lionesses, and three hundred bears. Lampridius[p] also mentions in the time of Gordianus the almost incredible number of a thousand bears, in addition to a hundred Lybian leopards.

To protect the people in the lower gallery from these wild beasts, a strong netting was provided (as has been mentioned); this was of gold wire, fixed in a wooden frame, and at the top was an ivory rod which turned round, so that if an animal should attempt to cling to it, he would necessarily fall back. This net was called *retia*, and at Puteoli or Pozzuoli it was either of gold, or gilt; and this was the case in the Colosseum also, and in other instances. Our authority for this is Calpurnius in his Eclogues[q].

The naval fights with the larger vessels were sometimes held in the Circus Maximus, which could be flooded to the depth required by stopping up at the lower end the stream that runs through it, which is in fact a branch of the small river Almo, but was in this

---

the men who fed the wild beasts, and threw down their food from the small passage before mentioned. (See p. 17.)

[m] "Addidit alia die in Amphitheatro una missione centum jubatos leones, qui rugitibus suis tonitru excitabant; qui omnes e POSTICIS interempti sunt, non magnum præbentes spectaculum quo occidebantur. Neque enim erat bestiarum impetus ille, qui esse e caveis egredientibus olet." (Vopisci Probus,

c. 19, ap. Script. Hist. Aug.)

[n] "Ut sæpe faciunt amphitheatrales feræ diffractis tandem solutæ POSTICIS." (Ammianus Marcellinus, lib. 27.)

[o] "Stat. CARDINE aperto — Infelix cavea." The door opening on a hinge or a pivot.

[p] "Feras lybicas una die centum exhibuit, ursos una die mille." (Julii Capitolini, i. c. 3, ap. Script. Hist. Aug.)

[q] ". . . . Auro quoque torta refulgent
Retia, quæ totis in Arenam dentibus extant.
. . . . nec non, ubi finis Arenæ,
Proxima marmoreo peragit spectaculo muro:
Sternitur adjunctis ebur admirabile truncis,
Et coit in rotulam, tereti qua lubricus axis
Impositos subita vertigine falleret ungues
Excuteretque feras." (Calpurnii, Ecl. 7.)

part called the Euripus. This name was also given to the canals for the *naumachia*, as in the Colosseum. This must have been the case, because the Emperor Heliogabalus upon one occasion filled these canals with wine, which could not have been done in the Circus Maximus, where the Euripus was a natural running stream of water; but in the Colosseum a canal supplied with water from an aqueduct, which could be let in or drawn off at pleasure, might very well have been filled with wine during an abundant season, when in Rome the wine is sometimes worth less than the vessel that holds it, so that large quantities are frequently wasted for want of casks to put it in. In all wine-growing countries, the same thing occurs from time to time in superabundant seasons. It is true that these naval fights were called Circensian games, because they were sometimes held in a circus (as has been said), but the same name was given to them when they were held in the amphitheatre, as in this instance, by Lampridius[r]. Martial[s] distinguishes very clearly both the one and the other, and makes it evident that the *stagna* of Nero were used for the *naumachia* of the Cæsars.

That the vaults under the arena were called *caveæ*, caves (or cavities), has been already mentioned, and is evident from many passages in classical and mediæval authors; as in Tertullian and in Prudentius[t], when describing the scenes that had taken place in the amphitheatre as the wicked rites in which the gladiators were killed on the arena, and the impious games in which the sad

---

[r] "Fertur in euripis vino plenis Navales Circenses exhibuisse." (Lampridii Antoninus Heliogabalus, c. 23, ap. Script. Hist. Aug.)

[s] "Quidquid et in Circo spectatur et amphitheatro,
  Dives Cæsarea præstitit unda tibi :
Fucinus et pigri taceantur stagna Neronis :
  Hanc norint unam sæcula Naumachiam."
      (Martialis de Spect. Ep. 28.)

That is, the *stagna* in the amphitheatre were supplied by an aqueduct from the lake of Fucino. This lake has been drained in 1874-75 by Prince Torlonia, by carrying out the project of the great engineers of the time of the Emperor Claudius, and making an *emisarium*, on even a grander scale than the one partially made in the time of Claudius, on a similar plan to those of the lakes of Albano and Nemi.

[t] "Respice terrifici scelerata sacraria Ditis,
Cui cadit infausta fusus gladiator arena,
Heu male lustratæ Phlegetontia victima Romæ.
Nam quid vesani sibi vult ars impia ludi?
Quid mortes juvenum, quid sanguine pasta voluptas
Quid pulvis Caveæ semper funebris et illa
Amphitheatralis spectacula tristia pompæ?
Nempe Charon jugulis miserorum se duce dignas
Accipit inferias, placatas crimine sacro.
Hæ sunt deliciæ Jovis Infernalis : in istis
Arbiter obscuri placidus requiescit Averni."
      (Aur. Prudentius Clem. contra Symmachum, 379—389.)

spectacles of funereal character were brought up from the caves, worthy only of the infernal Jupiter (whom the Christians call Satan).

THE ARENA.

That one of the modes of putting criminals to death in Rome was to throw them to the wild beasts to be torn to pieces on the arena, to glut the savage taste of the Roman people, is notorious; but that many of the gladiators and other actors were also frequently killed on the arena is not so generally known, and yet the evidence for it is too distinct to be doubted. Seneca mentions distinctly, in one of his Epistles [u], that a number of the bodies were exposed to view, of men who were unable to defend themselves by their swords or their shields. He justly says that the men were as savage as the lions or the bears, and the usual end of these fighting men was death on the arena. There is a representation of them in a fine mosaic picture in the Villa Borghese, with the letter θ, and others on two of the *graffiti* found in the Colosseum in 1875 [v].

It is well known that the Roman people sometimes called upon the emperor to produce the most celebrated gladiators, who had been named in the programme for the show. Horace [x] alludes to this in his Epistles; and Martial [y] speaks of two of these gladiators, one called Myrinus, and the other Triumphus (a name which has misled some of the commentators). Another gladiator of that period was named Columbus, and was called for by the people under Claudius, who promised that he should be exhibited if he could be found, as is related by Suetonius [z]. Under Gordianus we

---

[u] 2. "Casu in meridianum spectaculum incidi, lusus expectans et sales et aliquid laxamenti, quo hominum oculi ab humano cruore acquiescant. 3. Contra est : quidquid ante pugnatum est, misericordia fuit. Nunc omissis nugis, mera homicidia sunt. Nihil habent quo tegantur ; ad ictum totis corporibus expositi, nunquam frustra mittunt manum mittunt. Hoc plerique ordinariis paribus et postulatitiis præferunt non galea, non scuto repellitur ferrum. Quo munimenta? quo gladii artes? Omnia ista mortes meræ sunt. Mane leonibus et ursis homines, meridie spectatoribus suis objiciuntur. 4. Interfectores interfecturis jubentur objici, et victorem in aliam detinent cædem, exitus pugnantium mors est ferro et ignores geritur. Hæc fiunt dum vacat arena." (Sen., Epistolæ ad Lucilium, 7.)

[v] See Photos., Nos. 3273, 3274, and Plates XXIII., XXIV.

[x] "Prima dicte mihi, summa dicende Camœna,
 Spectatum, satis et donatum jam rude quæris,
 Mæcenas, iterum antiquo me includere ludo."
(Horatii Epist., lib. i. 1.)

[y] "Dum peteret pars hæc Myrinum, pars illa Triumphum ;
 Promisit pariter Cæsar utrâque manu."
(Martiali de Spectaculis, Epig. 20.)

[z] "Fuerunt sub Gordiano Romæ elephanti triginta et duo, gladiatorum Fisculium paria mille." (Julii Capitolini Gordianus tertius.)

are told that thirty-two elephants, and about a thousand gladiators were exhibited; it is probable that many of these were killed in the fight. It has already been stated that Commodus fought himself with the gladiators on the arena.

There was a particular costume for the athletes, and also for the emperor when he went on to the arena, and Commodus gave offence by not complying with the custom which had been established by Titus at the opening, as is mentioned by Suetonius[a]. The carrying out of the dead bodies from the arena is also mentioned by Quintilian[b] as done with pomp. Lampridius[c] expressly says that Commodus acted contrary to the established custom, and was not dressed in the proper manner; and that his helmet was carried out of the theatre by the gate by which the dead bodies were usually carried out, which was considered a bad omen, and he was murdered soon afterwards. This is also mentioned by Dio Cassius (as quoted on page 23).

The Gates.

There were naturally four gates to this enormous structure, one at each end, and one in the middle of each side; and the same arrangement was followed in all the other amphitheatres. By what names these gates were called, and whether these names were special for each particular building, or general for all, is a question still undecided, and also which was the state entrance. It is commonly said that in the Colosseum the state entrance was on the northern side, next the Esquiline Hill, because there is no number over that arch as there is over the other arches, but this was probably the case with all the four entrances; the other three gates are destroyed. The excavations in 1875 have been supposed to shew that the passage on the southern side towards the Cælian did not lead direct to the palace of Commodus, but was carried round the outer line of the building to the south-east end, near S. Clemente; the natural entrance from the palace of Nero would be from the gate at the east end, and not on the north side. The names of the gates are not easily fixed; one was called Porta Libitinensis, and from this door the bodies of those who were killed were carried out, as we learn from Lampridius in the life of Commodus[d]. They were carried

---

[a] Suetonii Titus, c. 9.

[b] "Jam ad spectaculum supplicii nostri populus convenerat: jam ostentata per arenam periturorum corpora mortis suæ *pompam* duxerant." (Quinctil., Decl. 9.)

[c] Lampridii Commodus Antoninus, 16.

[d] "Contra consuetudinem (Commodus) pænulatos jussit spectatores, non togatos ad munus convenire, quod funeribus solebat, ipse in pullis vestimentis

out of this gate on a special bier provided for the purpose, called *sandapila*, as is mentioned by Juvenal[e], and explained by the old Scoliast. This name is sometimes written *sanavivaria*, as in the *Acta Martyrum Felicita et Perpetua*[f]. The word *libitina* signifies death, or a funeral, or a bier; it is used also by Horace in his Odes[g], and explained by the Scoliast in the same manner, and by Martial in his Epigrams[h]. It appears that the name of *sandapilaria* and *libitinensis* were synonymous. Another gate was called Porta Prætoria, probably that at the south-east end, opening from the road to the Vivarium at the Prætorian Camp. Another, Porta Sacra, probably that at the north-west end, opening to the Via Sacra. The Meta Sudans was close to this gate, and was supplied with water by tubes, as Seneca mentions in his Epistles[i]. His fifty-seventh letter is full of lamentation for the fate of the athletes.

The name of *cochlea* is given to one of the doors of the amphitheatre, which led from the *cavea* to the arena. This name is used by Varro[k], and has puzzled all the commentators; it need hardly be said that *cochlea* is literally "a snail," and the name has been supposed to apply to some narrow doorway; but the name is well known in mediæval Latin as applied to a winding or newel staircase, popularly called a corkscrew-staircase, and there are two such staircases leading from the substructures or *cavea* to the level of the arena, one on either side, at the south-east end of the great central passage in the Flavian amphitheatre, to which there can be no doubt that this name was applied. Trajan's column is frequently called *columna cochlea*, because there is such a staircase inside of it.

---

præsidens. Galea ejus per portam Libitinensem elata est." (Lampridii Commodus Antoninus, ap. Script. Hist. Aug., c. 16.) This circumstance is also mentioned by Dio Cassius, as quoted previously.

[e] "Inter carnifices et fabros Sandapilarum." (Juvenal, Sat. viii. 175.)

[f] "Ruinart Acta Martyrum Sincera." (ap. Grævii Thesaurus, tom. ix.)

[g] "Non omnis moriar, multaque pars mei
    Vitabit Libitinam." (Horatii Odæ, lib. iii. ode 30.)

[h] "Effert uxores Fabius, Christilla maritos,
    Funereamque toris quassat uterque facem.
    Victores committe, Venus, quos iste manebit
    Exitus, una duos ut Libitina ferat."
        (Martial. Epig., lib. viii. 43.)

[i] "Ferrarium vicinum, aut hunc qui ad Metam sudantem tubas experitur et tibias." (Senecæ, Epist. 56.)
Some of the tubes or leaden pipes have been found (as before mentioned).

[k] "Ostium humile et angustum, et potissimum ejus generis, quod *cochleam* appellant, ut solet esse in *cavea* ex qua tauri pugnare solent." (Varr. de Re Rustica, iii. 5.

The Games in the Arena.

The importance attached to the public amusements, both by the people and by the emperors, appears extraordinary to modern ideas. Caligula[1] was present from morning to evening, and had a series of the various kinds of hunting in different countries exhibited, such as the hunts of the Africans and of the Trojans; on these occasions, the arena was strewed with red and green foliage. At this period Suetonius also mentions that the people assembled at midnight for the shows of the following day, when they were gratuitous[m]. The Emperor Claudius himself would go at daybreak to the amphitheatre, and see the wild beasts fed, and again at mid-day[n]. The same practice is mentioned by Pliny as used in the time of Nero[o]. Petronius also mentions the custom for two old negroes to sprinkle the arena with scents from small bottles, which they brought for the purpose[p]. Tacitus gives an account of the games performed under his own direction in the time of Claudius[q].

"During the same consulship, in the year of Rome eight hundred, the secular games were celebrated, after an interval of sixty-four years since they were last solemnized in the reign of Augustus.

"Being at that time one of the college of fifteen, and invested with the office of prætor, it fell to my province to regulate the ceremonies. Let it not be imagined that this is said from motives of vanity. The fact is, that in ancient times the business was conducted under the special directions of the quindecemviral order, while the chief magistrates officiated in the several ceremonies. Claudius thought proper to revive this public spectacle. He attended in the circus, and, in his presence, the Trojan game was performed by the youth of noble birth. Britannicus, the emperor's son, and Lucius Domitius, who by adoption took the name of Nero, and afterwards succeeded to the empire, appeared, with the rest of the band, mounted on superb horses. Nero was received with acclamations, and that mark of popular favour was considered as an omen of his future grandeur."

---

[1] "Edidit et Circenses plurimos a mane usque ad vesperam, interjecta modo Africanarum venatione, modo Trojæ decursione: quosdam præcipuos, *minio* et *chrysocolla* constrato circo nec ullis nisi ex senatorio ordine aurigantibus." (Suetonii Caligula, 18.)

[m] "Inquietatus fremitu gratuita in Circo loca de media nocte occupantium, omnes fustibus abegit; elisique per eum tumultum viginti amplius Equites Romani, totidem matronæ, super innumeram turbam ceteram." (Suetonii Caligula, cap. 26.)

A similar mania has sometimes been heard of in recent times in Paris and in London.

[n] "Bestiariis meridianisque adeo delectabatur, ut et prima luce ad spectaculum descenderet et meridie dimisso ad prandium populo persederet præterque destinatos, etiam levi subitaque de causa, quosdam committeret, de fabrorum quoque ac ministrorum atque id genus numero si automatum, vel pegma, vel quid tale aliud parum cessisset. Induxit et unum ex nomenclatoribus suis, sicut erat togatus." (Suet. Claudius, c. xxxiv.)

[o] "Visumque jam est Neronis principis spectaculis arenam Circi chrysocolla sterni cum ipse concolori panno aurigaturus esset." (Plinii Nat. Hist., xxxiii. 27.)

[p] "Subinde intraverunt duo Æthiopes capillati, cum pusillis utribus, quales solent esse qui ARENAM *in amphitheatro* spargunt." (Petronii Sat., cap. 34.)

[q] Taciti Annales, lib. xi. c. 11.

APPENDIX.

Scaurus.

The meaning of the word Scaurus is "club-footed," and no doubt the first member of the family had that peculiar formation of the foot; but this family was a branch of the great Gens Æmilia, one member of that family built the Basilica Æmilia in the Forum Romanum, and another was one of the second Triumvirate. The Scaurus who built this great amphitheatre was a man of enormous wealth, and a great builder; he is mentioned by several of his contemporaries, of whom one was Cicero; he was an ædile, and was noted for his great liberality in his ædileship. His father was an orator, and was consul in the year of Rome 688 (B.C. 35); his mother, when a widow, married Sylla the dictator. Pliny mentions him several times in his Natural History[a]; he calls his buildings *insane* works, on account of the enormous sum expended upon them, which must have exceeded the equivalent of two millions sterling of our money. The temporary amphitheatre which he built would hold 80,000 persons, it was three storeys high, and had 360 marble columns in it; these were on the ground-floor, and it is mentioned that those on the first floor were of glass[b], a luxury before unheard of (and apparently not repeated), on the upper storey they were of gilt wood. Pliny thus describes this building of Scaurus:—

"Mosaic pavements were first introduced in the time of Sylla; at all events, there is still in existence a pavement[c], formed of small segments, which he ordered to be laid down in the Temple of Fortune, at Præneste. Since his time, these mosaics have left the ground for the arched roofs of houses, and they are now made of glass. This, however, is but a recent invention; for there can be no doubt that, when Agrippa ordered the earthenware walls of the hot baths, in the thermæ which he was building at Rome, to be painted in encaustic, and had the other parts coated with pargetting, he would have had the arches decorated with mosaic in glass, if the use of them had been known; or, at all events, if

---

[a] "Lithostrota acceptavere jam sub Sulla: parvulis certe crustis exstat hodieque, quod in Fortunæ delubro Præneste fecit. Pulsa deinde ex humo pavimenta in cameras transiere, e vitro: novitium e hoc inventum. Agrippa certe in Thermis quas Romæ fecit, figlinum opus encausto pinxit: in reliquis albaria adornavit: non dubie vitreas facturus cameras, si prius inventum id fuisset, aut a parietibus scena, ut diximus, Scauri, pervenisset in cameras. Quamobrem et vitri natura indicanda est." (Plinii Nat. Hist., lib. xxxvi. 64.)

[b] Friedländer says that a compact floor of glass was found at Veii, (vol. iii. p. 103).

[c] This remarkably fine pavement is still preserved (1876) at Præneste, now called Palestrina.

from the walls of the theatre of Scaurus, where it figured, as already stated, glass had by that time come to be used for the arched roofs of apartments. It will be as well, therefore, to give some account also of glass[d]."

"It may possibly be observed, that this was because marble was not then introduced. Such, however, is not the fact; for in the ædileship of M. Scaurus, three hundred and sixty columns were to be seen imported, for the decorations of a temporary theatre, too, one that was destined to be in use for barely a single month. And yet the laws were silent thereon, in a spirit of indulgence for the amusements of the public, no doubt. But then, why such indulgence? or how do vices more insidiously steal upon us than under the plea of serving the public? By what other way, in fact, did ivory, gold, and precious stones, first come into use with private individuals?

"Can we say that there is now anything that we have reserved for the exclusive use of the gods? However, be it so, let us admit of this indulgence for the amusements of the public; but still, why did the laws maintain their silence when the largest of these columns, pillars of Lucullan marble, as much as eight-and-thirty feet in height, were erected in the atrium of Scaurus? a thing, too, that was not done privately, or in secret; for the contractor for the public sewers compelled him to give security for the possible damage that might be done in the carriage of them to the Palace. . . . . Already had L. Crassus, the orator, he who was the first to possess pillars of foreign marble, and in this same Palatium too, received from M. Brutus, on the occasion of a dispute, the nickname of the 'Palatine Venus,' for his indulgence in this kind of luxury. The material, I should remark, was Hymetian marble, and the pillars were but six in number, and not exceeding some twelve feet in height . . . . These particulars, and others in the sequel, will shew that we are so far improved; for who is there at the present day that has, in his atrium, any such massive columns as these of Scaurus[e]?" . . . .

"I will not permit, however, these two Caiuses, or two Neros, to enjoy this glory even, such as it is; for I will prove that these extravagant follies of theirs have been surpassed, in the use that was made of his wealth by M. Scaurus, a private citizen. Indeed, I am by no means certain that it was not the ædileship of this personage that inflicted the first great blow upon the public manners, and that Sylla was not guilty of a greater crime in giving such unlimited power to his step-son, than in the proscription of so many thousands. During his ædileship, and only for the temporary purposes of a few days, Scaurus executed the greatest work that has ever been made by the hands of man, even when intended to be of everlasting duration; his theatre, I mean. This building consisted of three storeys, supported upon three hundred and sixty columns; and this, too, in a city which had not allowed without some censure one of its greatest citizens to erect six pillars of Hymetian marble. The ground-storey was of marble, the second of glass, a species of luxury which ever since that time has been quite unheard of, and the highest of gilded wood. The lowermost columns, as previously stated, were eight-and-thirty feet in height; and, placed between these columns, as already mentioned, were bronze statues, three thousand in number. The area of this theatre afforded accommodation for eighty thousand spectators; and yet the theatre of Pompey, after the city had so greatly increased, and the inhabitants had become so vastly more numerous, was considered abundantly

[d] Pliny, Nat. Hist., bk. xxxvi. 2, 3.   [e] Ibid. xxxvi. 24, 7.

large, with its sittings for forty thousand only. The rest of the fittings of it, what with Attalic vestments, pictures, and the other stage properties, were of such enormous value that, after Scaurus had conveyed to his Tusculan villa such parts thereof as were not required for the enjoyment of his daily luxuries, the loss was no less than three hundred millions of sesterces, when the villa was burnt by his servants in a spirit of revenge.... C. Curio, who died during the civil wars, fighting on the side of Cæsar, found, to his dismay, that he could not, when celebrating the funeral games in honour of his father, surpass the riches and magnificence of Scaurus—for where, in fact, was to be found such a step-sire as Sylla, and such a mother as Metella, that bidder at all auctions for the property of the proscribed? Where, too, was he to find for his father, M. Scaurus, so long the principal man in the city, and one who had acted, in his alliance with Marius, as a receptacle for the plunder of whole provinces? Indeed, Scaurus himself was now no longer able to rival himself; and it was at least one advantage which he derived from this destruction by fire of so many objects brought from all parts of the earth, that no one could ever after be his equal in this species of folly. Curio, consequently, found himself compelled to fall back upon his own resources, and to think of some new device of his own."

The points on which this account agrees with the Colosseum are so remarkable, that there can hardly be a doubt that the enormous building of Scaurus was on this site, and the old tufa walls of the substructure must have belonged to his building. This was the earliest amphitheatre, and in none of the other amphitheatres built in imitation of it do we find similar old tufa walls, although in other respects some are exact copies of the Colosseum.

AMPHITHEATRE OF NERO.

SOME persons interpret a passage in the Annals of Tacitus[f] to mean, that the amphitheatre of Nero was in the Campus Martius, but this is only a wrong interpretation of the passage; he is speaking of the great wooden amphitheatre which Julius Cæsar built there, and which was repaired and restored to use in the second consulate of Nero (A.D. 56). He mentions foundations and beams only, and especially says it was of little importance. The time of Nero was a great building era in Rome, and he no doubt repaired all the public buildings that required it.

[f] "Nerone secundum, L. Pisone consulibus, *pauca memoria* digna evenere: nisi cui libeat, laudandis fundamentis et trabibus, quis molem amphitheatri apud Campum Martis, Cæsar exstrux- erat, volumina implere: cum ex dignitate populi Romani repertum sit, res inlustres annalibus, talia diurnis urbis actis mandare." (Taciti Annales, lib. xiii. c. 31.)

The Great Drain.

THERE is considerable difficulty at the present time (in 1876) in obtaining correct information on the subject of the great drain, which carried off the water from the substructures. The entrance to it from the south-east end, under the entrance for animals, has been mentioned before, with the sluice-gate, which lifted up like a portcullis, and the grooves for it remain. Openings into it, covered with modern iron gratings, are seen in the floor of the passage, and across the mouth of it is an ancient iron grating. This great and deep drain carried the water in a straight line beyond the outer wall of the building, and just at this point a steam engine was placed in the years 1874 and 1875 to pump out the water, which gushed out of the earth a little further on, in the direction of the church of S. Clement, with a divergence to the south towards the Cœlian Hill. This water was very abundant, but it appeared more like the continuous stream of an aqueduct than a natural spring of water; it was at a very low level, quite 30 ft. underground. At a considerably higher level, and near the surface of the ground, was an aperture into the brick *specus* or conduit of an aqueduct of the third century, in which the water was flowing steadily along from west to east; this continued all the summer of 1874, and the water was always flowing. This aperture was closed in the summer of 1875, and the whole *specus* buried again; where the water was sent to is not known to any one but the persons employed, and they say that this water had little to do with the other water which they pumped out, although both were always good clear limpid streams of drinking water. The water was pumped out and conveyed in an open channel, parallel to the building, to the Arch of Constantine, where it made a small flood during all the spring of 1875, and was then carried into a modern drain under the road between the Cœlian and the Palatine, after passing over the road and washing the base of the Arch of Constantine for several months. The old drain, at a great depth, was traced the whole length of the Colosseum, parallel to it, close under the foot of that part of the Cœlian Hill on which the Claudium stood, and under which the two *piscinæ*, one of the time of Nero, the other of Alexander Severus, have been mentioned. The workmen employed to clear out the old drain were alarmed at the great depth; an enormous quantity of earth had been thrown upon it, and they were afraid of its falling in behind them, and blocking up their only mode of exit; deep wells were made down into it, but after they had gone nearly as far as the Arch of Constantine at this depth, they were stopped for want of air. Another well, or air-pipe, was necessary, but the works were then all suspended for want of funds. It is known that an ancient drain, at a great depth, went under the road, and at a much lower level than a modern drain, which passes near the monastery or church of S. Gregory on the Cœlian, between that and the Palatine; and there can be little doubt that this was a continuation of the same drain, and that it might all be cleared out and repaired, but unless air-pipes can be put down by boring the expense would be enormous.

Another small ancient drain has also been found coming from the Summa Sacra Via, apparently for the fountains at the four corners of the Porticus Liviæ. The workmen had been told that they were to find the great drain passing under that part, and going on to the Cloaca Maxima in the Forum Romanum, but this could not be found, and did not appear practicable.

Father Mullooly, the excellent Prior of S. Clement, says he has observed that the water under this church always rises and falls at the same time as that under the Colosseum, and he is convinced that they both come from the same source. It seemed probable that this source, or at least one of the sources of this water, is the great reservoir of the earliest aqueduct, the Aqua Appia, under the garden of the Villa Cœlimontana, formerly called Villa Mattei, which is now the property of the Baron Hoffman, at the west end of the Cœlian Hill, on a high level. The Baron wanted to make this old vaulted reservoir into a wine-cellar, but found it impossible to get rid of the water, which is always two or three feet deep, and as fast as he pumped it out it filled again to the same level, but no higher; this shews that there must be some outlet to it, but so deep underground that no one knows which way it goes. This old reservoir is nearly under the great reservoir of Nero for the Anio Novus, which was fifty feet higher, and carried on his arches, for which also the Arch of Dolabella was used as a substructure only. We have found in our examination of the aqueducts that the later ones always followed the same course as the earlier ones, not exactly over them, but by the side of them, each succeeding aqueduct being always on a higher level, and there is always a subterranean reservoir of one of the earlier aqueducts nearly under those of the later period. The Appia was made nearly four centuries before the Anio Novus, still it is very probable that the same plan was followed in both cases. We have found that the aqueduct of Claudius and Nero, called the Anio Novus, was divided into three branches at this point; one went straight on over the Palatine to the Capitoline Hill, another branch went to the left, or south, of the Aventine, and a third to the right, or north, to the Colosseum. It seems extremely probable that the same plan had been followed with the Appia, both were carried along the high ground of the Cœlian Hill as far as could be done, and then each was divided into three branches. We traced one branch of it over the Porta Capena to the Aventine and the Tiber; this is now necessarily out of use, the gate on the arch of which it was carried having been destroyed. A landslip in the garden of the Marchese Rappini, in February, 1876, between the Villa Cœlimontana and the Palatine, served to shew that a *specus* or conduit passed there, now also out of use. An excavation was made there in April of the same year, but all that came to light was a deep well, an ancient quarry of tufa, also at a great depth, and the *specus* of the aqueduct coming from the reservoir under the Claudium, called a *vivarium*, and going in the direction of the valley in which was the Porta Capena. This *specus* has been long out of use, and could not have had any connection with the flood in the Colosseum, which was the object of the search. The water conveyed in this *specus* originally must have been one of those that passed over the short *agger* of Servius Tullius from the Cœlian to the Aventine, found in the excavation of 1868, and traced also in 1876 in the cave under S. Sabba, by the side of the Aqua Appia, in the same tunnel, but in a terra-cotta pipe, not in the stone *specus*. The third branch, in the direction of the Colosseum, may still be in use, though so deep as to be unknown, supplying wells only, and this may be the one tapped by the workmen employed by Signor Rosa, and which now floods the Colosseum, and S. Clement's also. The only outlet from a large reservoir, in which the water is always three feet deep, must afford a very abundant supply of water, and the account given by the workmen who made this branch of it agrees with this. They say it was a steady constant stream of water, and it did not gush out of the earth in the manner that a natural spring does; the spring must therefore be at some distance. If this view is correct, it would be comparatively easy to turn the stream into a drain under the Clivus Scauri, and into the one made by the Municipality about 1865, under the road near the church of S. Gregory, between the Cœlian and the Palatine, and to carry it in that manner to the Tiber.

It is however probable that this spring alone, which was only a subsidiary spring to the Appian aqueduct, is not sufficiently abundant to supply the quantity of water, which now rises to the height of about ten feet, or quite three metres, in the substructures of the Colosseum. There is another spring, or perhaps more than one, in the ancient stone quarry under the garden of the monks of SS. John and Paul, on the other side of the Clivus Scauri, on the site of the Claudium, or that square part of the Cœlian Hill which is nearest to the Colosseum. This site is marked on an old plan of Rome, of the sixteenth century, as a reservoir of water, and there are no less than ten wells that descend into this old stone quarry. In the eighteenth century, and down to the middle of the nineteenth, this was called a *vivarium*, and was supposed to be the place where the wild animals were kept for exhibitions in the Colosseum, but there is no visible communication from one to the other. A plan of the old quarry, which was made for this work some years since, shews that this was not a *vivarium*. There are three ponds, but perhaps only one spring of water in it, and if the outlet for this water was stopped, the whole of the quarry, or caves as they are called, would soon be full of water. It seems probable that this is the place from which the greater part of the water comes that floods both the Colosseum and the cave of Mithras, nearly under the church of S. Clement. It seems also quite practicable to remove the water by an iron pipe into the drain under the road between the Cœlian and the Palatine, made by the Municipality about 1866. The level of the quarry is eight metres above that of the Colosseum; the soil there is on the level of the arena, and that is seven metres above the original pavement; the water in the old quarry is therefore fifteen metres, or about 45 ft. above the level of the old drain of the Colosseum, and nearly six metres above the drain made by the Municipality.

This opportunity may be taken to say, that great credit is due to the Municipality of Rome for the energy and perseverance with which they have carried on an admirable system of new drainage for the city; and not only the new city on the hills on the site of the city of the Kings and of the Empire, but also of the modern city of the Popes, built in the swamp between the hills and the Tiber, the draining of which is by no means easy. Nothing can be better than the old Cloaca Maxima, which is still the chief drain to this part of Rome, or for that of part of the old city; it drains the water of the streams that run down from three hills, the Palatine, the Capitoline, and the Quirinal, on this side. But on the northern side of the Capitoline Hill, in which was the Campus Martius, the mediæval drains are by no means equally good with those of the

Kings; the mouths of these drains are always open to the Tiber, and when there is a flood of the river the water runs up the drains, and the Pantheon, which stands on very low ground, is always the first place in Rome to be flooded. Surely a sluice-gate might be placed at the mouth of each drain, suspended from a bar at the top, and worked on pivots only, which would let the water out, but would not let any in, as in the common *traps* of a drain in daily use in England.

The Roman authorities say that the water of the Tiber would close the doors, and not let any of the water in the drain pass out, but if the door was placed obliquely, and let the water flow past it with as little pressure upon it as possible, the water in the drains, which runs rapidly and with considerable force, would very soon force open the door that was suspended at the mouth of it. Any embankment of the Tiber would be money thrown away; if the great engineers and architects who built the wall of Aurelian, could not make it secure on the bank of the Tiber, no modern engineers or architects will do so. We see that nearly the whole of the great wall of Aurelian, on the bank of the Tiber, has been swept away by the great floods; the substructures of the towers, under water, remain, and are visible when the water is low in the river, but all along the bank has been swept away. When the water rises at the rate of a foot in an hour, and continues to do so for twenty hours consecutively, and runs at the rate of nine or ten miles an hour, no wall can stand against it that offers any resistance to it; smooth walls parallel to the course of the river might stand, as the quay of the Ripa Grande does, because it offers no resistance to the water.

AFTER the greater part of this chapter was written and in type, I thought it necessary to go to Capua and Pozzuoli again to examine the remains of these amphitheatres, and I did so in November, 1875; it was my intention at the same time to have gone to Pompeii, to examine the amphitheatre there also, but the weather was so bad at that time I found it quite impracticable to do so; I therefore did so in May, 1876, and I find that the amphitheatre at Pompeii is of the time of Sylla the Dictator, and that the arrangements are not the same as those of the Roman amphitheatre; there are no substructions under the arena, and it appears there never could have been any, as in the centre there is the top of an original well, and the floor seems always to have been of earth only; there are no preparations for *Naumachia*, and the dens for the wild beasts are on the same level as the arena, and behind the *podium*. In the principal entrances there are sockets for a wooden balustrade, to separate the people from the wild beasts. The corridor round at the back of these dens has the original walls of brickwork, of good hard bricks, but rather thick, somewhat similar to those of the Pantheon at Rome, but much thicker than those of the time of Nero; the brick vaults of this corridor, or passage under the lower gallery, are modern or mediæval repairs. Many of the seats have been preserved or restored, they are of stone of volcanic character, the stone of the country, in fact, but they are of a convenient height, and comfortable to sit upon, though closely packed; the seat is raised two or three inches above the place for the feet of those in the next seat above. The construction of the outer wall is of blocks of lava, about the shape of English bricks, but rather larger, and with *opus reticulatum*, the pattern of large size, enclosed in a sort of framework of these quasi-bricks, very similar to the Muro Torto at Rome. The fresco of the first century found on a wall here, and now preserved in the Museum at Naples[g], is a caricature of the building; and the *vomitoria*, which form a conspicuous object in the front of the picture, are greatly exaggerated, made much more lofty and more long and narrow than they really are. They are said to be the ladies' entrance to their gallery, which was the upper gallery at the back; but as the slope was very gradual, and the building not nearly so high as the Colosseum, they would be able to see perfectly well, and their entrance and exit being entirely on the exterior of the building, while that of the men was from the interior, was a very convenient arrangement. It seems probable that Scaurus, the stepson of Sylla, had seen this building in progress, and as the Romans always had the idea of making Rome the most magnificent city in the world, he built the far more magnificent amphitheatre in Rome; but as the upper part was built of wood, though magnificently decorated with columns of marble, of glass, and of gilt wood, as we have said, it seems to have offended the Republican notions of the Romans, and this upper part was entirely destroyed, or this may have happened from an accidental fire; but as the substructures were of tufa they were everlasting, as Pliny says, and they still remain as the principal foundations of the Colosseum, with brick walls and galleries erected upon them in the time of Nero, and the whole enclosed by the magnificent stone front and double corridors of the Flavian Emperors.

[g] See Plate XXVII.

ALPHABETICAL INDEX.

THE COLOSSEUM.

ACTORS, space required for, under the stage, 47.
Alexander Severus, Piscina of, 5; walls of, 6.
Amphitheatres a Roman invention (?), 4;—of Nero not in Campus Martius, 56, 58;—represented on coins, 21;—described as perfect by Ammianus Marcellinus, A.D. 357, 26;—restored by Lampadius, A.D. 445, 27;—again by Venantius Basilius, A.D. 508, *ib.*;—used for shows of wild beasts by Theodoric, A.D. 519, *ib.*;—again used in 523, the last occasion mentioned, *ib.*;—again damaged by earthquake, A.D. 1703, 30;—consecrated as a church, A.D. 1724, *ib.*;—north-western side nearly perfect, *ib.*;—Arch of lower storey restored by Gordianus, A.D. 220—238, 31.
——— at Arles, 46.
——— at Bordeaux, 46.
——— at Capua, 40, 41.
——— at Nismes, 46.
——— at Pompeii, 63.
——— at Pozzuoli, 42, 65.
——— of Scaurus, on this spot, 56.
——— at Verona, 43, 65.
Animals brought from vivaria in cages, called *pegmata*, 15.
Apollodorus told Hadrian he *ought to have* provided space for the machinery, 34.
Apuleius mentions *pegmata* in amphitheatre, 49.
Arch of tufa shaken by an earthquake, supported by brick wall of Nero, 14.
Arena, for the gymnasium, 1;—of wood covered with sand, and full of trapdoors, 7, 11;—no open space under the, 21;—criminals torn to pieces upon it, 52.
Arles, Amphitheatre at, 46; no substructures visible, *ib.*
Augustus intended to build an amphitheatre here, but did not, 15.
Awning of Nero mentioned by Pliny, 23; contrivances for supporting it, *ib.*; at Pompeii, shewn in a fresco, 24; an intermediate passage for sailors to manage awning, 47; cords for it, strong enough to carry an elephant, called *catadromus*, 48.

Battles of sailors with swords, not with boats, 47.
Benedict XIII. consecrated area of amphitheatre as a church, A.D. 1728, 30.
Benedict XIV. erects cross and stations in amphitheatre, A.D. 1749, 30.
Boards removed from arena placed on corbels provided for them, 34.
Bordeaux, Amphitheatre at, 47; Remains called the *Arènes*, it had a boarded floor, *ib.*
Brick-work of Nero here, 6.
Building apparently perfect in time of Bede, 27;—made part of fortress of Frangipani, A.D. 1130, 28;—half given to Annibaldi by Frederick II., grant rescinded by Innocent IV. in A.D. 1244, *ib.*;—much damaged by an earthquake, A.D. 1349, *ib.*;—made common property as a stone-quarry, A.D. 1362, 29;—several palaces made out of this quarry, *ib.*

Calpurnius mentions *pegmata* in amphitheatre, 49.
Canals brought to light in 1812 and 1875, with substructures, 10;—great cisterns under boards, 14; about 10 ft. deep, but not always the same width, *ib.*;—walls to support unusually thick, *ib.*;—lined with lead, one on arches, the other on beams of wood, *ib.*
Capitals fallen from upper gallery, 21.
Capstans, sockets for, 7.
CAPUA, Amphitheatre almost the same size as that of Rome, 40;—Substructures more perfect, *ib.*;—Aqueduct and drain, *ib.*;—Remains of aqueduct, 13;—Dens under the *podium*, 40;—Sockets for pivots for cages, *ib.*;—Arena of brick, not wood, but apertures for trap-doors, *ib.*;—Grooves for covers over them to make them water-tight, *ib.*;—Building of the time of Hadrian, *ib.*;—Inscription, 41;—Machine for lifting vessels, as in the Colosseum, 47.
Castra Misenatium, for sailors employed in furling awning, or *vela*, or *velaria*, 24.
Catadromus, cords for awning, 48.
Cavea, name for an amphitheatre, 3; and for vaults under it, 51.

E*

Alphabetical Index.

Chambers, narrow and lofty vaulted, on each side of central passage, 38.
Circensian games, name retained in amphitheatre, 51.
Circus Maximus, sometimes used instead of amphitheatre, 50.
Claudian mentions *pegmata* in amphitheatre, 49.
Clivus Scauri, Arcade to this amphitheatre, 3.
Colossus visible from gulf in amphitheatre, 49.
Columns and capitals fallen from upper gallery on to arena, and into *cavea*, 21.
Commodus, acts of, in this building, described by Dion Cassius, 22.
Comparison and construction, 40;—one of the first principles of archæology, *ib*.;—especially useful for this amphitheatre, *ib*.
Construction, here made visible by demolition of outer corridor, 30.
Corbels or brackets for placing boards of arena upon, 11, 36.
Corridors, open channels for running water, in amphitheatre, 11;—water supplied by aqueducts, *ib*.
Cradle, or dry-dock, in central passage, 18, 38.
Culprits executed by being thrown to wild beasts in this amphitheatre, 3.

Dens under the *podium* have arches of Neronian brickwork, 12;—small stream of water in front of them, 17.
Drain, large, under passage, 35, and in Appendix, 56, 59; ancient iron grating at mouth of, 36; place for flood-gates visible, *ib*.

Emperors went to see wild beasts fed, 55.
Evidence of construction, and comparison, 40.
Excavations begun by the French, A.D. 1810, 31; not deep enough, 33; shew channels for water, 32;—made in search of treasure, A.D. 1864, 1865, 33;—A.D. 1874, 1875, 1; results of them a great surprise, 37.
Exhibitions by Julius Cæsar in circus required a separate building, 5.

Framework, curious wooden, on floor of central passage, a cradle, or drydock, 18.
Frangipani make amphitheatre part of fortress, A.D. 1130, 28.
Front of three periods, upper storey added a century later, 19.

Gallery, upper, of wood, destroyed by fire, 12; restored in stone, completed A.D. 240, under Gordianus, *ib*.
Games on arena, 55; great importance attached to them, *ib*.
Gates, usually four to each amphitheatre, 53; names of, not easily ascertained, *ib*.; one called *sandapila*, *ib*.; others called Porta Prætoria, Porta Sacra, Porta Cochlea, 54.
Gaudentius employed upon it, not the architect of it, 20.
Gladiators often killed, 52;—called for by the people, *ib*.
Gordianus completed the building, and restored arch of lower storey, A.D. 220—238, 31.
Grooves in walls for lifts, 7.
Gulf, or central passage, in all amphitheatres, 47.
Gymnasium on the arena, 1; of Nero also here, 6.

Hadrian and Apollodorus, 34.
Herodian mentions 100 lions leaping on to the arena in amphitheatre, 50.

Icarus, an actor playing part of, fell dead at feet of Nero, 48.
Inscriptions record dates of later walls, 7;—give the word THEATRUM for Amphitheatre, *ib*.

Jerusalem, view of, century xvi., 29.
Joints, straight vertical, between the brick galleries and stone corridors, 6.
Josephus mentions *pegmata* in amphitheatre, 49.
Julius Cæsar, Amphitheatre of, 2.
Julius Capitolinus mentions 100 lions in amphitheatre, 50.

Lampadius restores amphitheatre, A.D. 445, 27.
Lampridius mentions 100 lions in amphitheatre, 50.
Lifts for men and dogs on both sides of central passage, 14; grooves for, remain in walls, 7.
Lions, 100 killed at once in the shows, 26.

Machine for raising stones for walls, 21.
Machines required, numerous and large, 48.
Martial's first book, *De Spectaculis*, relates to this amphitheatre, 4;—mentions *pegmata* in amphitheatre, 49.
Martyrdom of early Christians on sand of arena, not on soil 21 ft. below, 36.
Mass celebrated in amphitheatre by Cardinal Vicar, A.D. 1756, 30.
Masts, or poles, and corbels for awning, 24.

Alphabetical Index. 67

Miracle plays performed in amphitheatre, A.D. 1540, 29.
Mixture of stone and brick in construction, 19.

Naumachia, the new, those of Augustus in Trastevere, 9;—the old, in this building, 1, 8, 10;—none in amphitheatre of Taurus, 10;—and Stagna, names used indifferently, 12;—the two sides were flooded, not the central passage, 14;—vessels employed in usually *rates*, 47.
Naval fights held sometimes in Circus Maximus, 50;—must have been in canals of Colosseum, as Heliogabalus filled them with wine, 51;—called Circensian games, *ib.*;—Martial distinguishes them, *ib.*
Nero, substructures part of the time of, 1, 12;—gymnasium and naumachia of, on site of this amphitheatre, 5;—remains of aqueducts and piscina, *ib.*;—gymnasium of, on the arena, 6;—brickwork of time of, *ib.*;—supper of, in the amphitheatre, 7;—exterior of brick unfinished by him, and finished by Flavian Emperors in stone, 11;—two small chambers of brick, of his time, enclosed in travertine walls, 15;—awning of, mentioned by Pliny, 23;—amphitheatre of, not in Campus Martius, 56;—his Stagna were canals of aqueducts, 8.
Netting to protect lower gallery of gold (or gilt) wire, called *retia*, 50.
Nismes, amphitheatre still has a wooden floor with trap-doors in it, 46; arrangements below quite different, *ib.*

Palaces, several made out of amphitheatre, 29.
Passage, great, found at S.-E. end, 34.
Passages, small special, for messengers, intermediate between the great ones at Pozzuoli, and in Colosseum at Rome, 47;—central, or gulf, in all the amphitheatres, *ib.*
Pavement, original here, 21 ft. below level of arena, 35.
Pegmata, cages for wild beasts, 15;—described by Seneca, 16;—not only cages, but wooden machines, 49.
Piers of travertine, introduced to support floors, 12;—from top to bottom, to carry upper gallery, 39.
Piscinae, remains of two, 11.
Pit for a man to descend to feed the animals, 17.
Plan, general, is oval, with galleries, vomitoria, &c., 18.
Pliny mentions Scaurus and his *insane* works, 56.

Podium protected by wire netting and bars, 16.
Pola, in Istria, Amphitheatre at, 45, 46;—built of white stone, *ib.*;—two tiers of arches remain, *ib.*;—A curious stone parapet, with indications of awning, *ib.*;—Built against rocky mountain, *ib.*;—Substructures in lower part, *ib.*;—Canal for water visible, *ib.*;—Square towers (for musicians?), 46.
Pozzuoli (Puteoli), Arena of brick full of trap-doors, 13, 42;—Surface there flooded for *naumachia*, 13;—An intermediate passage for messengers, 47;—Building much smaller than those of Rome and Capua, 42;—Substructures more perfect and more highly finished, *ib.*;—Arena of brick, with apertures for trap-doors, *ib.*;—Arrangement for fixing masts for awning, as in Rome, 43;—Building also of time of Hadrian, *ib.*;—Vaults preserved and used, *ib.*

Rhodope, mountain of, represented as a scene here, 4.

Scaurus, Family of Æmilius, 56;—name means club-footed, *ib.*;—one of the family built Basilica Æmilia, *ib.*;—*insane* works of, so called from their enormous cost, *ib.*;—his theatre to hold 80,000 people could only be on site of Colosseum, *ib.*;—no other theatre three storeys high, *ib.*;—extract from Pliny, *ib.*;—walls of, 15;—buildings of, parts temporary, other parts eternal, according to Pliny, on site of present amphitheatre, 3;—Clivus of, leads to this site, *ib.*
Sea-water (?) used in canals, 8.
Seneca, *pegmata* described by, 16.
Severus, Alexander, piscina of, 5; wall of, 6.
Sockets in the pavement for pivots of capstans, 7, 35.
Stagna, or old *naumachia*, under the arena, 1, 12;—of Nero supplied by three aqueducts, 9;—boarded over for gladiators and wild beasts, but boards removed easily. 10;—two, each 300 ft. long, and about 50 wide, 14.
Stagnum of Nero, "like a sea," when surface was flooded, 9, 12.
——— Navale of Tacitus, 9.
——— of Agrippa near the Pantheon, 9.
Statilius Taurus, Amphitheatre of, 1.
Storey, upper, an addition and an afterthought, 6.
Substructures, part of the time of Nero, 1;—evidently retained and used when upper part was built, 39;—compared with others, 47.

Suetonius does not mention the beginning of the work, 1.

Tacitus gives an account of games here under his own direction, 55.
Taurus, Statilius, Amphitheatre of, 1.
Theatrum and Amphitheatrum, names used indifferently for this building, 7.
Theodoric uses amphitheatre for shows of wild beasts, A.D. 519, 27.
Titus, wall of, 6;—exhibitions of, at the dedication, 8.
Trap-doors in the arena numerous, 7.
Travertine piers cut through older wall, of tufa and brick, to carry upper gallery, 19.
Tufa, much used to fill up between piers of travertine, 18;—taken from second wall of Rome, ib.
Tusculum, canals in amphitheatre, as in Rome, 14.

Upper storey, of stone, an addition to the plan, 6, 12; damaged by lightning, A.D. 230, 26;—of wood, burnt, A.D. 217, 25; restored by Heliogabalus, Al. Severus, and Gordianus, ib.

Vaults under arena called *caveæ*, 51.
Venantius Basilius restores amphitheatre, A.D. 508, 27.
VERONA, Amphitheatre at, 43, 44:—Outer wall almost destroyed, 43;—Arcade of two lower storeys preserved, 44;—Comparison of the number that each amphitheatre would contain, ib.;—Seats remarkably well preserved, ib.;—Dimensions of the three principal amphitheatres, Rome, Verona, Capua, 45;—and Capua, remains of aqueducts, 13.

Vertical joints, open, between brick walls of galleries, and stone walls of corridors, 6.
Vespasian and Titus, Walls of, 6.
Vessels employed in *naumachia* usually *rates*, 47.
View of Jerusalem, century xvi., 29.
Views on coins, and in sculpture on tomb of Aterii, 20.
Vivaria outside walls of Rome, 15;—one at Prætorian camp, 16;—the other at Sessorium, ib.
Vopiscus mentions *pegmata* and 100 lions in amphitheatre, 49.

Wall, the outer, of three periods, Vespasian, Titus, and Alexander Severus, 6.
Walls, original, of tufa, interfered with by later work, 7;—of tufa in substructure older than time of Nero, 13;—of front, and of the corridors in the superstructure, are of travertine, ib.;—of tufa, round edge of substructure for lifts, not for canals, 14;—of tufa, probably of Scaurus, time of Sylla, 15;—grooves in, for lifts and cages, 15, 35;—of tufa, in parts supported by brick walls of Flavian Emperors, 17;—part destroyed by being used as a stone-quarry, 18;—north side only part perfect, ib.;—weeded by the French in 1812, this repeated 1870, 31;—upper, hastily built under Gordianus, 33;—lower, of brick, belong to repairs after earthquakes in A.D. 442, and 508, 37.
Water, shallow open channels for, remain, 33;—reservoirs in principal gallery, ib.;—two *piscinæ* or ——, under Cœlian, ib.
Wild beasts brought to Rome, B.C. 251, 3;—number kept for shows, 25.

THE COLOSSEUM.

PLATE I.

SUPERSTRUCTURE.

EXTERIOR, FROM THE THERMÆ OF TITUS.

COLOSSEUM.

DESCRIPTION OF PLATE I.

SUPERSTRUCTURE.

EXTERIOR, FROM THE THERMÆ OF TITUS.

This view shews the only part that is at all perfect of the magnificent work of the Flavian Emperors, consisting of the grand front and the splendid corridors, built around the brick theatre of Nero, with the galleries for spectators, which are surrounded by these stone corridors. These are of the best building stone to be had in Rome,—the travertine from the quarries near Tibur, now Tivoli.

The front had evidently been left unfinished by Nero, as we find no traces of any brick front according to the fashion of his time, when the brick-work was the finest that the world has ever seen.

It will be observed that the lower part of the ground-floor is concealed in the view by the bank of earth on which the modern road is carried, and the parapet wall of that road. It will also be observed that each storey is different; the lower storeys have different orders of architecture, but with scarcely any difference of plan or of construction, whereas the upper storey is quite different from the rest. There are no arches in it, but flat pilasters instead of columns, small square windows, and a row of corbels projecting boldly from the wall, and a prominent cornice over it. These corbels were for the purpose of carrying the feet of the masts that supported the awning over the heads of the spectators in the galleries, and these masts passed through holes left for them in the cornice, as will be seen more plainly in Plate XII.

This upper storey is more than a century later in date than the lower parts of the building; it replaces a wooden gallery for the common people, which had been made upon the top of the great corridors, which was too tempting a place for the purpose to be lost, although this wooden gallery does not appear to have formed part of the original design,—to judge from the representations of the building on the coins, which are probably made from the designs of the architects before the work was executed. There are six designs extant on the coins, and no two of them are exactly alike, especially for this upper storey[a].

[a] See Plate XXV.

THE COLOSSEUM IN 1874.

EXTERIOR N.E. SIDE FROM THE THERMAE OF TITUS.

THE COLOSSEUM.

PLATE II.

SUPERSTRUCTURE.
VIEWS OF PARTS OF THE BUILDING.

COLOSSEUM.

DESCRIPTION OF PLATE II.
SUPERSTRUCTURE.
VIEWS OF PARTS OF THE BUILDING.

A. The upper view is taken from the top gallery looking down, and shewing the ruins of the lower brick galleries, with the windows of the corridors. Behind the wall in which these windows are placed is seen part of one of the corridors without its roof or vault, but with the steps of one of the *vomitoria*, and at the back of that the arches can be seen of the outer corridor; for it must be remembered that there was a *double* corridor all round this enormous fabric. The object of this was to facilitate ingress and egress from the rest of the building, and the galleries were divided into many distinct parts, each with its own passages and steps, so that there would be no more confusion or pressure in emptying this enormous building than from the emptying of an ordinary room that would hold fifty people. In the upper part of this view, on the right hand, is seen in the distance the church of S. Stefano Rotondo and the trees on the Cœlian Hill.

B. The lower view is taken from the inner side of the chief gallery on the first floor, looking outwards, through one of the arches of the corridor. In this particular compartment was one of the reservoirs of water supplied by the aqueducts. The evidence for this is seen on the right-hand side of the picture, where the lower part of a *specus* or channel for the water remains, with some of the peculiar cement used only for the aqueducts, against the wall and lining the *specus*. Half way along this brick wall is seen a part of one of the narrow piers of travertine which go from the top to the bottom of the building, to carry the upper gallery at that enormous height, as the engineers were afraid to trust the soft tufa wall with the facing of brick. A little further on the right is seen the opening between the brick wall of the gallery and the stone wall of the corridor; the light is seen shining through the opening, which is here about three inches wide, and there is no bonding anywhere between the brick wall of the gallery and the stone wall of the corridor. Towards the south end of the building on this level, in at least two instances, the stone piers have been carried away for building materials, and the lower part of the brick wall, through which it had been cut, stands just as well without it as with it. The object of this tall stone pier was to carry the upper gallery only, not to support the old walls of the lower galleries [b].

[b] See Plate XX.

THE COLOSSEUM.

PLATE III.

SUPERSTRUCTURE AND SUBSTRUCTURE.

Description of Plate III.
SUPERSTRUCTURE AND SUBSTRUCTURE.

THE INTERIOR AS IT APPEARED IN 1812, when *partially* excavated by order of the French Government. This view, taken from an engraving of the period, helps to explain what follows, but the excavations at that time were only carried to the depth of ten feet, and the original pavement was found only (in 1874) at the depth of twenty-one feet from the foot of the *podium*, which is on the ordinary level of the soil. Consequently, we only have here visible the surface, with the central passage and the two canals on each side of it, and the side passage round the edge just under the *podium*. The square openings for the lifts for men and dogs are seen on each side of the central passage. The ruins of the brick galleries are also seen much as they remain now.

The view is taken from above, at the north end. It is singular that the engineers at that time did not see that they had excavated the tops of arches of which the lower parts were still buried, yet the same thing is clearly seen in the excellent set of drawings made for the French Government at the time, and now preserved in the British Museum. In these all the details are given with exact measurements, and yet they appear not to have seen that they had excavated the tops of a series of arches and left the rest buried.

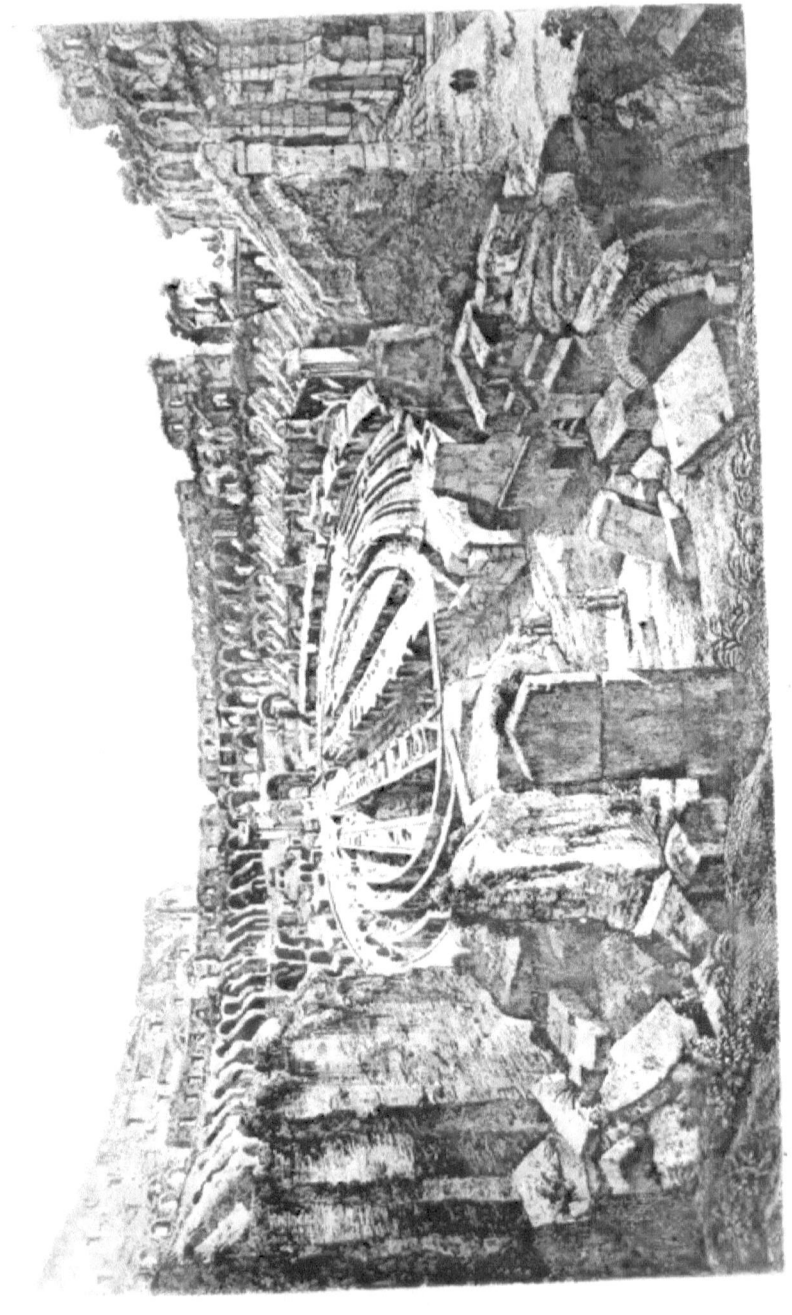

THE COLOSSEUM IN 1812

THE COLOSSEUM.

PLATE IV.

SUBSTRUCTURES IN 1874.

Interior, at the South-east end.   View in the Passages.

DESCRIPTION OF PLATE IV.

THE COLOSSEUM IN 1874.

SUBSTRUCTURE.

INTERIOR, AT THE SOUTH-EAST END. VIEW IN THE PASSAGES.

In the centre of the view, at the foot, are seen the boards for the wheelbarrows of the workmen, leaning against the top of the arch of the great subterranean drain to carry off the water when it was let off with a rush after the naval fights. Under the boards are remains of an ancient iron grating, to prevent any object being carried off into the drain by the force of the water. On each side of these boards are traces of the flood-gate, by which the water could be stopped, or the rate of it regulated.

Beyond this, on each side, is a wide arch of stone parallel to the great central passage. These arches open into two large and lofty vaulted chambers of considerable length, passing under the galleries. In the pavement of the floor in each of these is a line of seven sockets for pivots to work in, some of which retain the bronze socket, in others it has been torn out.

Between the two great round-headed arches is seen a square-topped opening at the end of a long passage over the great drain. This was the passage for the animals that were brought through it in their cages, excepting the elephants, which were led into the large dens provided for them, two on each side of the passage further on.

Above this was the state entrance from the south towards S. Clement's and the Lateran, and on each side are the ruins of the galleries as before.

THE COLOSSEVM IN 1871.

INTERIOR S.E. END. - THE PASSAGES

THE COLOSSEUM.

PLATE V.

INTERIOR, TOWARDS THE SOUTH-WEST,
WITH THE SUBSTRUCTURES IN 1874.

DESCRIPTION OF PLATE V.

INTERIOR, TOWARDS THE SOUTH-WEST,

WITH THE SUBSTRUCTURES IN 1874.

IMMEDIATELY to the right, and nearly in the centre of the picture, is seen the earth not then excavated when this view was taken. In front of this, as shewn to the right of the picture, is one of the ancient walls of tufa faced with brick, which carries on its right-hand side one of the canals of water. To the left of the view, close under the *podium*, is seen another wall of tufa, but cut, and with vertical grooves clearly seen in it; these were for the lifts. Behind this are the arches of the dens of the wild beasts, under the path in front of the *podium;* then the *podium* itself, with square recesses in it, usually said to have been for men to take refuge in, should the animals be able to spring over the net-work in front; but this is not probable, when we see the precautions taken: they were more likely for the athletes, or for the attendants or guards under the state gallery. Behind this are the ruins of the galleries and the windows of the corridors, as before.

THE COLOSSEVM IN 1874

INTERIOR S.W. – THE SVBSTRVCTVRE

THE COLOSSEUM.

PLATE VI.

INTERIOR, AT THE SOUTH-EAST END.

With the early Walls of Tufa.

Description of Plate VI.

INTERIOR, AT THE SOUTH-EAST END.

With the early Walls of Tufa.

In this view the grooves in the walls are clearly seen on both sides of the passage between them, and the arches of the dens behind the outer wall. The lions, or other wild animals about that size, passed from the dens through an opening in the wall into the cages provided for them in this passage. The cages were placed upon lifts, and when the word was given by the emperor, were all pulled up at once to the arena, or floor of boards, with trap-doors in it all along over this passage. We are told by Herodian (as has been shewn in the text, p. 26) that on one occasion a hundred lions leaped on to the stage or arena at the same time, and appeared to the spectators in the gallery to "leap out of the earth;" the sand with which the floor was covered over would have that appearance when the trap-doors, and lifts, and the tops of the cages along with them, were opened from below. In the passage is a long series (one behind the place for each cage and lift) of sockets seen in the pavement, apparently each for a capstan to wind the twenty-one feet of cord upon, when the cage was pulled up to the top, and the trap-doors opened.

THE COLOSSEVM IN 1874.

INTERIOR S.E. END: WITH THE EARLY WALLS.

THE COLOSSEUM.

PLATE VII.

VIEW AT THE SOUTH-EAST END.

Description of Plate VII.

VIEW AT THE SOUTH-EAST END.

This plate is from an excellent drawing of Signor Cicconetti, made chiefly from the photographs, in order to explain them more clearly. The photographs are evidence of historical facts, which no drawing alone can be, because drawings are always liable to errors, accidentally or otherwise. Unfortunately drawings are very often made to suit the idea either of the artist who draws the object as he thinks "it must have been," or to suit the view of the person who orders the drawing. These drawings can be compared with the photographs throughout, and make them more easy to understand.

A. Wooden framework (?), cradle (?), or dry dock (?).

B, B. Marble slabs placed upright, to serve as struts to support the galleys standing on the frame.

C, C. Walls of the central passage.

D. Line of one of the canals.

E, E. Ancient tufa walls, with the dens behind them.

F, F. Podium and state gallery.

G, G. Principal gallery.

H, H. Second gallery.

I. Top gallery, added after the fire.

K. Drain or cloaca.

L. Passage for animals.

M. State entrance and corridor.

N. Modern buttress.

THE COLOSSEUM 1875.

VIEW OF SOUTH EAST END

THE COLOSSEUM.

PLATE VIII.

PLAN OF THE SOUTHERN HALF, AT THE LOWEST LEVEL,

Shewing the Excavations in 1874 and 1875.

Description of Plate VIII.

PLAN OF THE SOUTH-EASTERN HALF, AT THE LOWEST LEVEL,

Shewing the Excavations in 1874 and 1875.

A, A. The frame, cradle, or dry dock, for the galleys to stand upon when not wanted for use.

F, F. The *podium*.

L. The passage for animals.

T, T. Lofty vaulted chambers, with seven sockets in a line in each.

V. Subterranean side-passage, called of Commodus.

a. The dens for wild beasts.

b. The shaft for a man to descend and feed the animals.

c. The drain and flood-gate at the mouth of it.

e, e. Small brick chambers of the time of Nero.

All the sockets that are visible are shewn in the plan, whether in the passages or in the chambers.

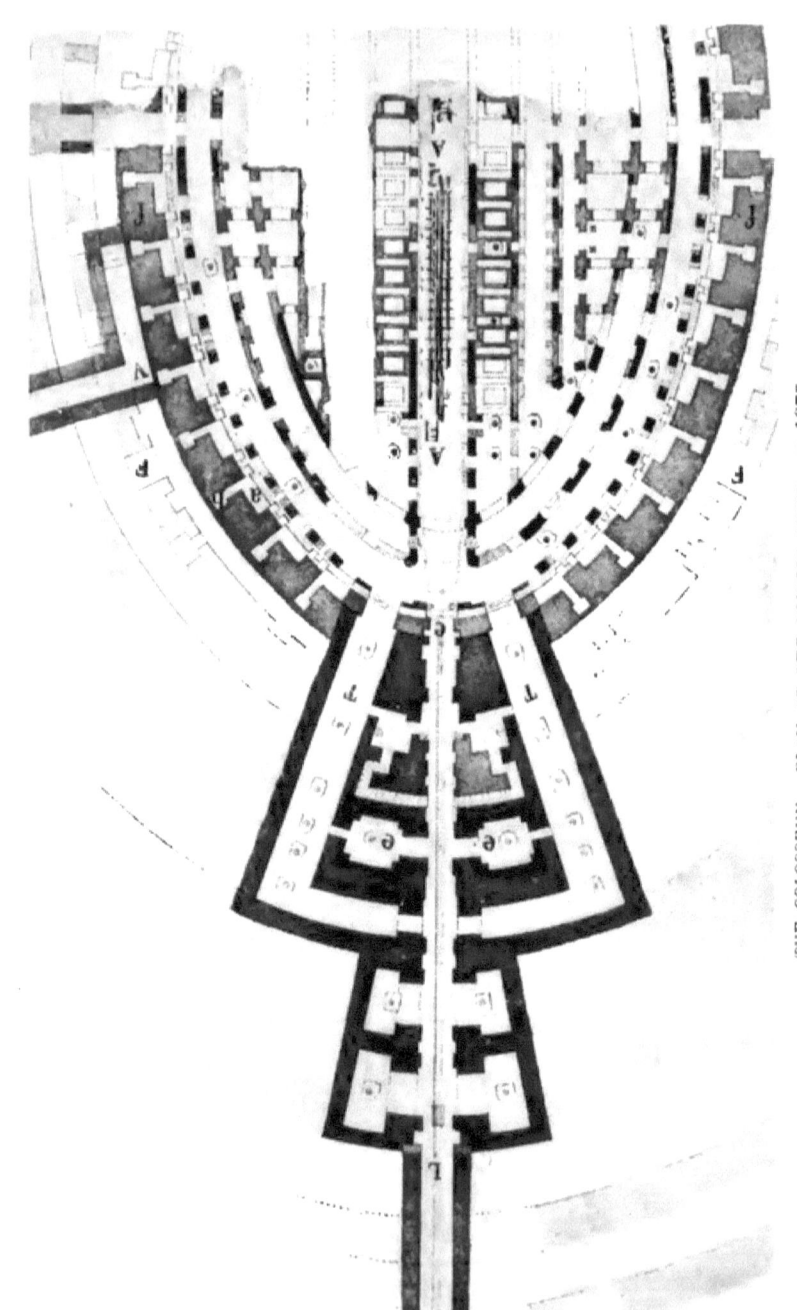

THE COLOSSEUM – PLAN AT THE LOWEST LEVEL, IN 1875.

THE COLOSSEUM.

PLATE IX.

ARCHES IN THE SUBSTRUCTURE.

DESCRIPTION OF PLATE IX.

1. ARCH OF THE SECOND CENTURY IN THE SUBSTRUCTURE.

IN addition to the two ancient walls of tufa parallel to each other round the edge, with the grooves for lifts in them, there are some remains here and there of a third wall of tufa within the other two, and this appears to have been much shaken by an earthquake. In this, little is perfect, but in the parts that remain there are arches, and these arches are supported by brick walls of different periods. The upper arch in this plate is supported by a brick wall of the second century, as is seen by the thickness and quality of the bricks and of the mortar between them. This is shewn by the six-foot rule, each foot painted alternately black and white, by which the bricks can be counted the same as on the spot.

2. ARCH OF THE FIRST CENTURY IN THE SAME.

This small arch is in the same wall, but in this case the brick arch that supports the tufa is clearly of the time of Nero[e]. The long, thin bricks of his time, nine or ten to the foot, are well known to all Roman archæologists, and are so marked that there is no mistaking them: they are thus good evidence that the amphitheatre of Nero, mentioned by Pliny, was on the same site as the Flavian Amphitheatre. A segment of another arch of the same period abuts against it, to support it like a flying buttress, and is seen in the plate.

[e] The photo-engraver has unfortunately turned this photograph upside down, but it is not of much consequence, as the size and thickness of the bricks of Nero can be seen just the same. The space is so narrow that it was difficult to get a photograph of it at all; but this is just one of the cases in which a photograph is of great importance, because there is nothing in which artists are so careless as in the thickness of the bricks and of the mortar between them; there is nothing in which it would be more easy to play tricks, if they wished to do so.

COLOSSEUM.

Arch of the Second Century, in the Substructure.

Brick Arch of Nero, in the Substructure.

THE COLOSSEUM.

PLATE X.

SUBSTRUCTURES.

Remains of two Canals, one supported on Timbers, the other on Brick Arches.

DESCRIPTION OF PLATE X.

SUBSTRUCTURES.

REMAINS OF TWO CANALS, ONE SUPPORTED ON TIMBERS, THE OTHER ON BRICK ARCHES.

THESE two canals, parallel to each other, to be supplied with water by the aqueducts, and used for the *naumachia* or naval fights, are among the most curious discoveries brought to light in the recent explorations. They shew how completely the whole of the great public exhibitions of the ancient Romans were theatrical displays, with all the usual tricks of a theatre, just the same as in a Christmas pantomime.

This shews also that *stagna* do not necessarily mean ponds; any reservoir of water is a *stagnum*, whether supplied by a natural spring or by an aqueduct. Neither of these now remaining are of the time of Nero, they belong to later repairs or alterations; but the great thickness and strength of the wall of so little height could only have been made to support the weight of water. This is especially evident in the upper view, where the wall is nearly as thick as it is high. In this passage the canal, lined with lead, was supported on massive wooden beams; in the lower view the canal in that passage, which is wider than the other, was supported on the brick arches of the second or third century, shewn in this view.

It is even probable that the *stagna* of Nero were in the same place as these, as a good deal of brick-work of his time is on a higher level than these walls, and the two sheets of water, one on either side of the great central passage, would have been magnificent sheets of water, about three hundred feet long and fifty or sixty or more wide in the central part, though narrow at both ends. It is still possible, though not probable, that the *stagna* of Nero were on a lower level, cut through a bed of tufa, which is not generally very thick, to the clay of the Tiber valley beneath. This would account for the central passages on the site of the *stagna* having suffered so much from the earthquakes, while the great corridors of the Flavian Emperors, standing on the bed of tufa, have not suffered at all.

COLOSSEUM — SUBSTRUCTURES

A. REMAINS OF A CANAL SUPPORTED ON TIMBERS
B. ———— OF ANOTHER CANAL SUPPORTED ON ARCHES

THE COLOSSEUM.

PLATE XI.

TWO CAPITALS.

A. From the Upper Storey.
B. From the lower one, or the Podium.

Description of Plate XI.

TWO CAPITALS.

A. From the Upper Storey.
B. From the lower one, or the Podium.

It will be seen at once that this capital (A) is intentionally left in a rude state to be seen from a distance[d], the upper gallery being nearly a hundred feet above the level of the arena. A great number of these capitals, and of the white marble columns to which they belonged, have rolled down from the top of the building to the bottom in an earthquake, crushing all the seats of the galleries in their fall; as many as forty of them have been found, and a still larger number of broken columns, which have evidently fallen with great force; some of them have been found passing quite through the walls in the substructure, and can be still seen with one end on one side of the wall, and the other on the opposite side.

B. is a highly-finished capital of the Corinthian order: of this kind only three or four have been found, but much more perfect than most of the others. They were probably on the short columns of the *podium* by the side of the state entrance.

---

[d] The fragment of sculpture placed upon this capital has nothing to do with it, being merely placed there by the workmen, but a photograph necessarily reproduces things exactly as they were found at the time the photograph was taken.

COLOSSEUM — TWO CAPITALS

A. OF UPPER STOREY — B. OF LOWER

THE COLOSSEUM.

PLATE XII.

RESTORATION OF ONE COMPARTMENT OF THE SUPERSTRUCTURE.

Description of Plate XII.

RESTORATION OF ONE COMPARTMENT OF THE SUPERSTRUCTURE.

SHEWING the colonnade of the third century, on the upper storey, after the burning of the wooden upper floor; to this colonnade the capitals and columns that have fallen down in an earthquake have belonged, — shewing also the arrangement of the seats, the corridors, and the *vomitoria*.

COLOSSEUM — SUPERSTRUCTURES

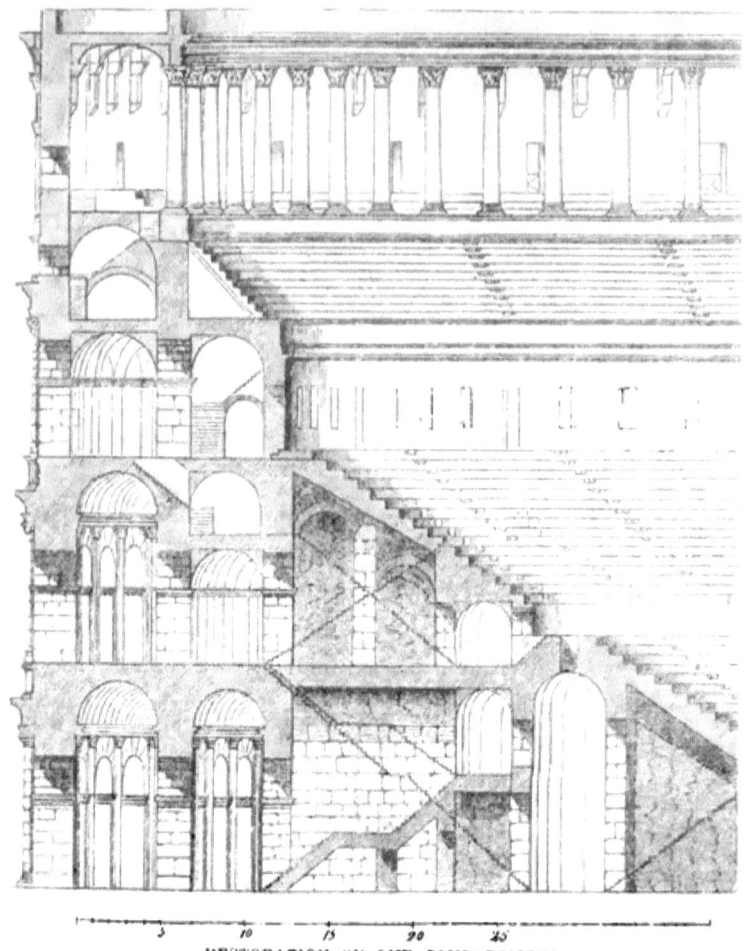

RESTORATION OF ONE COMPARTMENT

THE COLOSSEUM.

PLATE XIII.

SECTION AND DETAILS OF ONE COMPARTMENT,
Including the Substructures below, and
the Awning above.

DESCRIPTION OF PLATE XIII.

SECTION AND DETAILS OF ONE COMPARTMENT,

INCLUDING THE SUBSTRUCTURES BELOW, AND THE AWNING ABOVE.

A, A, A. The wooden framework.
C. Wall of central passage.
D. Wall of central passage.
E, E, E. The ancient tufa walls.
F. The *podium*.
G. First gallery.
H. Second gallery.
I, I. Upper galleries.
K. The drain or cloaca.
L. The passage for animals.
M, M. The state corridors.
O, O, O, O. Corbels at the foot of the masts.
P, P. The dens, and vertical shafts for a man to descend to feed the animals.
R, R, R, R. Corbels to stiffen the masts, and to carry the boards or planks of the arena.
S. Passage from the den to the cage.
a. Series of lattice-work to protect the lower gallery from the wild beasts.
b, b, b. Masts to carry the awning.
e. Place for the counter-weight in the tufa wall.
f, f. Sockets in the pavement of the passage, for the pivots of the capstans to work in.

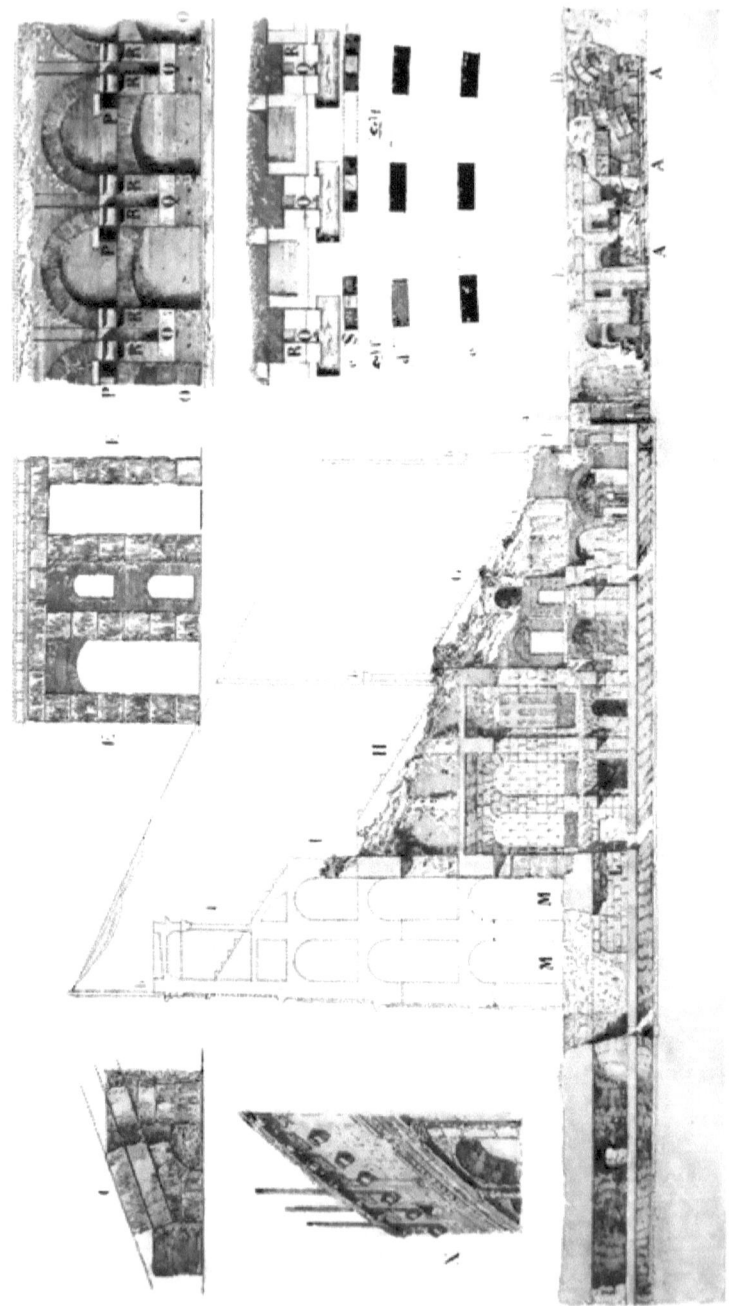

THE COLOSSEUM.

PLATE XIV.

SECTION OF ONE BAY OR COMPARTMENT, AND PLANS OF THE SIX STOREYS.

DESCRIPTION OF PLATE XIV.

SECTION OF ONE BAY OR COMPARTMENT, AND PLANS OF THE SIX STOREYS.

a. Ground-storey and corridor.
b. First storey and upper corridor.
c. Second storey and *vomitoria*.
d. Third storey, passage, and *vomitoria*.
e. Fourth storey with *vomitoria*.
f. Upper storey.

It has not been generally observed that there are so many floors or storeys in the Colosseum. Two of these are only subdivisions for the *vomitoria*, still, to give a complete idea of the whole building, it was necessary to have them.

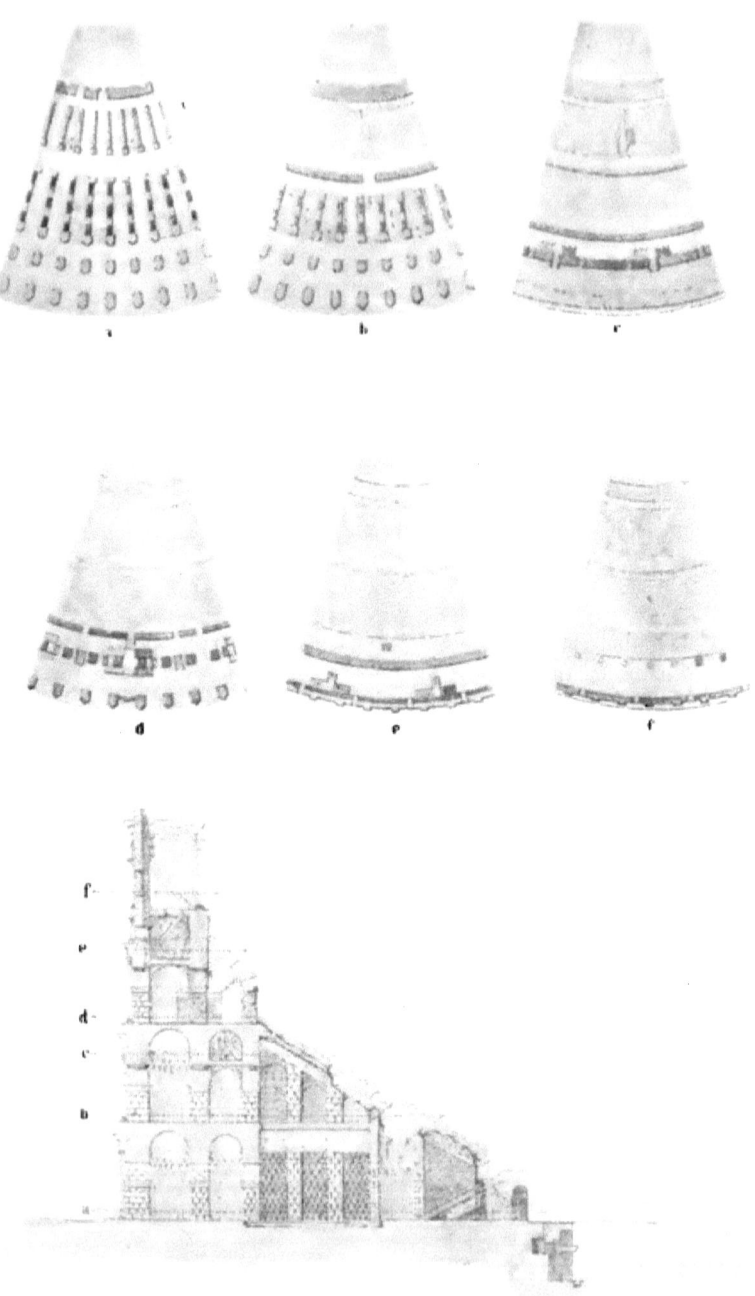

COLOSSEUM
PLANS OF THE SIX STOREYS

SECTION OF ONE BAY

THE COLOSSEUM.

PLATE XV.

SUBSTRUCTURES,
With probable Restorations of the Stagna, the Arena, &c.
Two Views.

DESCRIPTION OF PLATE XV.

SUBSTRUCTURES,

WITH PROBABLE RESTORATIONS OF THE STAGNA, THE ARENA, &C.
TWO VIEWS.

A. STAGNUM AND ARENA.

h, h. Stagnum.
i, i. Space between two canals, flooded at the time of the shows.
g, g, g. Passage under the canals.
A. The wooden framework.
F, F, F. Narrow platform and passage in front of the *podium*, and one of the dens.
I, I, I. The trap-doors for the lifts.
k, k. Smaller trap-door for lifts, (for dogs?).

B. BRICK ARCHES OF NERO SUPPORTING THE TUFA WALL AND ARCH.

n, n, n. Level of the original pavement.
o. Passage.
p. Ancient tufa wall.
q. Brick arch of Nero, under an arch of tufa.
r. Segment of another brick arch of Nero, abutting against the centre of the tufa arch to support it, like an arch-buttress or flying-buttress of the Middle Ages. (For the Phototype of this arch, see Plate IX.)
s. Socket for a pivot to work in.

BRICK ARCHES OF NERO SUPPORTING THE TUFA WALL AND ARCH

COLOSSEUM — SUBSTRUCTURES

h,h. STAGNUM — l,l. ARENA

THE COLOSSEUM.

PLATE XVI.

SUBSTRUCTURES EXCAVATED IN 1875,
With probable Restorations of the Lifts or Pegmata.

Description of Plate XVI.

SUBSTRUCTURES EXCAVATED IN 1875,

With probable Restorations of the Lifts or Pegmata.

The object of this plate is to make more clear to the eye what has previously been explained. An animal is represented first as coming out of the den behind the tufa wall into the cage, with the empty socket behind, as they actually remain, and a capstan with the cord is placed in the socket on the opposite side of the cage. The second is half-way up, to shew the action of the cords, which seems the only mode of explaining the things found. In the third the animal is leaping out on to the stage or arena, as described by Herodian. In front of the *podium* a piece of trellice-work is shewn in its place, taken from a graffito found on the spot.

WITH PROBABLE RESTORATION OF THE LIFTS OR PEGMATA

THE COLOSSEUM.

PLATE XVII.

VIEW IN THE SUBSTRUCTURES.

DESCRIPTION OF PLATE XVII.

VIEW IN THE SUBSTRUCTURES.

E. The Consoles, for placing the boards of the arena upon when not in use.

F. F. The Podium.   X. The level of the arena.

a a a. Doorways to small chambers, to descend to feed the wild beasts in their dens.

b b b. The dens for the wild beasts.

c c c. Blocks of travertine to support the foot of the masts.

d d d. Aperture at the foot of the small chambers, for feeding the wild beasts; these are ten feet from the ground.

e e e. Small water-course in front of the dens.

f. Socket for the pivot of a capstan.

g g. Original pavement of bricks, arranged herring-bone fashion.

h h. Sites of piers of tufa, (removed in the drawing to shew what is behind them).

VIEW IN THE SUBSTRUCTURES.

THE COLOSSEUM.

PLATE XVIII.

VIEW IN THE SUBSTRUCTURES.

Description of Plate XVIII.

VIEW IN THE SUBSTRUCTURES[c].

E. The consoles, for placing the planks of the arena upon.

E*. Consoles, now enclosed in the older tufa wall, in which holes are cut to insert them.

F. The podium.   X. Level of the arena.

a. Doorways of the small descending passages, for feeding the wild beasts in the dens below.

b. The dens for the wild beasts.

c. Blocks of travertine, to support the lower end of the masts for the awning.

d. Recesses for lamps.

e. Small drain for water, which runs round the building in front of the dens.

f. Sockets for the pivots of the capstans.

g. Brick pavement of the second century, in herring-bone pattern.

h. Line of the profiles of ancient tufa piers of arches. (These are represented by dotted lines only, as if transparent, to shew the consoles of the Flavian Emperor inserted in them.)

i*. Line of second arcade of tufa.

A. Plan.   B. Section.

The same letters of reference are used in the plan of this section.

[c] The piers of tufa are represented as transparent, to shew the insertion of the consoles in them. This insertion, with the irregularity of the plan of the tufa piers, contrasted with the mathematical accuracy of the work of the Flavian Emperors, proves that they belonged to an earlier building.

VIEW IN THE SUBSTRUCTURES.

THE COLOSSEUM.

PLATE XIX.

VIEW IN PART OF THE SUBSTRUCTURE, WITH PLAN AND SECTION.

Description of Plate XIX.

VIEW IN PART OF THE SUBSTRUCTURE, WITH PLAN AND SECTION.

E E. The consoles.
F F. The podium.
a. Entrance to the descent to feed the animals.
b. One of the dens.
c. The stream of water in front of the dens.
f f. The sockets for pivots for the capstan to work in.
g g. The original pavement.
h h. Piers of tufa in front of the dens.
k k. Long and lofty chamber under the gallery, in which are seven sockets for the pivots of the capstan to work in.
y. Mouth of the great drain, with the iron grating.
z. Site of the sluice-gate, and groove for it to work in, as a portcullis.
A. The Plan of this part.
B. The Section of it.

VIEW IN THE SUBSTRUCTURES.

THE COLOSSEUM.

PLATE XX.

PORTION OF THE SUPERSTRUCTURE IN THE PRINCIPAL GALLERY.

DESCRIPTION OF PLATE XX.

PORTION OF THE SUPERSTRUCTURE IN THE PRINCIPAL GALLERY.

A A. Walls of brick, dividing the different bays of the gallery.

B B. Arches of construction, to make the brick facing adhere better to the mass of tufa concrete behind it.

C C. A void space from which a pier of travertine has been carried away for building purposes[f].

D D. The great pier of travertine on one of the arches of the corridor of the Flavian Emperors.

[f] In other instances, the brick arches of construction appear to rest on the piers of travertine between them; but as these have been removed, and the brick walls stand equally well without them, it is evident that this is not the case. The tall piers of travertine reach the whole height of the building, to support the upper gallery. In the following plate the same remarkable construction is shewn more clearly, because in this instance the aperture left by the removal of the stone piers is visible in two storeys, and it is seen that three piers extended from the upper gallery to the ground, passing through all the other storeys.

PORTION OF THE SUPERSTRUCTURE IN THE PRINCIPAL GALLERY.

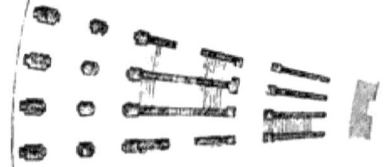

THE COLOSSEUM.

PLATE XXI.
VIEW IN THE UPPER PART.
Details.

DESCRIPTION OF PLATE XXI.

VIEW IN THE UPPER PART.

DETAILS.

A A.
A A. } Piers of the great corridor.

a a. Aperture from which a pier of travertine has been removed for building material, by the Barberini (?).

b b. Wall of brick, with arch of construction standing equally well without the support of the travertine pier.

c c. Wall of tufa, of a lower storey.

d d. Vault of a third storey, below.

e e. Remains of the vault of the stairs to the upper storey.

f f. Floor of the second corridor.

g g. Floor of the principal gallery.

The object of this plate is to make it still more clear that the brick arches of construction did not *really* rest on the piers of travertine, although at first sight they appear to do so. The Roman bricks of the first century are two feet square and one inch thick, but in these arches they are cut down from two feet to three or four inches at the impost, or springing of each arch, just where the greatest strength would have been required. They have evidently been cut through to admit the stone piers, which were required to carry the upper gallery, when that was built of stone instead of wood.

COLOSSEUM

DETAILS IN UPPER PART

THE COLOSSEUM.

PLATE XXII.

THE GRAFFITI,
OR SCRATCHINGS ON MARBLE BY THE WORKMEN OF
THE SECOND CENTURY.

DESCRIPTION OF PLATE XXII.

THE GRAFFITI,

OR SCRATCHINGS ON MARBLE BY THE WORKMEN OF THE SECOND CENTURY.

A. An athlete, commonly called a wrestler; but the athletes were more than merely wrestlers, they were often men of high rank, and fought with weapons also, sometimes with fatal results. This is a prize-man with his palm-branch in his hand.

B. Athletes.—On this fragment of marble the drawing is very indistinct, but there appear to be two figures only, with arms in their hands, and their heads bare, their helmets being on a table behind them. Inscriptions are scratched upon these, which are rather difficult to make out, but seem to be—on one, IVTOK (?); on another, LIMENI NIKÆ; on a third, OVIM. The rest are too indistinct to be read.

C. A hunt of wild beasts.—This is extremely curious, but not very distinct in the original, and therefore not in the photo-engraving, which admits of no *restorations*. There are five animals all of the same kind, but what animal they are intended for it is not easy to say; they have claws, the heads look like wolves'. Each has a broken cord hanging to its neck. There are two huntsmen with spears in their hands running after them; they are clothed in tight dresses, with bands round the waist and the knees, and with buskins on their feet.

COLOSSEUM — GRAFFITI

A. AND B. ATHLETES

C. WILD-BEAST HUNT

THE COLOSSEUM.

PLATE XXIII.
GRAFFITO OF THE PODIUM, &c.

DESCRIPTION OF PLATE XXIII.

GRAFFITO OF THE PODIUM, &c.

THIS is one of the four *graffiti* found during the excavations in 1874. It represents the front of the *podium*, with the framework for the netting to protect the spectators in the lower gallery, or state-gallery, from the wild beasts, if they should attempt to spring up into it when hunted on the stage or arena below, at the foot of the *podium*. This fragment shews the lower portion of the screen, which is recorded to have had a bar at the top that turned round, so that if any animal tried to cling to it he would fall backwards on the arena. This was level with the foot of the *podium*, and twenty-one feet above the pavement at the bottom, on the level of the dens for the wild beasts, and the floor of the passage between the two walls of tufa, with vertical grooves in them for the lifts, with the cages upon them. Behind the place for each cage in the paved floor of the passage, is a socket for a pivot to work in, at the foot of a capstan or post, to wind the twenty-one feet of cord upon, with the lift, when pulled up to the trap-door of the arena. This pavement is represented as resting on the top of a series of arches with bars across; these are probably intended for the doors of the wild beasts below, but rudely represented, and with some sort of performance going on in front.

THE COLOSSEUM.

PLATE XXIV.
REPRESENTATIONS ON COINS OR MEDALS.

Description of Plate XXIV.

REPRESENTATIONS ON COINS OR MEDALS[g].

1. Titus sitting upon a trophy of arms (A.U.C. 823, A.D. 80).

On the obverse the legend is, TIB. VESP. AVG. P.M. TR. P.P. COS. VIII. S.C.

On the reverse is the amphitheatre, with the Meta Sudans to the left, and on the right a double colonnade, one over the other, for the aqueduct (?).

2. Head of Alexander Severus, A.D. 224.

Legend:—IMP. CÆSAR DIVI SEV. ALEXANDER.

Reverse:—The Amphitheatre, with the Meta Sudans on the right, and two figures on the left, with the legend of the dates of his tribuneship and consulate.

3. Obverse:—Head of Alexander Severus (A.U.C. 937, A.D. 224).

Legend:—IMP. CAES. DIVI. SEV. ALEXANDER.

Reverse:—Amphitheatre, with a group of figures to the left, and a building of two storeys to the right[h].

Legend:—Dates of tribuneship and consulate.

4. Obverse:—Head of Gordianus III. (A.U.C. 997, A.D. 244).

Legend:—IMP. GORDIANVS PIVS FELIX AVG.

Reverse:—Amphitheatre, with a colossus on the left, and a small building on the right[i].

Legend:—MUNIFICENTIA GORDIANI. AVG.

[g] In this plate the coins are taken by photograph from the originals in the British Museum.
[h] Qy. Colonnade of Aqueduct, or Piscina Limaria.
[i] Qy. Reservoir (*castellum aquæ*) of the time of Alexander Severus, of which there are remains.

REPRESENTATIONS ON COINS OR MEDALS.

THE COLOSSEUM.

PLATE XXV.

DIAGRAMS OF COINS OR MEDALS.

DESCRIPTION OF PLATE XXV.

DIAGRAMS OF COINS OR MEDALS.

1. OBVERSE :—Head of Titus.
Legend :—VESP. GENS. T. CAES. IMP.
Reverse :—Amphitheatre, with Meta Sudans to the left, and double colonnade to the right. (Same as No. 1, Plate XXIV.)

2. Obverse :—Head of Domitian, with legend, IMP. CAES. DOMIT. AVG. GERM. P.M. TRP. XIIII.
Reverse :—Amphitheatre, with Meta Sudans and colonnade, probably of aqueduct from the Cœlian.

3. Obverse :—Head of Alexander Severus (same as No. 3, Plate XXIV.), with legend, IMP. CAES. M. AVR. SEV. ALEXANDER. AVG.
Reverse :—Amphitheatre, with group of figures on the left, and a small building on the right (*castellum aquæ?*).

4. Obverse :—Head of Gordianus III.
Legend :—IMP. GORDIANVS. PIVS. FELIX. AVG.
Reverse :—Amphitheatre, with a colossus and a building.
Legend :—MVNIFICENTIA GORDIANI. AVG.

COLOSSEUM — REPRESENTATIONS ON COINS

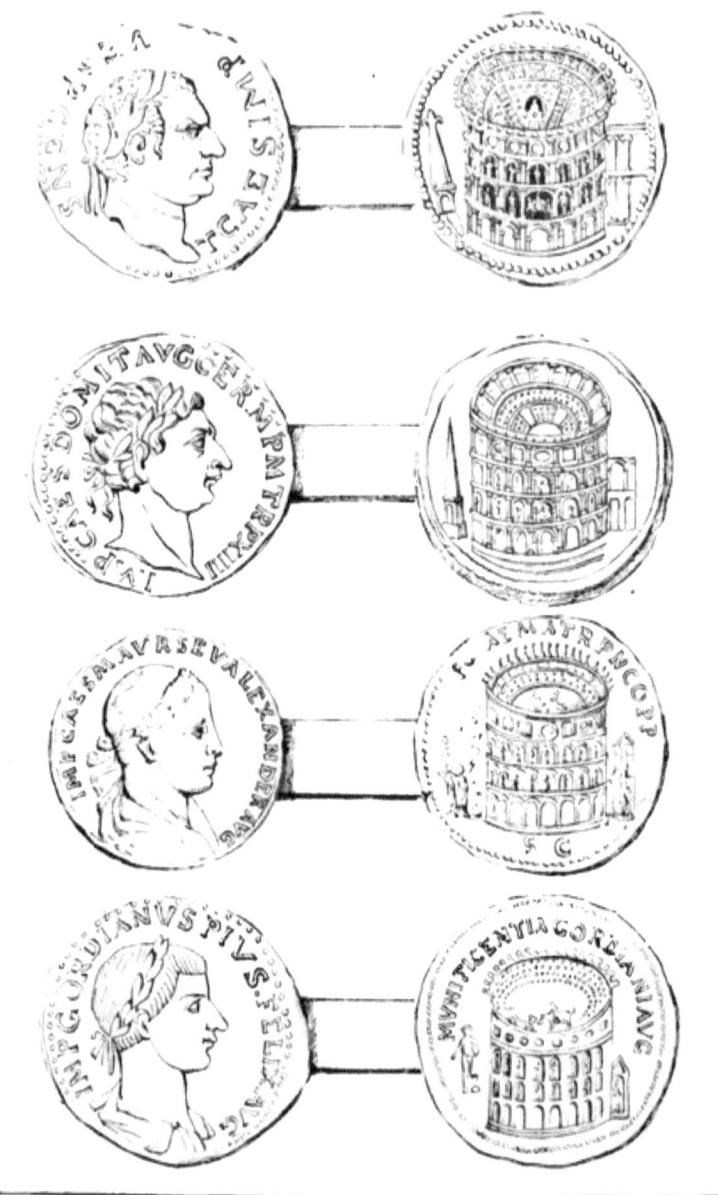

THE COLOSSEUM.

PLATE XXVI.

A ROMAN GALLEY ON A CRADLE FOR LAUNCHING.

Description of Plate XXVI.

A ROMAN GALLEY ON A CRADLE FOR LAUNCHING.

This is drawn from a restoration made by M. Viollet-le-Duc for Napoleon III. at Compiègne. It illustrates in a very remarkable manner the cradle found in the Colosseum, with the struts on each side. As this cradle was made from the best authorities long before the finding of the cradle in the Colosseum, it is particularly valuable for the purpose of comparison.

COLOSSEUM – A ROMAN GALLEY ON A CRADLE FOR LAUNCHING

THE COLOSSEUM.

PLATE XXVII.

AMPHITHEATRE OR COLOSSEUM AT CAPUA.

COLOSSEUM.

DESCRIPTION OF PLATE XXVII.

AMPHITHEATRE OR COLOSSEUM AT CAPUA.

This Plate is a reproduction of Photograph with no attempt at restoration.

THE resemblance between this and the Colosseum in Rome is so remarkable, that there can be no doubt one is a copy from the other. In this amphitheatre the two canals for water, on each side of the great central passage, and the curved passage round the outer edge, are distinctly visible. At Capua, the aqueduct for the water, and the drain to carry it off, remain.

AMPHITHEATRE AT POMPEII, FROM A FRESCO PAINTING.

The lower view is from a fresco at Pompeii. It shews the awning is drawn off behind. There is a front built out distinct from the oval building, with which it is connected by a curved wall at each end, and on which is a passage with persons upon it; there are two grand flights of steps leading up to the top, and persons going up them. These steps are carried on arches, increasing in height as they get nearer the top. The front passage is also carried on tall arches. All these arrangements for the entrance and exit seem to be a bad substitute for the *vomitoria* of the Roman Colosseum.

There appears to be another place of amusement of some kind by the side of the amphitheatre. A square space enclosed by a high wall, with two arches on one side or doorways (?), probably a school for gladiators, with an *impluvium* in the middle. There is an inscription on the wall, of which all that is legible is DIVCRET . . . ; there is also in the front of the picture a tent with persons under it, and two small square or oblong huts, evidently of wood, the planks being shewn in one with a door; this was probably a wine-shop.

There are a number of figures in active motion in all parts of the picture, many of them evidently fighting, and it represents a skirmish between the Nucerini and the Pompeiani; the inhabitants of a neighbouring town, called Nuceria or Nocera, having made a sudden inroad on Pompeii, the Pompeians are flying in all directions, closely followed, some dying and some dead. These hand-to-hand fights are seen on the arena, in the corridors or *ambulatories*, on the walls of the town, and on the esplanade round the building, which is planted with trees for shade [k].

---

[k] For further details see the *Descrizione di Pompeii per Giuseppe Fiorelli*, Napoli, 1875, 12mo., pp. 56 and 70. All who are interested in Pompeii should have this valuable little work.

AMPHITHEATRE OR COLOSSEUM AT CAPUA

AMPHITHEATRE WITH AWNING FROM A FRESCO AT POMPEI

THE COLOSSEUM.

PLATE XXVIII.

AMPHITHEATRE AT CAPUA.

DESCRIPTION OF PLATE XXVIII.

AMPHITHEATRE AT CAPUA.

A. Perspective view, looking down upon it, with a restoration of the canals for water.

d. The pavement.
g g. Walls to support the canals of water.
h h. Dens for the wild beasts.
i. Socket for a pivot.
k k. Canals for water.

B. One of the chambers in the substructure of the time of Hadrian, with the aqueduct, l, and an opening made in the vault.

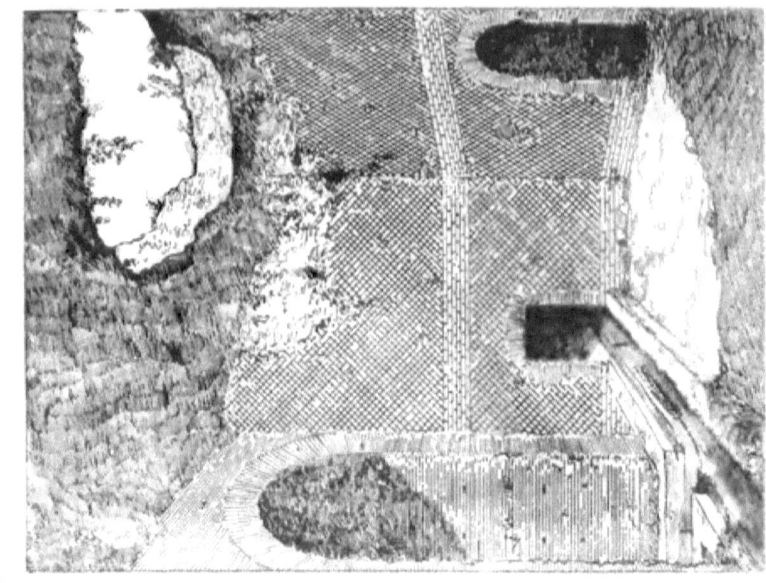

AMPHITHEATRE AT CAPUA — VIEW AND DETAILS

THE COLOSSEUM.

PLATE XXIX.

AMPHITHEATRE AT CAPUA.

Details.

DESCRIPTION OF PLATE XXIX.

AMPHITHEATRE AT CAPUA.

DETAILS.

o o o. Portion of the exterior,—all that remains of it being two arches of the arcade, with pilasters between them, and one pilaster of the upper storey.

A—B. Transverse section of the remains.

C. Four arches of the inner arcade.

h h h. Dens for wild beasts.

P P P. Corbels, or consoles, as in the Colosseum, Plate XVII.

l l. Aqueduct coming from the chambers of the time of Hadrian. (See the Plan.)

D. Plan of this portion of the building.

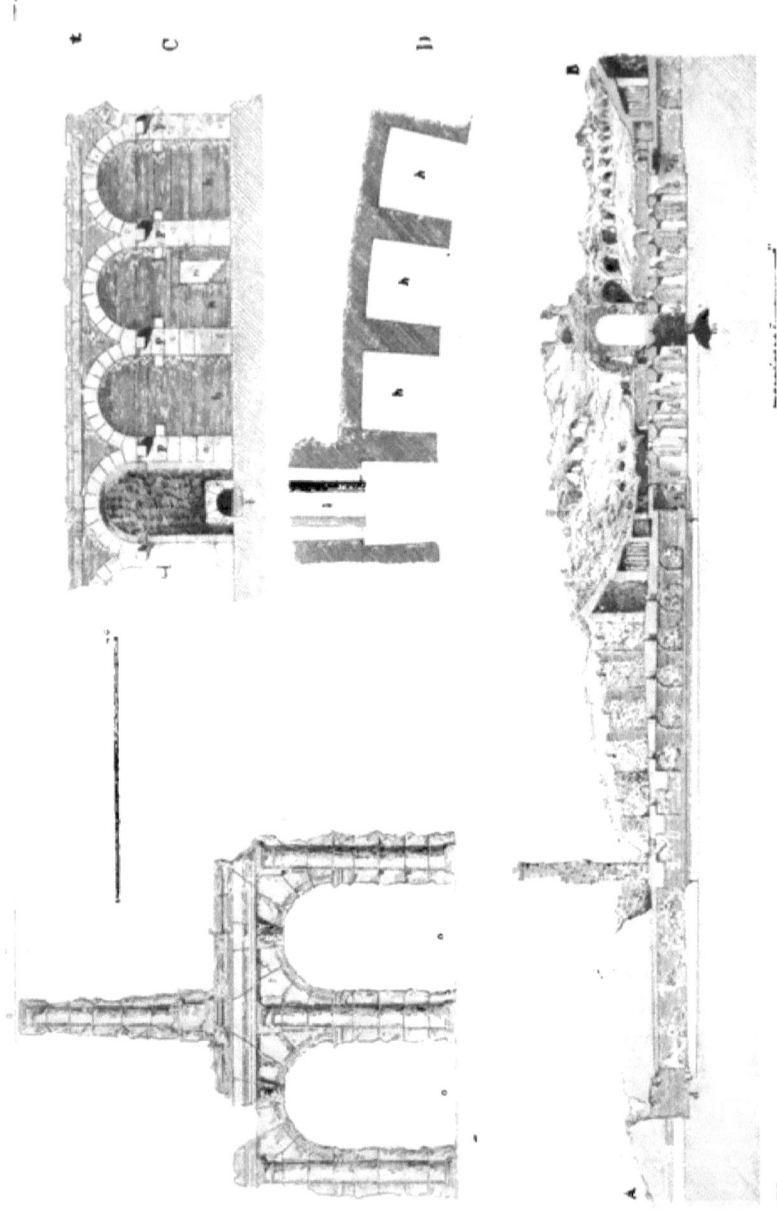

A. PORTION OF EXTERIOR
B. LONGITUDINAL SECTION
C. PORTION OF ARCADES AND DENS
D. PLAN OF THE SAME

THE COLOSSEUM.

PLATE XXX.

AMPHITHEATRE AT CAPUA.

Plan of the Substructures, with the Superstructures in dotted lines.

DESCRIPTION OF PLATE XXX.

AMPHITHEATRE AT CAPUA.

PLAN OF THE SUBSTRUCTURES, WITH THE SUPERSTRUCTURES IN DOTTED LINES.

a. North entrance.
b b b. Central passage.
c c c. Eastern passage.
d. Small chamber of the time of Hadrian.
e e. Western passage.
f f. The galleries.
g g. Substructures with water.
h h h. Dens for the wild beasts.
i i. Sockets for pivots, as in the Colosseum.
k k k. Canals for water.
l l. The aqueduct.
m m. The drain.
n n. Stairs.
o o. Superstructure. The only remains of the exterior façade.

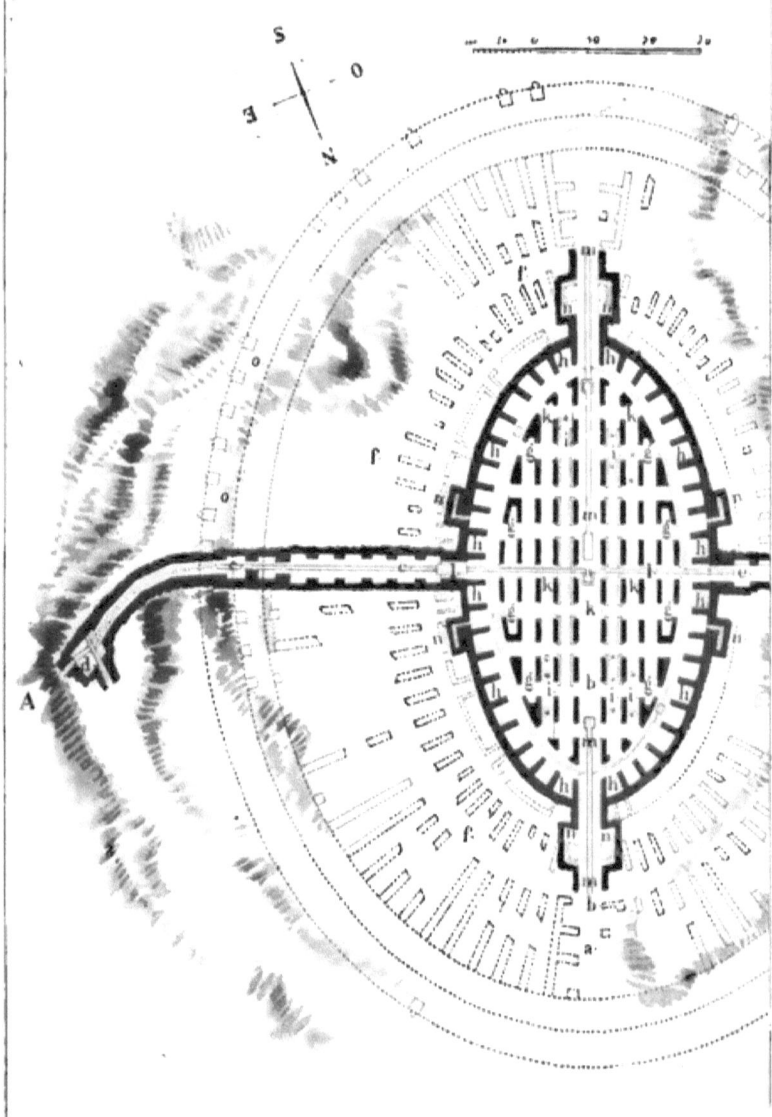

AMPHITHEATRE AT CAPUA

PLAN WITH THE SUBSTRUCTIONS

THE COLOSSEUM.

PLATE XXXI.
AMPHITHEATRE AT VERONA.

DESCRIPTION OF PLATE XXXI.

AMPHITHEATRE AT VERONA.
(*From Photograph.*)

A. EXTERIOR, with the double arcade,— and remains of the exterior front.

B. INTERIOR, with the marble seats. These are the most perfect that remain anywhere, and they shew what the Colosseum must have been when perfect.

AMPHITHEATRE OF VERONA

A. VIEW OF EXTERIOR WITH THE ARCADES
B. VIEW IN INTERIOR WITH SEATS

THE COLOSSEUM.

PLATE XXXII.

THE AMPHITHEATRE AT POZZUOLI, NEAR NAPLES.

Colosseum.

Description of Plate XXXII.

THE AMPHITHEATRE AT POZZUOLI, NEAR NAPLES.

In this instance the arena has fortunately been preserved, with the trap-doors in it; those round the edge being for wild beasts, the others for men and dogs, and the central passage as in the *Colosseum*. We see that the central passage has been boarded over also. The arrangement of the seats in the galleries is also the same, and the tufa wall behind probably indicates that there was an awning over the galleries in the same manner. This confirms one part of the history of the Colosseum, and the Amphitheatre at Capua confirms another part, the canals for the *naumachia* or naval battles, although these were evidently very different from what had formerly been supposed. At each end of the part that is uncovered of the central passage it will be observed that there is a short post, looking very much like a capstan for winding a cord upon, as in Rome, although in this instance they are square and on the surface, and not on the pavement below. Each of the openings to the trap-doors has a groove round it, for a cover to fit into; possibly this was made water-tight, so that the whole surface could be flooded. The central passage has the same sort of groove sunk round it. The same arrangement may have been used in the Colosseum, but in that case there is the difficulty of the interval between the *podium* of the lower gallery and the floor of the arena, which does not appear to have existed at Pozzuoli. This would have made it impracticable to flood the whole surface at Rome, which might have been done at Pozzuoli.

THE COLOSSEUM.

PLATE XXXIII.

AMPHITHEATRE AT POZZUOLI.
Plan.

DESCRIPTION OF PLATE XXXIII.

AMPHITHEATRE AT POZZUOLI.

PLAN.

A—B. Line of the Longitudinal Section.
C—D. Line of the view of the exterior.
a. Plan of the substructions.
b. With the superstructure in dotted lines.
c. Principal entrance from the west.
d. Eastern entrance.
e. Central passage.
f. Transverse Section.
g. Aqueduct.
h. Dens for animals.
i i. Part of the substructure not yet excavated.
k. Chambers commonly called "the Prison of Nero."
l l. Drain leading to the sea.

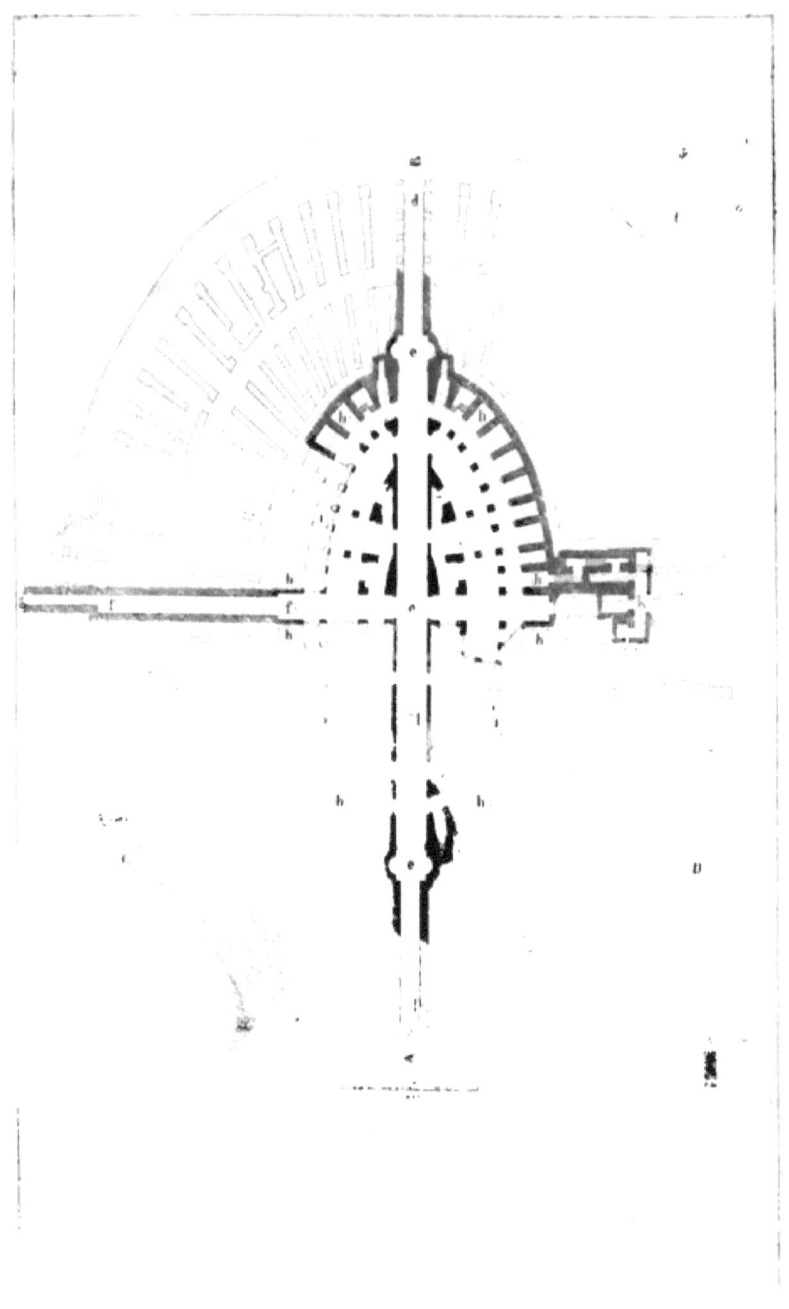

AMPHITHEATRE AT POZZUOLI — PLAN

THE COLOSSEUM.

PLATE XXXIV.

AMPHITHEATRE AT POZZUOLI.

DESCRIPTION OF PLATE XXXIV.

AMPHITHEATRE AT POZZUOLI.

A—B. Longitudinal Section.
c. Principal entrance from the west.
d. Eastern entrance.
  These two entrances are on sloping ground, descending to the central passage, e e e.
e. The drain to the sea.

C—D. View of the Exterior, from the principal entrance on the western side.

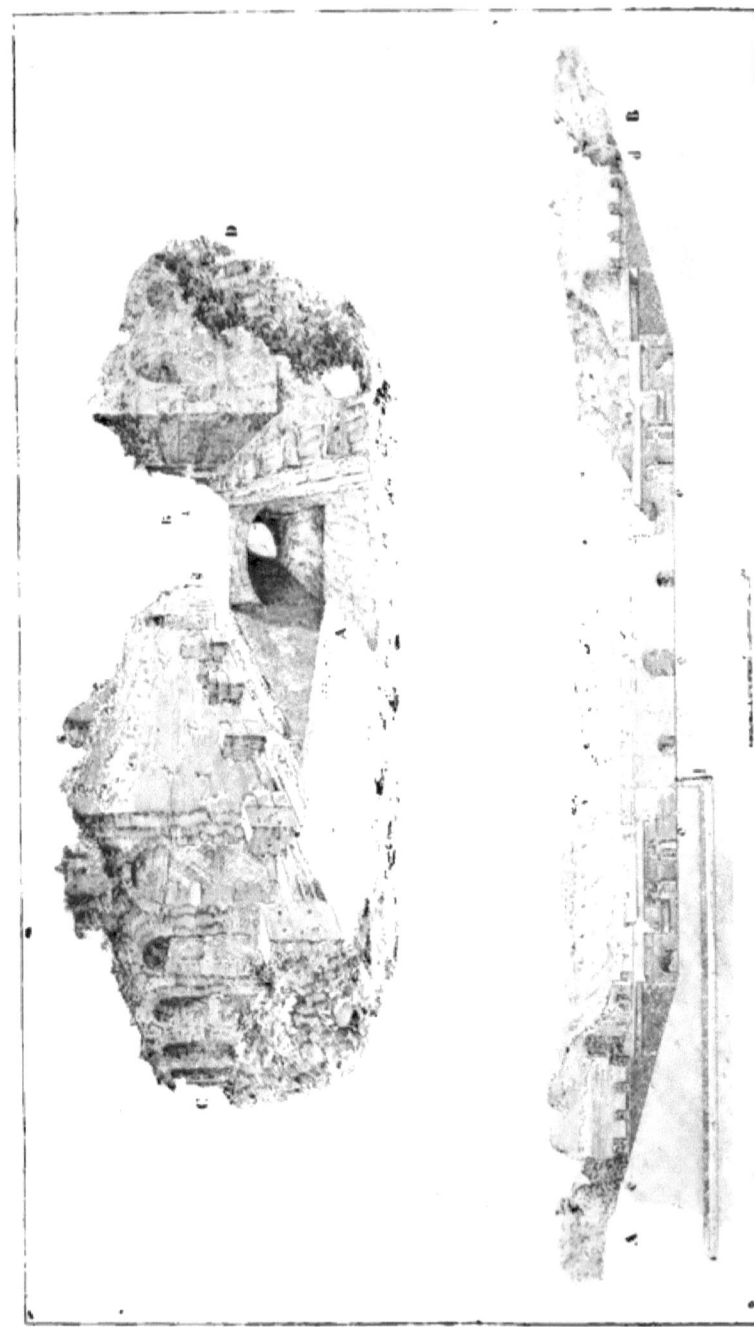

AMPHITHEATRE AT POZZUOLI

THE COLOSSEUM.

PLATE XXXV.
AMPHITHEATRE AT POZZUOLI.

DESCRIPTION OF PLATE XXXV.

AMPHITHEATRE AT POZZUOLI.

E. View in the principal corridor, with the receptacles to collect the water, m m m.

F. View in a subterranean corridor under the arena, shewing remains of the decorations thrown down by the hand of men, through the aperture, n.

It is here impossible that they could have fallen down in an earthquake, as was the case in the Colosseum. A garden was made here upon the arena, and these decorations were removed from the surface, as interfering with the cultivation of the garden, and thrown down into the substructures, and then arranged under the vault as we see them.

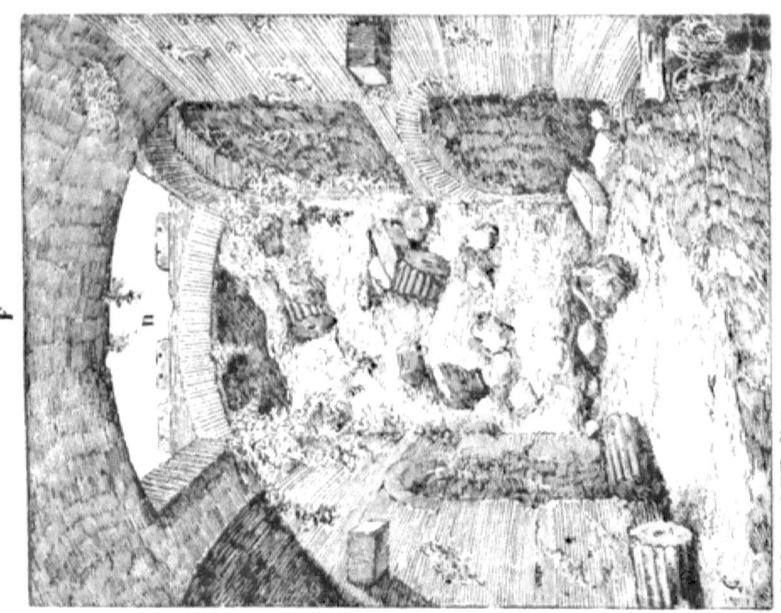
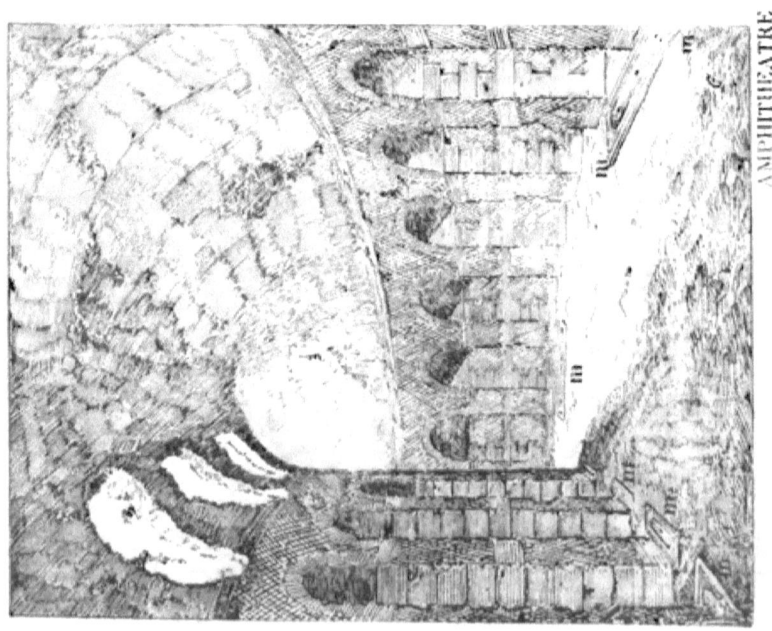

AMPHITHEATRE AT POZZUOLI — DETAILS

THE COLOSSEUM.

PLATE XXXVI.
PLAN OF THE GREAT DRAIN.

DESCRIPTION OF PLATE XXXVI.

PLAN OF THE GREAT DRAIN.

A. The Colosseum.
B. Part of the Cœlian Hill, on which the Claudium stood.
C. Part of the Palatine Hill.

a. Summa Sacra Via.
a*. Clivus Triumphalis.
b. Meta Sudans.
c. Arch of Constantine.
d d. Passage of Commodus.
e. Site on which the steam-engine was placed in 1874-5, to pump out the water coming from this point.
f. Piscina of the time of Nero.
g. Castellum Aquæ, or reservoir of Alexander Severus.
g*. Aqueduct of the third century.
h h. Exhedra of the Ludus Magnus.
i i i. Great Drain of the Colosseum, to convey the water to the Tiber.
k. The exact spot where the water runs down from the Cœlian into the Colosseum, called a natural spring, but not having the usual bubbling character of a spring.
l. Via di S. Giovanni in Laterano.
m. Via Cœlimontana.
n n n. Orto Botanico. Waste ground at the foot of the Cœlian Hill, planted with trees and shrubs, *called* the Botanical Garden, but not used as such.
o o. Via del Arco di Constantino. The road between the Cœlian and the Palatine Hill.
p. Podium of the colossal statue of Gordianus, 50 ft. high.

COLOSSEUM — PLAN OF THE GREAT DRAIN

THE ARCHÆOLOGY OF ROME,

BY

JOHN HENRY PARKER, C.B.

Hon. M.A. Oxon., F.S.A. Lond.;

KEEPER OF THE ASHMOLEAN MUSEUM OF HISTORY AND ARCHÆOLOGY, OXFORD;
VICE-PRESIDENT OF THE OXFORD ARCHITECTURAL AND HISTORICAL SOCIETY,
AND OF THE BRITISH AND AMERICAN ARCHÆOLOGICAL SOCIETY OF ROME;
MEMBER OF THE ROYAL ARCHÆOLOGICAL INSTITUTE,
MEMBRE DE LA SOCIÉTÉ FRANÇAISE D'ARCHÉOLOGIE,
HONORARY MEMBER OF THE ROYAL INSTITUTE OF BRITISH ARCHITECTS,
AND OF VARIOUS ARCHÆOLOGICAL SOCIETIES, ENGLISH AND FOREIGN.

PART VII.

THE FLAVIAN AMPHITHEATRE,

COMMONLY CALLED

THE COLOSSEUM.

OXFORD:
JAMES PARKER AND CO.

LONDON:
JOHN MURRAY, ALBEMARLE-STREET.
1876.

CATALOGUE OF PHOTOGRAPHS.—PART IV.

The Forum Romanum in 1872.   4to. 2959

Near the north end, shewing the column of Phocas in front of the Arch of Septimius Severus, and the fragments of the marble wall of the Comitium in front of the Church of S. Hadrian and S. Luke.

Sculpture—One side of one of the Marble Walls of the Comitium.   8vo. 2960

Shewing the Magistrate (?) or the Emperor (?) seated on his curule chair surrounded by the officers of the court, and the procession of voters coming up to vote, according to one interpretation; in the back-ground the entablature and cornice and panelling of a basilica, or market-hall, is represented. This is believed to be a view of the Forum Romanum itself at that period. It is of the time of Hadrian, and the figure seated on a throne is probably that Emperor.

Sculpture—One side of the second Wall of the Comitium, in fragments, as it was found, before it was put together.   8vo. 2961

A procession of persons carrying books or tablets is distinctly visible, they are supposed to represent the books of the taxes which Hadrian had cancelled, and they are bringing them up to be burnt; the sculpture thus representing an historical event of importance. In the background are seen the porticoes of two temples, with an arch between them, which there is reason to believe is also a view of the Forum. It is evident that the sculptures on these two marble walls of the Comitium must be considered as a continuation of the same subject, and this most probably is the great donation to the Roman people by the Emperor Hadrian.

In this view the original stone wall of foundation, of an earlier period, is seen under the marble wall.

Sculpture—Other fragments of the Marble Wall of the Comitium, as found.   8vo. 2962

This view shews the same wall as 2961 in perspective, and on the back of the other wall the three animals prepared for sacrifice—the Bull, the Ram, and the Boar, decorated with garlands of flowers. The Comitium is mentioned by Varro as a law court (de Ling. Lat., v. 154), and he says that the Græcostasis was near to it, and that above this (that is, on a higher level) were the Senaculum, the Temple of Concord, and the Basilica Opimia. The discovery of the Comitium on a low level, therefore, fixes the sites of the other buildings. Livy says that the Comitium was covered over at the time that Hannibal was in Italy, but the roof was probably of wood, or perhaps an awning only (Livii Hist., lib. xxvii. c. 36).

Fountain in the Piazza Tartaruga, near the Ghetto.   4to. 2963

The design is by Giacomo Della Porta, incorrectly attributed to Raphael. The figures by Taddeo Landini. The water flows from the mouths of toads standing on the margin of a circular basin; it is popularly called the toad fountain.

Primitive Fortifications—Sections of the Cœlian Hill.   4to. 2964

Excavations, 1872—Sculpture—Small Statue representing the young Hercules, found in the Campo Verano in the spring of 1872. 8vo. 2965

Excavations, 1872—Sculpture—Statue representing Tellus, or the Earth, seated, found in the spring of 1872 in the Campo Verano. 8vo. 2966

Excavations, 1873—Architectural Details—Gigantic Cornice, found at the Macceo, near the Prætorian Camp, in 1873. 4to. 2967

Excavations, 1873—Remains of a House of the time of the Antonines, shewing the Fountain or Cistern, on the ground-floor. 4to. 2968

Found in 1873, against the cliff of the Esquiline, at the point where the Via Nazionale touches the Via de Serpenti.

Excavations, 1873—Remains of a House of the time of the Antonines—View shewing the Construction, on the upper floor. 4to. 2969

Excavations, 1873—Mosaic Pavement of a House of the time of the Antonines. 4to. 2970

Excavations—Architectural Details—Base of a large Column of the fourth century, time of the Emperor Constantius. 8vo. 2971

Found in the Forum Romanum, and now placed at the entrance to the Palaces of the Cæsars, with sculptures representing the three animals for sacrifice, the same as on the wall of the Comitium.

Palatine—Palaces of the Cæsars—Part of the Palace of the time of Trajan. 4to. 2972

With square brick piers added in the time of Hadrian, to carry a lofty vault over the paved road that descends near the north-east angle of the Palatine Hill, called the Via Triumphalis. (This Palace is miscalled that of Tiberius.)

Palatine—Palaces of the Cæsars—Wall of a Chamber of the time of Hadrian, adjoining the paved road called the Via Triumphalis, at the north-east angle. 4to. 2973

This adjoins the paved road, and corresponds exactly with a similar wall in the Villa of Hadrian, at Tivoli.

Palatine—Part of the Palace of Tiberius against the west cliff, near the middle of the Palatine Hill. 4to. 2974

Palatine—Details of the Palace of Tiberius. 4to. 2975

These details correspond exactly with the sleeping-places of the guards inside the north wall of the Prætorian Camp, built in the time of Tiberius.

Excavations, 1872—Architectural Details—Fragments of Cornices and Bases of the second century, found in the Palazzo Fiano, and now in the courtyard of the same palace. 4to. 2976

Excavations, 1872—Architectural Details—Fragments of Cornices, with elegant foliage of the second century, found in the Palazzo Fiano, and now in the courtyard of the same palace. 4to. 2977

Excavations, 1872 — Architectural Details — Fragment of Sculpture on a Base, found in the Palazzo Fiano, and now in the courtyard of the same palace. 8vo. 2978

Excavations, 1872—Architectural Details—Base of a Pilaster, with foliage of the second century, found in the Palazzo Fiano, and now in the courtyard of the same palace. 8vo. 2979

Sarcophagus of the second century, with figures of actors and masks, now in the garden of the Villa Celimontana, formerly called Villa Mattei. 8vo. 2980

It was found in this garden on the site of one of the Cohortes of the Vigili, or barracks of the firemen and night police of the Empire.

Excavations, 1872—Fresco Painting in a subterranean chamber of the private house of Trajan, on the Aventine. 4to. 2981

Tombs—Fresco Painting of a female figure holding a crown, the Genius of Death(?), in the Pyramid of Caius Cestius, B.C. 30(?), outside the Porta S. Paolo. *Taken with magnesian light.* 8vo. 2982

Tombs—Fresco Painting of the Genius of Death holding a crown, in the Pyramid of Caius Cestius, B.C. 30(?), outside the Porta S. Paolo. *Taken with magnesian light.* 8vo. 2983

Crypt of S. Peter in the Vatican (34)—A fine picture of the fourteenth century, representing the Madonna and Child with two Angels. *Taken with magnesian light.* 4to. 2984

Crypt of S. Peter (8)—A fine Door-post of Marble, used in the Chapel of John VII., A.D. 706, with animals, birds, and foliage. *Taken with magnesian light.* 8vo. 2985

Crypt of S. Peter (8)—A fine Door-post of Marble, used in the Chapel of John VII., A.D. 706, with birds, foliage, and figures. *Taken with magnesian light.* 8vo. 2986

Crypt of S. Peter (8)—A fine Door-post used in the Chapel of John VII., A.D. 706, with birds, foliage, and figures. *Taken with magnesian light.* 8vo. 2987

Crypt of S. Peter—Fresco Painting of the old Basilica of S. Peter, before it was destroyed in 1570 under Paul V. *Taken with magnesian light.* 8vo. 2988

Crypt of S. Peter (67)—Ciborium of the Holy Lance (time of Innocent VIII., A.D. 1490), two Angels adoring the Holy Relic. *Taken with magnesian light.* 8vo. 2989

Crypt of S. Peter (22) — Sculpture from the Tomb of Cardinal Berardus Herulus, of Narni, A.D. 1479. *Taken with magnesian light.* 8vo. 2990

It represents the Almighty in the act of blessing, holding a book, and surrounded by Angels with eight wings.

Crypt of S. Peter (53)—Sculpture in white marble representing S. John the Evangelist. *Taken with magnesian light.* 8vo. 2991

This sculpture was ordered by Innocent VIII., A.D. 1490, to decorate the Ciborium of the Holy Lance, with the other three Evangelists.

Crypt of S. Peter (156)—Antique Sarcophagus of red granite used for the body of Pope Hadrian IV., A.D. 1159, the only English Pope (Breakspear). *Taken with magnesian light.* 4to. 2992

Crypt of S. Peter (37)—A Bas-relief made at the end of the sixteenth century, under Pope Sixtus V. *Taken with magnesian light.* 4to. 2993

This splendid bas-relief was made to decorate the front of the Altar of the Pope. It represents the Judgment of the Apostles by Nero.

Crypt of S. Peter (18)—Cross of white marble, formerly on the gable of the front of the old Basilica. *Taken with magnesian light.* 8vo. 2994

Crypt of S. Peter (16)—The celebrated Statue of S. Peter, with decoration of Cosmati-work, formerly under the portico of the old Basilica. *Taken with magnesian light.* 4to. 2995

The Apostle is represented seated, holding the keys. The figure, which recalls the statues of the Consuls, is antique; the head is of the sixteenth century, and the hands are modern.

Crypt of S. Peter (221)—Bas-relief from the Ciborium of Pius II., A.D. 1460. Two angels holding the head of S. Andrew. *Taken with magnesian light.* 4to. 2996

Crypt of S. Peter (231)—The celebrated Sarcophagus of Junius Bassus, prefect of Rome, five times Consul, deceased A.D. 359. *Taken with magnesian light.* 4to. 2997

The subjects represented in the upper part are:—
1. The Sacrifice of Abraham.
2. The Capture of S. Peter.
3. Christ seated between Peter and Paul.
4. The Capture of Christ.
5. Pilate washing his hands.

In the lower part are:—
1. Job on his mat, insulted by his Wife and his Friends.
2. Temptation of Adam and Eve.
3. Entrance of Christ into Jerusalem.
4. Daniel in the lions' den.
5. Capture of S. Paul.

Construction—Brickwork of the Pantheon, B.C. 26.   8vo. 2998
Construction—Brickwork of the Palace of Caligula, A.D. 40.
   8vo. 2999
Construction—Brickwork of the Arches of Nero on the Cœlian, near S. Stefano Rotondo, A.D. 60. *The best period of construction.*   8vo. 3000
Construction of the upper part of the Prætorian Camp, Tiberius, A.D. 20.   8vo. 3001
Construction—Brickwork at the Prætorian Camp, Tiberius, A.D. 20.   8vo. 3002
Obelisk in the Garden of the Villa Cœlimontana (Mattei).   8vo. 3003
Excavations, 1873—Agger of Servius Tullius—View of part of the "Mons Justitiæ," destroyed near the Railway Station in 1873, with remains of houses built upon it, and into it.   4to. 3004
Excavations, 1873—Agger of Servius Tullius, shewing a portion of his wall between the Railway Station and S. Maria Maggiore.   4to. 3005
Castle of S. Angelo—Fresco Painting on the left side of an external Loggia—the Mausoleum of Hadrian, as it appeared in the sixteenth century.   4to. 3006
Castle of S. Angelo—Fresco Painting on the right side of an external Loggia—the Cupola or Dome of S. Peter's, as originally designed.   4to. 3007

Series of Paintings by the Pupils of Raphael.

Castle of S. Angelo—Fresco Painting by Siciolante, (da Sermoneta, A.D. 1504), representing Alexander the Great visiting the Temple of Jerusalem.   8vo. 3008
Castle of S. Angelo—Fresco Painting by Siciolante, A.D. 1504, representing the triumph of Alexander the Great.   8vo. 3009
Castle of S. Angelo—Fresco Painting by Siciolante, A.D. 1504, representing King Pyrrhus on the Elephant.   8vo. 3010
Castle of S. Angelo—Fresco Painting by Siciolante, A.D. 1504, representing a battle-scene.   8vo. 3011
Castle of S. Angelo—Fresco Painting by Siciolante, A.D. 1504, representing Alexander the Great with the Jewish high-priest.   8vo. 3012
Castle of S. Angelo—Fresco Painting by Pierino del Vago, A.D. 1540; St. Michael, &c.   4to. 3013
Castle of S. Angelo—Fresco Painting by Pierino del Vago, A.D. 1540; King Pyrrhus, &c.   4to. 3014

Castle of S. Angelo—Fresco Paintings and Stuccoes by
Giulio Romano, A.D. 1540; Mythological subjects. 4to. 3015

Castle of S. Angelo—Fresco Paintings and Stuccoes by
Giulio Romano, A.D. 1540; Mythological subjects. 4to. 3016

Castle of S. Angelo—Fresco Paintings and Stuccoes by
Giulio Romano, A.D. 1540; Mythological subjects. 4to. 3017

Castle of S. Angelo—Fresco Paintings and Stuccoes by
Giulio Romano, A.D. 1540; Mythological subjects. 4to. 3018

Castle of S. Angelo—Fresco Painting and Stuccoes by
Giulio Romano, A.D. 1540; Mythological subjects. 4to. 3019

Castle of S. Angelo—Fresco Painting and Stuccoes by
Giulio Romano, A.D. 1540; Mythological subjects. 4to. 3020

Castle of S. Angelo—Fresco Painting and Stuccoes by
Giulio Romano, A.D. 1540; Mythological subjects. 4to. 3021

Castle of S. Angelo—Fresco Painting and Stuccoes by
Giulio Romano, A.D. 1540; Mythological subjects. 4to. 3022

Castle of S. Angelo—Fresco Paintings by Pierino del Vago,
A.D. 1540; Mythological subjects. 4to. 3023

Castle of S. Angelo—Fresco Paintings by Pierino del Vago,
A.D. 1540; Mythological subjects. 4to. 3024

Castle of S. Angelo—Fresco Paintings by Pierino del Vago,
A.D. 1540; Mythological subjects. 4to. 3025

Church of S. Paul f. m.—View of the Interior, and the
Mosaic over the Arch of Triumph. 4to. 3026

Out of Rome—Mausoleum of the time of Hadrian, called
the "Torrone," two miles from Frascati, with part of
a Castle of the Savelli of the fifteenth century. 4to. 3027

Grotta-Ferrata—Tower and part of the fortified Monastery
of the fifteenth century. 4to. 3028

Aqueducts—Source of the Aqua Tepula, the arch made
B.C. 126, on the hill of Marino, under Grotta Ferrata. 4to. 3029

Albano—Distant view of the Castle of the Savelli. 4to. 3030

Albano—Remains of the Roman Amphitheatre. 4to. 3031

Albano—Original Viaduct of the Via Appia, near Ariccia, B.C. 312. 4to. 3032

Palazzuola (Alba Longa)—Scarped cliff, with a Tomb of a Roman Consul cut upon it. 4to. 3033

Alba Longa—Scarped cliff at the lower end of Alba Longa, (under the Monastery of Palazzuola, behind a wall). 4to. 3034

Alba Longa—Rocca di Papa.—Fortress shewing the scarped cliffs at the upper end of Alba Longa. 4to. 3035

Alba Longa—Rocca di Papa.—View of one side of it. Part of the town of Alba Longa. 4to. 3036

Civita Lavinia (Lanuvium)—Part of the wall of the Citadel of the time of the Empire, with a distant view of the scarped cliffs and earthworks of the older City. 4to. 3037

Civita Lavinia (Lanuvium)—View of a Castellum Aquæ of the time of Sylla. 4to. 3038

Tivoli (Tibur)—Temple of the Sybil and of Vesta. 4to. 3039

Tivoli (Tibur)—The Cascades from the opposite Hill. 4to. 3040

Tivoli (Tibur)—Portion of a large Castellum Aquæ of the time of Sylla, on the road to the Cascatelle. 4to. 3041

Villa or Farm of HORACE in the Sabine Hills—View of the country, shewing the village of Licenza, with small portion of Civitella. 4to. 3042

Villa or Farm of HORACE—Villages of Licenza and Civitella. 4to. 3043

Villa or Farm of HORACE, in the Sabine Hills, near Vico-Varo—View of the Hill called "Rocca Giovane." 4to. 3044

Tivoli (Tibur)—Village of Castel Madama on the hill near Tivoli, with a tomb in the foreground. 4to. 3045

Vico-Varo—View of the Church called the "Tempietto." 4to. 3046

Vico-Varo—A fine Sarcophagus of the first century, discovered in 1872. 4to. 3047

Vico-Varo—Portraits of the defuncts on the Sarcophagus of the first century, discovered in 1872. 4to. 3048

Vico-Varo—View from the River Anio. 4to. 3049

Villa or Farm of HORACE—View of a small Medieval Castle in a hill near Vico-Varo, called "Castellaccio." 4to. 3050

Aqueducts—Aqua Marcia Pia.—Stone Specus on arches, between Vico-Varo and Tivoli. 4to. 3051

Aqueducts—Claudia and Anio Novus, A.D. 50.—Reservoir of Nero over the Arch of Dolabella on the Cœlian. 4to. 3052

Temple of Fortuna Virilis, B.C. 90, and A.D. 10, from the north-west—The columns of the Portico walled up with a Medieval wall, to make the Church of S. Maria Ægyptiaca. 4to. 3053

Church of S. Thomas in formis on the Cœlian, as rebuilt in the twelfth century. 4to. 3054

Walls of Rome—Prætorian Camp, north-east corner, part of the original brickwork of the time of Tiberius, A.D. 20. 4to. 3055

Excavations, 1872—Villa Celimontana (Mattei)—Shewing a Brick Arch of the second century in the cliff under the house, apparently the entrance to a subterranean passage. 4to. 3056

Thermæ of Trajan—Fresco Painting found in excavations in 1872 near the Church of SS. Martin and Silvester. A dancing figure. 8vo. 3057

Thermæ of Trajan—Fresco Painting of a dancer found in excavations in 1872 near the Church of SS. Martin and Silvester. 8vo. 3058

Thermæ of Trajan—Fresco Painting found in excavations in 1872 near the Church of SS. Martin and Silvester. 8vo. 3059

It is of the time of Trajan, and represents the rape of Europa.

Church of S. Pudentiana—Doorway as restored in 1872. 4to. 3060

The columns and the shallow sculpture of the heads are ancient, representing the family of Pudens.

Church of S. Pudentiana—Sculpture, in the Gaetani Chapel, behind the altar. 4to. 3061

The offering of the Magi in fine alto-relievo, c. A.D. 1600.

Church of S. Pudentiana—Mosaic Picture of the sixteenth
century, in the Gaetani Chapel. 8vo. 3062
The sisters Pudentiana and Prassede collecting the blood of the Martyrs with sponges, c. A.D. 1600.

Church of S. Paul alle tre Fontane—View of the Exterior
of the Transept, A.D. 800, and East End, c. A.D. 1150. 4to. 3063

Mosaics in the Church of S. Maria Scala Cœli, at S. Paul
alle tre Fontane, sixteenth century, representing the
Ascension of the Virgin above, with four Saints below. 4to. 3064

Mosaic Pavement from Ostia, c. A.D. 250, representing the
four Seasons, now in the Church of S. Paul alle tre
Fontane. 8vo. 3065

Lucca—Portion of the Roman Amphitheatre. Cent. II. 4to. 3066

Lucca—Front of the Duomo, A.D. 1204, Pisan style, with
the small arcades and detached colonettes. 4to. 3067

Lucca—Bas-relief with Inscription, under the Portico of the
Duomo. Cent. XII. Representing the legend of S. Martin,
with allegorical figures of six of the months under arches
in panels. 4to. 3068

Lucca—Bas-relief with Inscription, over the principal Door
of the Duomo. Cent. XII. 4to. 3069
It represents S. Maria and the twelve Apostles, with their names under each, in sculpture of the thirteenth century. In the tympanum above is the ascension of Christ in an aureole, supported by two angels.

Lucca—Base of the Campanile, with part of the Apse of the
Church of S. Frediano, A.D. 1151. 4to. 3070
This portion shews three periods of construction, Centuries XI., XII., and XIII.

Lucca—Church of S. Frediano. View of the Apse and Campanile. Cent. XII., built of old materials. 4to. 3071

Lucca—Church of S. Frediano. View of the Façade with
Mosaics. Cent. XII.,—XIII. 4to. 3072

Lucca—Church of S. Christopher. Principal Door, with
fine mouldings and capitals. Cent. XII. 4to. 3073

Lucca—Church of S. Julia. Cent. XII. View of the Façade.
4to. 3074

Lucca—Church of S. John. Principal Door, with fine Sculpture. Cent. XII. 4to. 3075

Lucca—Church of S. Michael. View of the left Side, with double Arcade and Tower, A.D. 1188. 4to. 3076

Lucca—Church of S. Giusto. Cent. XII. Front view. 4to. 3077

Lucca—View of a part of the Palazzo Guinigi, with remains of a large brick Tower, A.D. 1380—1413, in the Via di S. Andrea. 4to. 3078

Lucca—Chapel of the Madonna della Rosa, A.D. 1280—1304 (?). Side view. 4to. 3079

Lucca—Church called the "Oratory," curious Bas-relief over the Door. 4to. 3080

This is a very curious and early piece of sculpture of about the middle of the twelfth century, apparently representing the legend of S. John Baptist. In the centre is the saint in the cauldron of boiling oil; on either side is a small temple, with a domical vault, and shafts having twisted fluting round them. It may probably be the work of the same sculptor as the celebrated font in S. Frediano, who has there inscribed his name and date, Robertus, 1151.

Pisa—General View of the Baptistery, A.D. 1153, and 1278—1350 (?), and Front of the Cathedral, thirteenth cent. 4to. 3081

Pisa—Construction of the left side of the Duomo, shewing the junction of two periods, A.D. 1067—1118. 4to. 3082

Pisa—Inscriptions on the right angle of the Duomo. 4to. 3083

Pisa—Inscription on a Tomb now in front of the Duomo. 4to. 3084

Pisa—Church of S. Paul. View of the Side and Transept. 4to. 3085

This view shews three periods of construction, and the cupola over the central space. This church served for a model of the cathedral, and is a few years earlier in each part. It has been raised higher, and lengthened in all directions.

Pisa—Church of S. Paul (Duomo Vecchio). View shewing the construction, and the junction of three periods, A.D. 1156, 1230 (?), and 1300 (?). 4to. 3086

Pisa—Medieval Tower of the Fortifications near the Church of S. Paul, part of the Wall of the City with fine bold machicolations. 8vo. 3087

Pisa—Leaning Tower, A.D. 1174—1350, and Cathedral. The Pisan style of the twelfth and thirteenth centuries. 4to. 3088

This view shews the southern transept, and east end of nave, with the junctions in the construction, when the building was carried to a much greater height, and lengthened one-half at the west end in the thirteenth century; also the cupola of the fourteenth over the central space. The leaning tower is on the right hand, and an apse at the end of the transept. There are three distinct periods visible in the construction.

Florence—Church of S. Maria Novella. View from the south. 4to. 3089

For the First Series, see Photographs 1476, 2712, 2713, 2714, 2715, 2716, 2717, 2718, 2719, 2720.

Second Series of (25) *Photographs from the Illuminations and Initial Letters of the Bible given to the Basilica of S. Paul, by* CHARLES THE BALD, A.D. 850, (*now in the monastery of S. Calixtus*), *Rome*.

Initial Letter F and the commencement of the Preface to the entire Bible, by St. Jerome, "FRATER AMBROSIUS."	3090
Title-page of the Book of Genesis, "INCIPIT LIBER BRESIT, ID EST GENESEOS."	3091
Commencement of the Book of Exodus, "HAEC SUNT NOMINA."	3092
Illumination at the commencement of the Book of Leviticus. Moses placing the Ark within the Tent or Tabernacle, guarded by Cherubim, below which is the seven-branched Candlestick, with Moses offering up a burnt sacrifice before the children of Israel.	3093
Commencement of the Book of Leviticus, "VOCAVIT AUTEM MOYSEN ET LOCUTUS EST."	3094
Commencement of the Book of Numbers, "LOCUTUS QUE DNS AD MOYSEN IN DESERTO SINAI IN TABERNACULO FOEDERIS."	3095
Illumination at commencement of the Book of Deuteronomy. Moses receiving the Tables of the Law from the hand of God on Mount Sinai, and describing the same to the children of Israel.	3096
Commencement of the Book of Deuteronomy, "HAEC SUNT VERBA QUAE LOCUTUS EST MOYSES AD OMNE ISRAHEL TRANS JORDANEN."	3097
Illuminated Page at the beginning of the Book of Joshua. Moses marshalling the Israelites to pass over Jordan, over which the Ark has already been borne; the twelve stones borne on men's shoulders, and the destruction of the walls of Jericho.	3098
Commencement of the Book of Joshua, "ET FACTŪ EST POST MORTE MOYSI SERVI DNI"—"Now after the death of Moses, the servant of the Lord, it came to pass."	3099

Illuminated Page at the commencement of the third (first) Book of Kings. Solomon anointed by Zadok and Nathan. The wisdom of Solomon, seated on his throne giving judgment between the two women.   3100

Commencement of the third (first) Book of Kings, "**E**T REX DAVID SENUERAT" — "Now king David was old and stricken in years."   3101

Illumination at the beginning of the second Book of Samuel (or second Book of Kings). David tearing his clothes on hearing of the death of Saul, and slaughter of the messenger, who accused himself of Saul's death.   3102

Commencement of the fourth (second) Book of Kings, "**P**RAEVARICATUS EST AUT MOAB IN ISRAHEL POST QUA MORTUUS EST ACAB CECIDITQ. OHOZIAS PER CANCELLOS CAENACULI QUOD HABEBAT"—"Then Moab rebelled against Israel after the death of Ahab, and Ahaziah fell down through a lattice in his upper chamber."   3103

Illumination at the commencement of the Apocryphal Book of Judith. The story of Judith and Holofernes, in three compartments. Judith attended by her maid leaving Bethulia; brought before Holofernes; and cutting off his head.   3104

Commencement of the Psalter, "**B**EATUS VIR QUI NON ABIIT IN CONSILIO IMPIORUM"—"Blessed is the man that walketh not in the counsel of the ungodly."   3105

Commencement of the Book of the Prophecies of Jeremiah, "**V**ERBA HIEREMIAE FILII HILLCHIAE DE SACERDOTIBUS" —"The words of Jeremiah, the son of Hilkiah, of the priests."   3106

Commencement of the Book of Daniel, "**Anno** TERTIO REGNI IOACHIM REGIS IUDAE"—"In the third year of the reign of Jehoiakim king of Judah."   3107

Illumination at the beginning of the Gospel of S. Matthew. The Evangelist writing, his symbolical angel in the upper angle of the drawing. On a large rainbow-like scroll is inscribed: "✠ MATTHEUS AGENS HOMINEM GENERALITER IMPLET"—"Matthew, for the most part, fills up the story of the Actions (of Christ) as a Man."   3108

Illumination at the beginning of the Gospel of S. Mark. The Evangelist seated writing, with his symbolical Lion in the clouds; on a similar scroll, dividing the design into two parts, is inscribed: "MARCUS UT ALTA FREMIT VOX PER DESERTA LEONIS"—"Mark raises his voice aloud, like a lion in the wilderness." (ch. i. ver. 3.)   3109

Illumination at the beginning of the Gospel of S. Luke, who, with his symbolical Bull, is represented writing on a long roll from a book on a stand before him. The scroll is inscribed: "JURA SACERDOTIS LUCAS TENET ORA JUVENCI"—"Luke holds the laws of the priests in the mouth of a bullock," in allusion to the priestly office of Christ set forth in his Gospel.   3110

Commencement of the Gospel of S. Luke, "Q̄m QUIDEM MULTI CONATI SUNT"—"Forasmuch as many have taken in hand (or have endeavoured)."   3111

Illumination at the commencement of the Gospel of S. John. The Evangelist seated, about to write in a book at the dictation of his symbolical eagle, also holding an open book in the clouds. The long rainbow-like scroll is inscribed: "MORE VOLANS AQUILE VERBO PETIT ASTRA IOHANNES"—"In the manner of a flying eagle, John seeks the stars for THE WORD," in allusion to the doctrinal character of his Gospel.   3112

Commencement of the Gospel of S. John, "IN PRINCIPIO ERAT VERBĀ"—"In the beginning was THE WORD."   3113

Illumination at the beginning of the Acts of the Apostles. Above is the Ascension of Christ, ASCENDIT XPS IN ALTUM—"Christ ascendeth on high." Below is the Gift of Tongues. The Twelve Apostles seated in a circle, within a walled and battlemented enclosure, each with a flame of fire on his head; the Virgin in the centre, with only a plain nimbus round her head.   3114

Porticus of the Thermæ of the Antonines and of Caracalla, begun by that Emperor and finished by his successor, Heliogabalus.—One of the bath-chambers excavated in 1873.   3115

Thermæ of Caracalla—Wall of the private house of Hadrian, on this site, before the Thermæ was built, at the northeast corner (now 20 feet below the surface), excavated in 1873.   3116

Thermæ of Caracalla—Remains of a Temple (?) or of a Tomb (?) on the side of the Via Appia, behind the Church of SS. Nereus and Achilleus, and torso of a Greek statue, found in the Vineyard of Sig. Pietro Brocard, between the Porticus and the present road, in 1873. 3117

Thermæ of Caracalla—Porticus in front of the Thermæ, with Bath-chambers under the lower arches, now in the vineyard of Sig. Brocard. 3118

Kircherian Museum—Vase of the fourth century, with the offerings of the Magi in shallow sculpture, and good foliage-like capitals. 3119 A and B

Kircherian Museum—Sarcophagus of the fourth century, representing the Last Supper of our Lord. 3120

Primitive Fortifications—Scarped Cliff of the ancient fortress of the Vatican Hill, on the northern side. 3121

Primitive Fortifications—Scarped Cliff of the Vatican fortress, northern side of the hill or rock. 3122

Palatine—Palace of Domitian, Fountain. 3123
The oval basin, and remains of the building in the centre; with the veneering of marble and the channel in which the water flowed, are seen in the foreground; and in the background the lofty angle of the Basilica Jovis.

Statue of Pasquino in the Piazza di Pasquino, at the back of the Palazzo Braschi. 3124

Palace of the Cæsars—View through the Arch of Titus. 3125

Via Appia—Third Mile General View, with the Tombs. 3126

Via Appia—Third Mile General View, with the Tombs. 3127

The Pantheon—View of the Portico, with the Obelisk and the Inscriptions. 3128

Vatican Museum (86)—Statue of a Female of elegant style, with the attributes of Higeia or the goddess of Health. 3129

Vatican Museum (120)—Statue of a Greek Woman, found in the Villa of Hadrian. The left hand is restored. 3130

Vatican Museum (224)—Statue of Nemesis. 3131

Vatican Museum (533)—Statue of Minerva, with the shield. 3132

Vatican Museum (681)—Statue of Diana, restored, with the symbols of Minerva. 3133

Vatican Museum (582)—Statue of Apollo, said to be an imitation of the celebrated original of Scopes. 3134

Mausoleum of Hadrian, now Castle of S. Angelo—The south side, with the Mediæval Battlements and the figure of the Angel. 3135

Colosseum—Inscription on a base at the north end. 3136

Colosseum—Inscription on a tablet at the south end. 3137

Colosseum—Arch at the north-west end, *restored* probably in the time of the Gordians, A.D. 220—238. 3138

Arch of Constantine—Panels of Sculpture on the east side; the two round panels are from the Arch of Trajan, A.D. 111; the long flat panel represents the Forum Romanum in the time of Constantine, A.D. 326. 3139

Church of Ara Cœli—Ambo, with Cosmati-work. 3140

Church of Ara Cœli—Ambo, with Cosmati-work. 3141

Church of Ara Cœli—Panels of Ribbon Mosaics from the Ambo. 3142

Church of Ara Cœli—Mosaic Pavement of Opus Alexandrinum. 3143

Church of Ara Cœli—Octagonal Panels of the Mosaic Pavement. 3144

Forum Romanum—Temple of Concord, Marble Veneering in the north-west corner, A.D. 11. 3145

Forum Romanum—Temple of Concord, south-west corner, with the entrance to a subterranean passage under the platform, B.C. 303 (?), 216 (?), or 144 (?). 3146

Forum Romanum—Pavement of the Clivus Capitolinus, B.C. 174, with remains of the Gate of Saturn. 3147

Forum Romanum—West side of the Podium of the Temple of Saturn, A.D. 12, with the Doorway of the Steps of the Ærarium, B.C. 494. 3148

Forum Romanum—Via Sacra. Podium of the Temple of Vesta, B.C. 794, excavated in 1874. 3149

Temple of Fortuna Virilis— Architectural Details. The Cell
of Tufa, B.C. 90; the Portico of Marble, A.D. 16.   3150

Forum of Augustus—Cornice or Corbel-table of the east
wall, A.D. 19.   3151

Pyramidal Tomb of Cajus Cestius, A.D. 10, from the English
burial-ground.   3152

Forum of Augustus—Exterior of the Wall, B.C. 19.   3153

Forum of Augustus, B.C. 3—Interior of the wall at the south-
east corner in 1874, (Plin., Hist. Nat. xxxv. 10).
Taken with magnesian light.   3154

Here this part of the Forum has been left unfinished, and the interior
of the old round tower of the second wall of Rome, B.C. 741, is seen in the
background. This is now in a stone-mason's workshop; the six-foot rule
is seen against the Wall of the Kings.

Palatine—Shallow Hypocaust, Palace of Tiberius (Domus
Tiberiana; Regionary Catalogue; Dio, i. 57; Taciti
Hist., i. 27.)   3155

This is on the upper level, and on the edge of the western cliff, over the
Circus Maximus. The small hollow space under the bricks or tiles of the
pavement, the bricks to support them, and the flue up which the hot air
ascended, are shewn.

Forum Romanum—Podium or basement of the Temple of
Concord in 1874. Built B.C. 303, rebuilt B.C. 216, and
again A.D. 11. Construction of three periods is visible.   3156

West side, taken from the Temple of Saturn, with the pavement of the
area of Vulcan, between them and the wall of the Ærarium (or public
Treasury of the kings of Rome), with two of the windows in it, and the
base of an arch of the Tabularium or Public Record Office of the kings of
Rome—both in the Capitolium.

Forum Romanum—Podium of the Temple of Castor and
Pollux, or the Dioscuri, in 1874.   3157

This basement is of the time of the Kings (rebuilt B.C. 479; Livii Hist.,
ii. 20); the celebrated three columns, of which the lower part is shewn,
are of the time of the Early Empire (A.D. 4; Dio, xlvii. 18).

Forum Romanum—Remains of the Podium of the Temple
of Vesta and Fountain of Juturna in 1874.   3158

The basement of this temple is of the time of the Kings, built when the
two hills were united in one City (Dionys., ii. 50). The remains of the
fountain are of the time of Augustus. This is at the south end of the Forum
Romanum, and a step is seen between this and the temple, which is in the
Vis sacra, and not in the Forum.

Forum Romanum—Rostrum of Julius Cæsar in 1874. 3159

With the pavement in front of it, and his temple behind it. This is at the south-east corner, and nearly under the Temple of Antoninus and Faustina.

Forum Romanum—Marble Walls of the Comitium in 1874. 3160

On the wall to the left are seen the three animals prepared for sacrifice (the boar, the ram, and the bull,) called the *suovetaurilia*. On the right-hand wall, part of the procession going up to the Emperor Hadrian, with the tablets of their debts to be cancelled and burnt, some of them thrown in a heap on the ground. The other part of the procession is at the back of the other wall. The basement of these walls is of stone, of the time of the Republic, with a modern base of marble introduced upon it. This sculpture was found in fragments, and cleverly put together by Signor Rosa.

Palatine—Four Arches of the Porticus of Nero, on the Velia. 3161

These are the upper arches of his Porticus, which was an arcade of two storeys; this was one use of the word Porticus in Rome, as in the Thermæ of Caracalla. The Porticus of Nero was a mile long, and can be traced by remains of it from this point, which is against the cliff of the Velia (always reckoned as part of the Palatine), to the Exquiliæ. In front of the picture is seen the pavement of the Summa Via Sacra, and the north-west corner of the platform on which the Porticus of Livia was placed. On the right is a portion of the Monastery of S. Francesca Romana, and in the background the Colosseum.

Palatine—Four Arches of the Porticus of Nero. 3162

In this view they are taken close, to shew the beautiful brickwork of the time of Nero, the finest brickwork in the world. Ten bricks to the foot can here be counted.

Forum Romanum—Basilica Julia. 3163

In this part some of the walls built of travertine, of the time of Julius Cæsar, are seen, shewing also that the direction of this great hall was then from east to west, and some of the brick arches of the fourth century, or the modern imitation of them, in which the direction is from north to south.

Forum Romanum—Cloaca Maxima, (B.C. 615; Livii Hist., i. 38). 3164

This part is under the south end of the Basilica Julia, and on the site of the Lake of Curtius, to drain which this great drain was made. The brick arch in the foreground is of the time of the Early Empire, that behind it is one arch of the original vault, built of the large blocks of tufa of the time of the Kings, and it is evidently part of the original construction. The same early construction occurs in the subterranean passage connected with the Prison of the Kings, (B.C. 632; Livii Hist., i. 33).

Palatine—Palace of Tiberius (Domus Tiberiana), Mosaic pavement. 3165

This is on the lower level, on the platform on which that palace was built; although the upper part is above the level of the top of the hill. A considerable part of this house was carried away in a land-slip about 1830. It was behind and above the upper gallery of the Circus Maximus, with a road also in front of it.

Palatine—Palaces of the Cæsars, Passage of Caligula. 3166

This passage is corbelled out from an earlier wall, and *may have* led over the bridge of Caligula, on the western side of his palace below. It is richly ornamented with stucco patterns, and has a portion of the *transenna*, or pierced marble parapet, remaining in its place. A wall of the time of Trajan is built up against the front of it, as shewn in the right hand of the picture.

Forum Romanum — Basement of a Temple and gigantic Column in 1874. 3167

This is under the great bank of earth on which the modern road is made, and close to the Arch of Septimius Severus; the podium or basement is built of stone of the time of the Kings, probably taken from the wall of the old fortress of the hill of Saturn, and used for the foundations of a temple.

Forum Romanum—Sculptures from the Arch of Constantine. 3168

The two circular panels are taken from the Arch of Trajan, at the south end of his Forum, destroyed in the time of Constantine; the long flat panel is of the time of Constantine, and represents the Forum Romanum of that time; in the centre is the rostrum, with the idols or statues upon it, and the *transenna* in front in the centre. Behind these are the tall columns, with images of the gods on the top of them. The arcade or porticus, at the back, appears to be the Tabularium.

Forum Romanum—Podium or Base of an equestrian statue. 3169

This is near the centre of the Forum; the podium is of brick of the time of Constantine, and the very thick marble casing of it is seen in the foreground to the right—it was probably the basement of the horse of Constantine. On each side is one of the square brick structures of the third century. These are commonly called bases for the tall columns, but they are hollow, with a door in each, and were more probably wine-shops.

Forum Romanum—General View, from the Palatine. 3170

On the right, in the foreground, is the Palace of Caligula, with part of his bridge. Beyond that, in the centre of the picture, is the Arch of Septimius Severus; to the left the Temple of Vespasian, with the seven columns, and behind that the Capitolium.

Veii—The Isola Farnesi. 3171

The picturesque modern village, and the Farnesi Villa built upon the old walls.

Veii—The Ponte Sodo. 3172

A natural bridge or tunnel through the rock, for the river to pass.

Veii—Ponte dell' Isola. 3173

The bridge is built of *late* Roman brickwork, upon older foundations, on stone of the character called Etruscan.

Veii—Portion of the Wall of the City. 3174

This fragment of very early masonry is situated on an angle of the rock over the Ponte Sodo. The character is earlier than that of the earliest wall in Rome.

Veii—As seen from the ravine, to shew the remains of the ancient scarped cliffs, and the rocky bed of the river, which is often nearly dry. This very picturesque spot is called the washing-place. 3175

Veii—The Isola Farnesi, as seen from the south, with the church, and the road up to it. 3176

Veii—The Farnesi Villa on the rock, as seen from the east. 3177

Veii—The early and rude Columbaria, cut in the rock. 3178

Veii—The Roman Bridge, built of stone, and resting on earlier foundations. 3179

Palatine—Fresco Painting of the first century, with framework of stucco ornament, in the Palace of Caligula (?). 3180

Palatine—Fresco Painting of the first century, with stucco ornament, in the Palace of Caligula (?). 3181
The painting is much faded, but the design is visible.

Palatine—Aqueduct at the north end. 3182
On the upper platform, behind the round Church of S. Theodore, shewing the angle made by the Aqueduct, as was usual at each half-mile. The specus that turns to the left goes in the direction of the bridge of Caligula.

Palatine—Great oval Piscina and reservoir of water for the Palaces of the Cæsars, at the north end, near the House of Augustus; it was supplied with water from the Aqueduct of Nero. 3183

Palatine—Basilica Jovis: the Apse with the Cancellus, and columns of the south aisle. 3184

Excavations, 1874—Part of the great Agger and Wall of Servius Tullius, with ruins of houses of the first century built up against it and into it. 3185

Excavations, 1874—Part of the great Agger and Wall of Servius Tullius, near the Exquiliæ, with a House of the first century built up against it. 3186

Excavations, 1874—Part of the great Agger and Wall of Servius Tullius, near the railway station, which is seen in the background, with some blocks of houses of the new city. 3187

Excavations, 1874—Part of the great Agger and Wall of Servius Tullius, a tower on the inner side of it (apparently for a catapult), and remains of houses of the first century, near the Church of S. Antonio; the tower in the distance belongs to the Porta di S. Lorenzo. 3188

Tomb on the Via Appia, one mile from Rome, in the Vigna
   Colonna, with the Columbaria of the *liberti*, or freedmen
   of Livia Augusta.   3189

Tomb of the *liberti* or freedmen of Livia Augusta, in the
   Vigna Colonna, shewing the Construction of the period,
   similar to that of the Pantheon.   3190
   This tomb was described by Dr. Gori in the eighteenth century, and the
inscriptions found on it are given in his work.

Excavations, 1874—Palatine and Summa Via Sacra.   *3191 A
   The Platform on the summit, with substructure at the south end, of
rubble-work of the time of the Republic.
   Elevation, looking north, with *probable Restoration* of the Porticus
Liviæ and Colossus of Nero.

A. South-east corner of Palatine.
B. Lavacrum of Heliogabalus.
C C. Steps to Platform at each end.
D D D. Substructure of the Platform, to raise the south end to the level of the north.
E. Narrow street on east side.
F. Porticus of Nero.
G. The Velia, always reckoned as part of the Palatine.
The back of the Colossus is seen through the columns.

Excavations, 1874—Palatine and Summa Via Sacra.   *3191 B
   The Platform, looking east, with steps up to it at the north end, and
a substructure at the south end.
   Probable restoration of the Porticus Liviæ, longitudinal section, and
side of the Colossus of Nero.

A. Basilica of Constantine, south-west corner.
B. Part of the Velia, the earth supported by remains of the Porticus of Nero.
C. Porticus of Nero. Four arches of the upper story seen through the columns.
D. The Colossus of Nero, on its podium or basement, as shewn on the Marble Plan.
E. The Substructure, with the Aqueduct to supply the four fountains at the corners.
F. Pavement in front of the Colosseum.
G. The Velia.

Palatine—BASILICA JOVIS, and Section of Nave and Aisles,
   looking towards the Apse.   3192 A

A. Vault.
B. Clere-story.
C. Gallery.
D E. Aisle.
F. Steps to gallery.
G. Arch through the buttresses.
H H. Buttresses with pilasters.
I. Substructure in the foss.

Palatine—Central part over the great southern Foss of Roma
   Quadrata—BASILICA JOVIS, *probable restoration*.   *3192 B
   Perspective View of the Interior, looking towards the Apse.
      The existing remains are distinguished by the darker tint.

---

* These reductions from Drawings and Plans are made for special purposes, and are not to be considered a part of the Series of Photographs. They are included in the Catalogue for convenience, because some persons may wish to have them separately, and they can only be found by the numbers on the negatives.

Palatine—Central part, on the Platform over the great Foss of Roma Quadrata. Section and Plan of the BASILICA JOVIS, *with probable restorations.* *3193A

1. Section.

A. Vault.
B. Clere-story.
C. Gallery.
D. Aisle.
E. Column of aisle.
F. Steps to gallery.
G. Chamber between buttresses.
H H. Buttress with columns attached.
I. Wall of substructure in the foss.

2. Plan.

A. Buttresses.
B. Chambers between buttresses on north side.
C. North aisle.
D. End wall behind the Tribune or Apse.
E. South aisle.
F F F. Altars between buttresses on south side.
G. Seat of Emperor on the wall of the apse, above the wooden seats for his officers.
H. Altar for taking oaths.
I. Cancellus or *transenna*.
J. A low screen of pierced marble.
K. Old pavement.
L. Doorway.
M M. Portico.

Basilica Jovis—1. Section of Interior. *3193 B

A. Roof and Vault.
B. Clere-story.
C. Gallery.
D. Aisle.
E. Portico.
F. Substructure.

2. Elevation of north side.

A. Roof and Vault.
B. Clere-story.
C. Columns against buttresses.
D. Portico.
E. Substructure on walls across the foss.

Palatine—Central part, over the Foss of Roma Quadrata; Triclinium or Dining-room of the Palace of Domitian, with a small Temple of the same period. *3194

1. Section from north to south.

A. South-west corner of Roma Quadrata, built on the rock, at the corner of the great foss.
B. Subterranean passages cut in the rock under this old Citadel.
C. Part of the Villa Farnesi, of the seventeenth century, built upon a portion of the great palace of Domitian, in the foss.
D. Substructure—a building of the time of the later Kings or early Republic, constructed in the great foss, and built over in the time of Domitian.
E. Southern bank of the great foss, a vertical cliff.

Palatine—2. Section from west to east of the north-west corner of Roma Quadrata.

F. The rock, with platform cut upon it, at the foot of the wall.
G. The passage, with the wall over it.
H. The rock, with platform and wall upon it.
I. Remains of wall and buttress.
K. Remains of the Tower.

Palatine — 3. A. Plan, and B. Section of the same, Triclinium, &c., with transverse walls to carry the vaults under the level platform above.

1. Forum Romanum—South-west corner, Temple of Castor and Pollux, and Palace of Caligula, *with probable restorations*. *3195

A. Temple, with the celebrated three columns of the time of Augustus, A.D. 4, and the earlier podium or basement, B.C. 721.
B. Palace of Caligula.
C. Pier of Bridge of Caligula, with the springing of arches at two levels.
D. Part of the bridge under a shed, in the background Palaces.

2. Forum Romanum — Palatine, north-east corner, with modern Church of S. M. Liberatrice, Temple of Castor and Pollux, and Bridge of Caligula, looking west.

A. Palaces of the Cæsars, Hadrian and Trajan, and Caligula (?).
B. Podium of the Temple of Vesta.
C. Church of S. M. Liberatrice, on the site of the Regia, and the house of the Vestal Virgins.
D. Fountain of Juturna in the foreground.
E. Temple of Castor and Pollux.
F. Bridge of Caligula.

3. Forum Romanum and Palatine, north-east corner, Church and Temple, looking south.

    A. Palaces.   B. Church.   C. Temple—the three columns.

Excavations, 1874—The Colosseum. *3196

A. Section, and B. Plan of one Division, with the channels for water recently found (distinguished by a darker tint).

Excavations, 1874—A Slab of rude shallow Sculpture, chiefly incised lines only, representing the Mithraic worship, with the usual accompaniments. 3197

Radiated sun and moon, two busts.
Mithras (*pileata*) slaying the bull; dog, serpent, scorpion, torch-bearers, palm-tree, and rock.—(Inscription.)

C. P.
PRIMUS PATER FECIT

Pater was one of the seven degrees.
The pileated Mithras blessing, or lifting up, a nude man.
The pileated Mithras and a clothed figure grasp hands over an altar.

Excavations, 1874—A Slab of shallow Sculpture of the Mithraic worship. 3198

Similar to, but not the same as the last; the style and sculpture is not quite the same, and the accessories are different.

It is Mithraic, with the usual accompaniments.
Mithras (*pileato*) slaying the bull, serpent, dog, scorpion; the two torch-bearers, palm-tree, sun arising out of the rock, moon on the other side.
(Inscription)—Deo sancto Mitra (MKA), grat. (gratuiti), et de sua pecunia (H. D. S. P.), placidus Marcellinus Leo, antistites. . . .

The omission of the "et" between the two proper names, shews a good period, early in the Empire.

For gratuiti, see 1307, Zoll.; for Leo (one of the seven Mithraic degrees), see S. Jerome, epist. ciii. ad Lactam; Dr. Henzen's paper in the *Bullettino dell' Instituto* for 1868, pp. 97, 98.

See Orelli, 1955, 2552, 6042 b, "pater Leonum."

For antistes, as appropriated to Mithraicism, see De Rossi *Bullettino de Archeologia Christian*, pp. 156, 157, &c., "pater et antistes."

Basis Capitolina—One side of this celebrated Base of a Statue of Hadrian, with the Regionary Catalogue of Regiones XII. and XIII.   3199

The Prometheus Sarcophagus, from the Capitoline Museum. (No. 88.)   3200

    The man made by Prometheus endowed with life and faculties by the gods. It represents the complete story of the Soul, according to Neo-Platonic theories—the creation of the mortal tenement by Prometheus; the infusion of life in the form of a butterfly, by Minerva; death at the inevitable hour decreed by the Parcæ; the emancipated spirit first as a butterfly, then embodied in the figure of Psyche, and on its journey to the invisible world under the guidance of Mercury.

    The effigy placed upon this Sarcophagus in the Museum is believed to have no connection with it.

Excavations, 1874—The Colosseum, Subterranean passage at the south end.   3201

    About twenty feet below the present level of the area, with square-headed doorways or arches across it. This was one of the original entrances from the old foss-way, now filled up to the level of the ground. Perhaps this passage was for the wild beasts.

Excavations, 1874—Colosseum, several small chambers, and passage below the level of the area.   3202

    There is construction of different periods; that near the surface is of the fifth century, when the level was raised considerably, as recorded on an inscription found here.

Excavations, 1874—Colosseum under the area, shewing some passages and walls of different periods.   3203

    Part of these are evidently rebuilt of old materials when the level was raised. Some of the walls are of tufa, with vertical grooves, originally used for the lifts, the greater part are of brick. Some of the older portion belonged to the Vetera Naumachia, on the same site, before the great arcades of the Colosseum were built round it. Naval fights (that is, river fights) in the old Naumachia, at the time of the dedication, are mentioned by Dion Cassius.

Excavations, 1874—In the Colosseum, with a fragment of an Inscription.   3204

    IN . THEATR . LECEPLU . . .
    . ICET   P .   X I I

    This inscription is important as shewing that the Flavian amphitheatre was also called *a Theatre* indifferently. The classical authors frequently use the word Theatre for it.

Excavations, 1874—Colosseum under the area, shewing some walls of different periods.   3205

    One wall has vertical grooves in it for lifts for the cages of the wild beasts.

Sculpture—Villa Ludovisi (41)—The fine Colossal Head known as the Ludovisi Juno.   3206

Sculpture—Villa Ludovisi (28)—The group of Paetus stabbing himself, after his wife Arria had given him the example.   3207

    This group is considered by Winckelmann to represent Canace receiving the sword sent by her father, Æolus.

Sculpture—Villa Ludovisi (7)—The celebrated group considered by Winckelmann to represent Orestes discovered by Electra; bearing the name of a Greek sculptor, Menelaus, pupil of Stephanus. 3208

Sculpture—Villa Ludovisi (43)—Bernini's celebrated group of Pluto carrying off Proserpine; one of his finest works. 3209

Sculpture—Villa Ludovisi (1)—The fine group of the sitting Mars, reposing with a Cupid at his feet. 3210
It was found within the precincts of the Portico of Octavia, and restored by Bernini; it is supposed to have formed part of a group of Mars and Venus.

Sculpture—Excavations, 1874—General View of the objects of Sculpture, &c., found in building the new quarters for the City of Rome, preserved in the Warehouse of the Municipality. 3211

Sculpture—Excavations, 1874—Another View of remains of Sculpture, &c., found, and preserved in the Warehouse of the Municipality. 3212

Sculpture—Excavations, 1874—Bust of Plotius, or Plautius, found on the Esquiline. 3213

Sculpture—Excavations, 1874—Fragments of a Statue found on the Esquiline. 3214

Sculpture—Excavations, 1874—Bust of the time of the Flavian Emperors, of an unknown person, found on the Esquiline. 3215

Sculpture—Excavations, 1874—Bust of an unknown person, of the fourth century, found on the Esquiline. 3216

Sculpture—Excavations, 1874—Bust of Manlia Scantilla, found on the Esquiline. 3217

Sculpture—Excavations, 1874—Bust of Didia Clara, found in the Villa Palombara, on the Esquiline. 3218

Inscriptions—One side of the Basis Capitolina, giving the Catalogue of Regiones of Rome I., X., XIV. 3219
Now on the staircase of the Palazzo de Conservatori, on the Capitol, (for the other side, with Regiones XII. and XIII., see No. 3199).

Excavations, 1874—View of the remains of the Basilica and Catacomb of S. Petronilla—The Entrance and part of the Nave. 3220

Excavations, 1874—View of the remains of the Basilica and Catacomb of S. Petronilla—The Apse. 3221

Inscription of Pope Damasus on the left of the principal door of the Church of S. Sebastian. Twelve verses inscribed by that Pope to the martyr Eutychius. 3222

Inscription in the Church of S. Sebastian, stating that the bodies of S. Calixtus and 174,000 holy Martyrs are interred in that cemetery.   3223

Fresco Painting of the eleventh century, in a Chapel on the side of the staircase of the Crypt of S. Sebastian's Church.   3224

<small>With an inscription over an altar stating that the bodies of S. Peter and S. Paul had been deposited there.</small>

Fresco Painting of the eleventh century, in a Chapel on the staircase of the Crypt of S. Sebastian's Church.   3225

<small>The conventional heads of S. Peter and S. Paul.</small>

Sculpture in the Church of S. Francesca Romana—Bas-relief in the right-hand transept, representing the return of Pope Gregory XI. and his Court from Avignon in 1377, from the designs of Pietro Olivieri.   3226

Apse of a Basilica on the Summa Sacra Via, now in the garden of S. Francesca Romana, miscalled the Temple of Venus and Rome (?).   3227

<small>Taken from the interior to shew the exact similarity to that of the Basilica or Market-hall of Constantine adjoining to it.</small>

Excavations, 1874—Substructure of the Platform of the Porticus Liviæ (miscalled the Temple of Venus and Rome).   3228

Excavations, 1874—Forum Romanum—View of the Basilica Julia, with the modern bases, &c. from the Palatine.   3229

Temple of Vesta (?) and Fountain in the Piazza della "Bocca della Verita."   3230

Theatre of Marcellus—View, shewing the curve.   3231

Theatre of Marcellus—Details, shewing the actual state of the building.   3232

Excavations, 1874—View of objects—of Glass and Metal-work—found in building the new City, (now in the Warehouse of the Municipality).   3233

Excavations, 1874—View of objects found in building the new City—Busts, &c., (now in the Warehouse of the Municipality).   3234

Excavations, 1874—View of objects found in building the new City—Busts and Statues.   3235

Excavations, 1874—View of objects found in building the new City—Busts and Statues.   3236

Veii—View of the Arco del Pino, an Arch over a road cut in the Tufa rock.   3237

Veii—View shewing a Gate in the gorge cut in the Tufa rock.   3238

Tomb of the celebrated young English poet Keats, in the English burial-ground as it was before the restoration in 1875. The wall of Aurelian is seen in the background. 3239

House of Domitii in the Villa Esmeade—Plan and section of the subterranean Chambers. 3240AB*

Villa Esmeade—General Plan of one of the Camps of the Goths. 3241*

Aqueducts—Specus or reservoir of the Anio Vetus, in the Vigna Sbarretti near the Porta Furba, two miles from Rome. 3242*

Aqueducts—Two *cippi* found at the foot of the Mons Justitiæ near the Railway Station, with inscriptions on them, stating that *the three* Aqueducts passed between them (the MARCIA, TEPULA, JULIA). 3243

Primitive Fortifications—Agger of Servius Tullius in 1871, near the Railway Station, with houses of the first century built into the side of the bank, *now all destroyed*. 3244

Primitive Fortifications—Agger of Servius Tullius in 1871. The Mons Justitiæ with the figure of ROMA on the top, and houses built into the bank at the foot, *now all destroyed*. 3245

Inscriptions on the Jambs of the Porta Salaria, destroyed in 1872. 3246AB

Tombs—Tomb of Lady Emma Dorothea de Grey, April 6th, 1873, in the English burial-ground, near the Pyramid of Caius Cestius, with a Cross in imitation of the old Cosmati Work. 3247

Church of S. Maria Antiqua on the Palatine—Interior of the Apse and Altar, A.D. 847—855. 3248

This Church was made in the ruins of the Lavacrum of Heliogabalus, by Leo IV., A.D. 847, and enlarged by Benedict III., A.D. 855 (Anastas. 529 and 568).

Church of S. Maria Antiqua, exterior of Apse of the ninth century. 3249

The Plan of the original Church is of the Greek Cross, with a Portico, and a Sacred Well under it: to this a long nave was added. The construction of the wall of the ninth century is clearly seen in this photograph. Part of a brick wall of A.D. 224 is also seen on the left. The architect used the old walls when they suited his plan.

Architectural Details—Corinthian capital from the Temple of Romulus, the son of Maxentius, of A.D. 310.   3250

Architectural Details—Cornice and Entablature of the Temple of Romulus, the son of Maxentius, A.D. 310.   3251

With the end of the doorway under it, now the door of the Church of SS. Cosmas and Damian, brought up from the original level, twenty feet underground, the original floor of the Temple having been made into the crypt of the Church in the sixteenth century.

Arch of Titus—View through it.   3252

Shewing the caissons of the Vault and the sculpture of the Seven-branch Candlestick on the right, the Triumph on the left, and the Colosseum and Arch of Constantine in the distance.

Tarpeian Rock—Remains of it in 1875 behind the houses.   3253

Basilica of S. Petronilla—Remains of the Nave, and of the Apse and Columns in 1875.   3254

Basilica of S. Petronilla—The Arch of the Apse has been rebuilt in 1875. The bases of the Columns and the Sarcophagi of the fourth and fifth centuries, let into the floor, are still seen.   3255

Church of S. Sebastian f. m.—The Front, A.D. 1612.   3256

Church of S. Paul f. m.—The Front, with the Portico and the modern Belfry Tower.   3257

Monastery of S. Paul f. m.—Exterior, A.D. 1250 and 1575, with modern alterations.   3258

Catacomb of Prætextatus—Circular Chapel at the entrance, c. A.D. 350, called a Basilica—Exterior.   3259

This is a circular building of the fourth century, with a series of Apses round it.

Catacomb of Prætextatus—Square Chapel at the entrance, called a Basilica.   3260

This Chapel is built on the plan of a Greek Cross, and belongs to the fourth century.

Catacomb of Prætextatus—Basilica at entrance, interior of the circular Chapel with Apses.   3261

The exterior of this is No. 3259.

Catacomb of Prætextatus—Basilica at entrance, interior of the Cruciform Chapel.   3262

The exterior of this is No. 3260.

Colosseum—Ancient wooden frame-work on the Floor
in 1875. 3263

This is at the lowest level, twenty-one feet below the boarded floor covered with sand, called the Arena, which rested on the top of the cross-walls of the substructures.

Colosseum—Substructure of the Corridors of the Flavian
Emperors. 3264

In this are seen the Piers of Travertine at short intervals, to carry the Superstructure and the filling up with large blocks of Tufa, evidently used again, and probably taken from the second wall of Rome, under the south end of the Palatine, close at hand, not then wanted.

Colosseum—View of the Central Passage, from above, in
1875. 3265

It is taken from the Gallery on the south-east end, looking northwards. The Pavement is seen, and the small Chambers for lifts on each side of the passage for men to go up to the Arena.

Colosseum—View in the Gallery on the first-floor, with
remains of a Reservoir for Water supplied by the Aqueducts. 3266

The peculiar cement, called *Opus signinum*, or *Coccio-pisto*, is seen against the wall, and an open channel for water on the right hand. Also a Travertine Pier cut through the brick wall, and the stone wall of the Corridors of the Flavian Emperors, which have been built up against it.

Colosseum—View from the Upper Gallery. 3267

This looks down upon the remains of the lower Gallery for seats, and the Corridors where the vaults are broken across. The back of the upper wall of the third century, as rebuilt after the fire of A.D. 217, under Macrinus, completed A.D. 240, under Gordianus III.

Colosseum—View in one of the Passages of the Substructure. 3268

In this view are seen brick arches to carry one of the canals of water for the Naumachia, called *lacus* by Dio (l. LXII. c. 15). A *lacus* is a technical term used in his treatise on the Aqueducts by Frontinus, for a loch. On the right of this picture is seen the sloping wall forming a sort of a gable, apparently to support some great machine.

Colosseum—Another View in the Passage. 3269

Under the canal for water, shewing the walls supported by buttresses on both sides to receive the weight of the water.

Colosseum—View of one of the Vomitoria for ready exit, in
an upper Corridor of the Flavian Emperors. 3270

Colosseum—Details. Arch of the time of Nero, of his
usual long thin bricks, supporting an older Arch of Tufa,
damaged by an earthquake (?). 3271

Colosseum—Details. Side View from the Upper Gallery. 3272

    Shewing the state of the Excavations in April, 1875, taken from the north side looking towards the Cœlian. The numerous fragments of Columns and Capitals lying about, have rolled down from the upper Gallery in an earthquake.

Colosseum — Graffito of a Hunt of Wild Beasts on the Arena. 3273

Colosseum—Graffito of one of the Athletes on the Arena. 3274

Colosseum—Graffito of two of the Athletes in the Arena. 3275

Colosseum—Details. Capital of the Composite Order from the Upper Gallery, A.D. 240. 3276

    These great rude Capitals (unfinished) were intended to have been seen from below, and from a great distance.

Colosseum—Details. Wall built like a gable-end for great strength, to support some Machine for lifting up the Vessels from below (?). 3277

Colosseum — Details. Capital of the Roman Composite Order, highly finished. 3278

    This probably belongs to a short Column on the Podium, time of Alexander Severus (A.D. 230), at one of the entrances.

Colosseum—Details. Pier of Travertine inserted in Brick Wall. 3279

    To support the upper Gallery, A.D. 230, the bricks form an arch of construction, and are evidently cut through.

Colosseum—Details. Bases in the Upper Gallery, A.D. 230 3280

    With view of inside of upper wall, shewing the hasty construction in the time of Gordianus III., A.D. 240.

Colosseum—Details. Part of the Area in 1875. 3281

    On the level of the Arena at the foot of the Podium, with Columns and Capitals lying about, having fallen down in an earthquake.

Colosseum—Details—Part of the ancient Tufa wall with a square-headed opening partially filled with brick-work of the fifth century. 3282

Colosseum—Details—View in the Passage. 3283

    Between the two ancient Tufa walls, with grooves for lifts, and shewing also two of the sockets for pivots to work in.

Colosseum—Details—Arch in the third Tufa wall supported by a brick arch of the Flavian Emperors. 3284

Colosseum—Details—Small square chamber.   3285
    With arches of construction in brick walls of the time of Nero, enclosed in stone walls of the Flavian Emperors, with a socket in the floor and fragments of sculpture.

Colosseum—Details—Doorway in the chamber of Nero, shewing the wall, half brick and half stone.   3286

Colosseum—Details—Chamber of the work of the Flavian Emperors, under the lower gallery, with six sockets in the floor.   3287

Forum of Trajan—Second row of shops at the east end.   3288
    On a ledge of the rock, now in the garden of a Nobleman. The lowest row of shops is on the level of the Forum.

Forum of Trajan—Third row of shops at the east end, on the top of the Arch, now at the foot of the Torre delle Milizie.   3289

House of Mæcenas on the Esquiline—The Auditorium (?) or Green-house (?)   3290
    The apparent windows have always been sham windows, painted to represent a garden.

Garden of Sallust—Exterior of Nymphæum, and part of a house of the first century.   3291

Garden of Sallust—Interior of the Nymphæum, called by some the Temple of the Vestal Virgins.   3292

Garden of Sallust—Part of the Porticus *Milliarius*, of the Emperor Aurelian, built against the ancient horn-work.   3293

Garden of Sallust—Construction of ancient Horn-work, time of the Kings, in a peculiar kind of dark-coloured Tufa.   3294

Garden of Sallust—Sculpture—Marble Mask found in that Garden in 1874.   3295

Mosaic—Picture in the Apse or Tribune of the Church of S. Paul, f. m., A.D. 1216—1227.   3296
    It represents Christ seated on a throne with the cruciform nimbus, and with the book open in His left hand; at His feet is the Donor, Pope Honorius III., extremely small, not larger than the foot of Christ. On either side are two of the Apostles, each holding a scroll, with an inscription upon it. Under the feet is another row of small figures of Angels and Saints, also carrying scrolls with inscriptions. This Mosaic was considerably damaged in the great fire in 1823, but has been carefully restored.

Church of SS. Vincenzo ed Anastasio, built in 626 by Honorius I., and restored in 796 by Leo III., rebuilt in 1600 (?)   3297

Illuminations from a MS., in the Library of S. Paul, *c.* A.D. 800.   3298

Balaam and his ass stopped in the way by an angel. The story of the conspiracy and destruction of Korah, Dathan and Abiram. The plague stayed.

Illuminations from a MS. in the Library of S. Paul, *c.* A.D. 800.   3299

Moses blessing the assembled people of Israel, and the death of Moses in Mount Abarim.

Illuminations from a MS. in the Library of S. Paul, *c.* A.D. 800.   3300

The entry of Antiochus and the Maccabees into Jerusalem, the expoliation of the Temple, the order for the Jews to worship Idols, and the uprising of Mattathias and the Jews.

These complete the Set; for the others, see Nos. 2712—2720.

CORRECTION.

Inscription from the Church of S. Stephen, near the Painted Tombs on the Via Latina, two miles from Rome.   2101

This inscription is broken into two parts; the upper part had not been found when the photograph was taken. The Bishop of Limerick obtained an impression of it, and when the two parts are put together, it reads thus:—

[IN HONOREM] Stephani Primi S. Martiri Ego Lupo grigarius [ECCLESIAE] campanam (?) [campanarium?] expensis meis feci tempore Domini Sergii ter bea[ti]ssimi et coangelico[rum] junioris Pape. Amen.

The words between brackets are probable conjectures only.

Sergius I. was Pope A.D. 687—701.

" I Lupo Gregorius [a] (or gregarius = a soldier (?) in church militant) constructed the bell (?), or belfry (?), in honour of S. Stephen the proto-martyr, in the time of our lord Sergius thrice blessed, and junior of his co-angels [b], Pope A. M."

[a] Gregarius Miles.   [b] Youngest of his fellow angels (i.e. lately dead).

Orders for these Photographs, at One Shilling each, will be received and executed by Mr. Stanford, Charing Cross; or F. W. Maynard, Esq., Secretary to the Arundel Society, 24, Old Bond-street; or in Oxford, by Mr. Evans, Assistant at the Ashmolean Museum.

Specimens can be seen in London, at Mr. Stanford's, at the rooms of the Arundel Society, in the British Museum, and the South Kensington Museum. In Oxford there is a complete set in the Bodleian Library, arranged in volumes in numerical order, for reference; in the Ashmolean Museum another set, arranged in Portfolios according to subjects.

CATALOGUE OF PHOTOGRAPHS.—PART V.

Tombs—View of the Tomb of the Family of Statilius Taurus, B.C. 30.   3301

As excavated in 1875, at the expense of the Company of the Italian Fund. The Tomb, full of Columbaria, is here seen from above. It is situated near the Porta Maggiore, in the same large vineyard in which stands the fine building of the third century, called Minerva Medica.

Tomb of Statilius Taurus—Part of the Interior, with Columbaria and *ollæ* **or cinerary urns, in their original places.**   3302

Tomb of Statilius Taurus—One compartment of the early Frescoes, B.C. 30, between the Columbaria, much damaged by the surface being hatched for fresh plastering to paint upon, probably in the second century, when the upper part and the vault was painted.   3303

The subject is, the Messengers of the tyrant Amulius announcing to Rhea Silvia, while she is seated amidst other young maidens in a rural scene, that she has been named a Vestal Virgin.

N.B. It is quite possible that these paintings were intended to illustrate the Æneid of Virgil, and may have received the approbation of Virgil himself: they are of his time.

Tomb of Statilius Taurus—Fresco Painting on the walls of the Columbaria.   3304

Representing the foundation of the city of Lavinium, named after Lavinia, daughter of King Latinus, and second wife of Æneas. She is represented as seated on part of the new wall of the City, with a crown and veil on her head.—Virgil, Æneid i. 558, xii. 194; Dionys. Halicarn. i. 59; Dio. Cass. Fragmenta, iii. 5; Livii Hist. xliv. 57.

Tomb of Statilius Taurus—Fresco Painting on the walls of the Columbaria.   3305

It represents the Latins imploring and obtaining peace of Æneas; the inscription written on it was: LATINI IMPLORANT PACEM. Also a personification of the Numicus or Rio Torto, the river that runs near Lavinium, in which Æneas was drowned.—Virgil, Æneid vii. 45 and 150; xi. 213.

Tomb of Statilius Taurus—Fresco Painting on the walls of the Columbaria.   3306

The subject is the battle between the Trojans and the Rutuli; the Trojans represented as well-armed, and the Rutuli as savages, almost naked.—Virgil, Æneid xi. 630.

Tomb of Statilius Taurus—Battle between the Trojans and the Rutuli.   3307

Virgil, Æneid xii. 625.

Tomb of Statilius Taurus—Fresco Painting. Æneas, after the combat with one of the Rutuli at his feet, is crowned by Victory. 3308

Tomb of Statilius Taurus—Fresco Painting. The fight between the Trojans and the Æneids. Æneas kills King Turnus. 3309
    Liv. i. 2; Virgil, Æneid xii. 950; Dionys. Hal. i. 64.

Tomb of Statilius Taurus—Fresco. The twins Romulus and Remus exposed in a wooden cradle, and left in the flood of a stream that falls into the Tiber. The river is personified as seated with open arms to receive them. 3310
    Dionys. Hal. i. 79; Liv. i. 5.

Tomb of Statilius Taurus—Fresco Painting in the Columbarium. 3311
 Romulus (?) as a shepherd, or Faustulus (?), with sheep at his feet (of the figure of Remus, a slight remnant left). Faustulus and Acca Laurentia, who saved the infant twins from the flood, and educated them. The drawing of the figure, whether Romulus or Faustulus, is of the best style of art, reminding us of Raphael.—Liv. i. 5; Dionys. Hal. i. 79; Dio. Cass. xxxiv. 5.

Tomb of Statilius Taurus—Fresco Painting of the time of Hadrian or of the Antonines (?), on the upper wall of the sepulchre, representing a funeral feast. 3312

Tomb of Statilius Taurus—Fresco of the time of Hadrian, or of the Antonines (?). The figure of Pallas. 3313

Tomb of Statilius Taurus—Fresco of the time of Hadrian, or of the Antonines. The figure of Mercury addressed by a female. 3314

Tomb of Statilius Taurus—Fresco of the time of Hadrian, or of the Antonines. Hercules and a female figure. 3315

Tomb of Statilius Taurus—Fresco Painting on the vault. In the centre is Ceres with her attributes; on the sides, Apollo, a Muse, Hercules, and Mercury. In the corners, two Pegasi and a dove. 3316

Tomb of Statilius Taurus—Some of the very fine lamps with emblems and figures found in the Columbaria. 3317

The figure of Faustulus or Romulus as a shepherd, on a larger scale. (See No. 3311.) 3318

Mediæval Fountain in the courtyard of the Palazzo Antamoro, with the family shield. 3319

Construction—Brick Arch of Tiberius, in the Mamertine Prison. 3320

Part of the great Agger and Wall of Servius Tullius, near the railway station, in 1876, about to be destroyed. 3321

Another part of the great Agger and Wall of Servius Tullius, near the railway station, in 1876. 3322
Shewing that there was a stone wall on each side of the great bank of earth in this part.

Another part of the great Agger of Servius Tullius, opposite to the railway station, in 1876. 3323
Remains of houses of the second century are seen built upon it, and into the bank. The specus of an aqueduct, with a triangular head, is also seen in the foreground. These are on the inner side of the bank.

Another part of the great Agger of Servius Tullius, near the railway station. 3324
Here there was a house of the time of King Theodoric built into it, on the outer side of the bank, where it has been cut through obliquely by the railway.

Another part of the great Agger of Servius Tullius, near the railway station. 3325
This was in the ancient earthwork called the Mons Justitiæ, which was by the side of the central gate called Porta Viminalis.

Another part of the great Agger of Servius Tullius, in the act of being destroyed in the spring of 1876. 3326

Wooden Panels of Sculpture of the sixth century, in the door of the church of S. Sabina, on the Aventine. 3327
Scriptural subjects; the Miracles of Christ.

Other wooden Panels of Sculpture of the sixth century, from the door of the church of S. Sabina. 3328

Other wooden Panels of Sculpture, of the sixth century, from the door of the church of S. Sabina. 3329

Other wooden Panels of Sculpture, of the sixth century, from the door of S. Sabina. 3330

Construction—Basilica of Constantine, junction of the Apse of Constantine, with the wall of the great building of Maxentius, the Temple of Peace (?). 3331

General View from the roof of the Basilica of Constantine —The Forum Romanum. 3332

General View from the roof of the Basilica of Constantine —Villa Farnese, on the Palatine Hill. 3333

General View of Rome from the top of the Basilica of Constantine, looking north, to the Capitol, &c. 3334

Construction—Wall of the Kings on the Cœlian Hill, opposite to the Palatine (behind S. Gregory), within the line of Servius Tullius. 3335

General View of the Palaces of the Cæsars, from the Cœlian Hill (on the steps of the church of S. Gregory). 3336

General Views—Palaces of the Cæsars, from the Cœlian Hill, near the steps of the church of S. Gregory. 3337

Medieval—Grotto of the sixteenth century, on the Velia, behind the Basilica of Constantine.	3338
Church and Altar Decorations—Mosaic and Fresco Pictures in the church of SS. Nereus and Achilleus.	3339
Church and Altar Decorations—Candelabrum of the sixteenth century, from the church of SS. Nereus and Achilleus.	3340
*Church and Altar Decorations—Figure of an Angel, with the Crown of Martyrdom, from the Candelabrum in the church of SS. Nereus and Achilleus.	3341
*Church and Altar Decorations—Figure of another Angel, from the Candelabrum in the church of SS. Nereus and Achilleus.	3342
Temple of Mars Ultor, and Arch miscalled of Pantano.	3343
Quirinal Hill—Remains of Thermæ of the second century, near those of Constantine, with cascade fountain.	3344
*Out of Rome—Ferentino—Wall of the time of the Kings, with quadrangular masonry around a Doorway.	3345
*Out of Rome—Ferentino—Arches in the ancient Wall of the time of the Kings, making a Barbican to the Gate.	3346
*Out of Rome—Ferentino—Medieval Church of the fourteenth century.	3347
*Out of Rome—Alatri—Doorway of the Arx or Citadel, of very massive construction, called Pelasgic, or more correctly early Greek.	3348
*Out of Rome—Alatri—Niche in the earliest wall, of the same period and character as the doorway.	3349
*Out of Rome—Alatri—Doorway in the earliest wall, with two kinds of Construction—Greek below, Roman above.	3350
*Out of Rome—Alatri—Very massive Construction of the earliest wall, in the style called Pelasgic, Cyclopean, &c.	3351
*Out of Rome—Alatri—Roman Arches on earlier walls.	3352
*Out of Rome—Alatri—Medieval Church of the eleventh or twelfth century.	3353

The tower has mid-wall shafts. A rose-window, of the fourteenth century, is inserted over the west door.

Temple of Antoninus and Faustina, as excavated in 1876.	3354

Shewing the pavement of the Via Sacra, and the lower part of the steps of the temple, with the monolithic columns, now shewn of their whole height, forty-six feet, including the bases. On the right-hand side is seen the depth of earth excavated, about twenty feet.

*The Photographs marked * are of the octavo size, instead of the usual quarto or normal size.*

HISTORICAL PHOTOGRAPHS.—PART VI.

The following have been added to Mr. Parker's Series during the Season 1876-77.

Sarcophagi—Cinerary Urns and Cippi found in Columbaria in the Exquiliæ, by the Italian Fund Company, and preserved in their Museum near the Minerva Medica. 3355

Sepulchral Inscriptions found in the Columbaria of the Exquiliæ in 1875, chiefly in the Tomb of Statilius Taurus, B.C. 30, of the family of the Gens Statilia. 3356

Other miscellaneous Inscriptions from the Columbaria in the Exquiliæ, found in 1875. 3357

Other Inscriptions of the Gens Statilia, from the Columbaria in the Exquiliæ, found in 1875. 3358

Inscriptions of the Gens Statilia, and others, found in the Exquiliæ in 1875. 3359

Cippus and Inscriptions, chiefly of the Gens Statilia, found in the Exquiliæ in 1875. 3360

Since these Photographs were taken, this small local Museum has been abandoned, and the contents transferred to the great new Museum on the Capitoline Hill, belonging to the Municipality, in the hands of the Conservator.

THE GREAT AGGER OF SERVIUS TULLIUS—View in the foss, as excavated in 1876, with a house built in the foss against the foot of the lofty wall. 3361

Part of the Great Agger and Wall of Servius Tullius, as excavated in 1876, near the railway station, in the central mound called Mons Justitiæ. 3362

Remains of the Porta Viminalis, in the centre of the Great Agger of Servius Tullius, excavated in February, 1877, opposite to the railway station. 3363

The Porta Viminalis, in the centre of the Great Agger, front view, with the Specus of the Aqua Felice, A.D. 1575, introduced on the middle wall, between the two roads that met at this Gate. 3364

One corner of the new Custom-house, with the scaffolding, is seen to the left of the picture, and the new building for the Finance Department in the distance. There is great probability that all these remains of the Great Agger will be destroyed by the railway company.

Part of the Great Agger and Wall of Servius Tullius, excavated in 1876, with the new building for the Finance Department.	3365
Another part of the Great Agger (or bank of earth), and stone Wall of Servius Tullius, with a brick wall of a house of the Early Empire built up against it.	3366
Pantheon of Agrippa—Details of Construction, shewing part of the original circular building.	3367

With the brick front behind the marble portico added on soon afterwards, but having a vertical joint clearly distinguishing this addition.

Pantheon of Agrippa—Details of Construction, at the back of the circular building.	3368

With two walls added on to connect it with other parts of the Thermæ.

The fine hexagonal Nymphæum of the third century, miscalled the TEMPLE OF MINERVA MEDICA; part at the back, with bath-chambers, excavated in 1876.	3369
Thermæ of Diocletian—One of the Exhedræ made into the Church of S. Bernard.	3370
CORNETO—General View of part of the Mediæval City, with one of the Towers and the Church.	3371
Corneto—General View of one of the Streets, with a picturesque Mediæval House, and one of the Towers in the distance.	3372
Corneto—West end of the Church of S. Maria in Castello, with the Bell-gable for three bells, one of the Towers, and one of the Gates of the city.	3373
Corneto—The Palazzaccio, or House of Cardinal Vitelleschi, c. A.D. 1420, Exterior, front with Gothic Windows, and Porticus or *Loggia*.	3374
Corneto—Interior of the House of Cardinal Vitelleschi, Courtyard, view in the Gallery, and of the Porticus on the inner side.	3375

The style of architecture is that of French Gothic of the thirteenth century, although it was built in the fifteenth.

Corneto—The Cardinal's House, another view in the very picturesque Gallery looking across the Courtyard.	3376
Corneto—The Cardinal's House, view in the Courtyard, with the Arcade below, the Gallery and Loggia above.	3377
Corneto—The Cardinal's House, another view in the Courtyard, looking the opposite way.	3378

Architectural Details—Roman Composite Capital, now in
the Piazza di Spagna.   3379

Architectural Details—Late mediæval Doorway of the Palace
of the Antamora family.   3380

Sculpture in the Forum Romanum, on the Marble Wall.   3381

   A group of figures—the Emperor Marcus Aurelius? or an orator? standing on the rostrum and addressing the people, the two foremost figures of whom are holding up their hands, one shewing five fingers, the other three.
   This is supposed to represent the scene described by Dio Cassius, (lib. lxxii. c. 52), when the people all cried out "octo," demanding eight gold pieces each, which were given to them.

Sculpture in the Forum Romanum, on the Marble Wall—
Another group of figures.   3382

   This is supposed to be the Emperor seated, and addressing a lady standing, with a baby on her arm, supposed to be Roma, in commemoration of the foundation of an orphanage by him; the building in the background is probably the Tabularium, at the north end of the Forum.

Stone-quarries, travertine, at Tivoli—General View, to shew
the character of the stone.   3383

Stone-quarries, travertine, at Tivoli—A Detailed View, with
the large blocks of hard limestone almost submerged by
water.   3384

Stone-quarry of travertine, near Tivoli or Tibur, from which
the stone was brought for the buildings of Rome in the
time of the Early Empire.   3385

   The different character of this stone from that of tufa is clearly seen. In this view the curious ancient machine for turning off the water is shewn. This is still in use, as it probably was in the days of the Early Empire.

Stone-quarry of Selci or Silex, or *hard lava*, near the Tomb
of Cecilia Metella, Rome.   3386

   This stone is used for the pavements in Rome, being peculiarly hard and durable. It was used also in the time of the Empire. The different character of the stone from either the travertine at Tivoli, Nos. 3383, 3384, 3385, or the tufa of the banks of the river Anio, used for the great Walls of the Kings, Nos. 866, 867, is very evidently seen.

Church of the Apostles, A.D. 1490.   3387

   It is always called by this name, but is really dedicated to two of the Apostles only, SS. Philip and James. It is a good example of the style of the fifteenth century in Rome, as far as the height of the porticus or arcade, built by P. Pintelli, who died in 1494. But the upper part is a modern addition, A.D. 1724.

Chapel of the Seven Sleepers—General View of the Interior. 3388

Chapel of the Seven Sleepers—Details, with Fresco-paintings. 3389

This chapel is within the walls of Rome, and near the tomb of the Scipios. It had been long forgotten, until it was re-discovered in 1875 by the proprietor, being then a house for firewood. The frescoes are believed to be of the eighth century, but they are in a very bad state.

Tomb of Cecilia Metella, on the Via Appia. 3390

With the fortified battlement of the Guelphs on the top, and the castle of the Gaetani added to it, as seen from the Circus of Maxentius and Romulus. Cecilia Metella was the wife of the rich Crassus, one of the Triumvirs with Julius Cæsar and Pompey, B.C. 56. A Roman married lady retained her maiden name; she was the daughter of Cæcilius Metellus, who was Consul B.C. 60.

Tomb of Cecilia Metella, on the Via Appia. 3391

From the road, with the chapel of c. A.D. 1300, which is considered to have somewhat of the character of the English Gothic of fifty years earlier. This view is taken from exactly the opposite direction from the previous one. The two views give a tolerably complete idea of this remarkable and well-known structure, which is popularly called *Capo di Bove*.

www.ingramcontent.com/pod-product-compliance
Lightning Source LLC
Chambersburg PA
CBHW032001230426
43672CB00010B/2225